MARK ABBOTT STERN

Beyond the Tunnel

THE SECOND LIFE OF ADOLPH SUTRO

Mark Abbott Stern

ISBN 13:   978-1-7325517-0-1

for IRENE GREENBERG STERN,
who inspired this text

Contents

Preface and Acknowledgments

In springtime 2010, The Pennsylvania State University Press conducted its final reviews of my book *David Franks; Colonial Merchant* and, soon after, printed copies of the hardback version were sent to a large number of university and college libraries worldwide. I must confess having had a sense of bewilderment at the time; I had never encountered a copy editor in my past and was still somewhat awestruck over the labors of Suzanne Wolk whose incredible service had such a profound impact on my volume. Along the ten-year path to completion, I had purchased three revisions of the *Chicago Manual of Style* trying my best to get the story line written and the rules observed. With all of that book learning, it could still not have been completed successfully without Ms. Wolk. Also, there was that exultant feeling of success - I had plunged into a strange world and emerged largely unscathed.

In retrospect, the Franks project had been a huge pleasure but it was over. What was I going to do next? Certainly there were other deserving American Jews who either had no biographies or whose biographical treatments needed expansion and more personal attention. I discussed the question with Bill Pencak and let him know that while I had enjoyed the process, I did not enjoy the seven cross-country journeys to Philadelphia, New York and Harrisburg. The sources of documentary information about Franks were just too diverse geographically; I would look for a candidate personality closer to home... maybe in the West.

Pencak was up to the challenge and sent me to visit history department colleagues in and around Los Angeles. A group of serial referrals led me to Adolph Sutro whose only "complete" biography was not at all complete. The authors, a husband and wife team of historians, had been captivated by the scientific beauty of Sutro's tunnel concept and by the vigor and determination with which he took on the world to complete the project.

The Sutro Tunnel was not known to me at that time. When I saw the variety and significance of the other phases and successes of his life, I became a victim - it was another story that needed to be told because everyone had just left it behind – untold, at best offered half-heartedly as a supplement to the tunnel story.

The beginning was easy - some 27,000 documents of Sutro's reposed in the Huntington Library which had already accorded access to me for the Franks project and was continued for Sutro. My sincerest thanks are extended to Peter Blodgett, the H. Russell Smith Foundation Curator of Western American History at the Huntington. Ten years earlier, Blodgett had placed great faith in Bill Pencak's nomination of me as a Reader and continued to support my research on a new project. I will always be grateful. A virtual army was there to back up the Curator including Laura Stalker, Christopher Adde, Gina Giang and numerous others who each had a hand in finding or reproducing fundamental documents in the vast collection. During one year, I made the 100-mile round trip from Thousand Oaks to San Marino every Tuesday and every Saturday from early March to late June in order to explore the details of Sutro's final eighteen years. I never came away empty handed. In the process, I was aided by librarians, photocopiers, restoration experts and others too numerous to mention other than to say the Huntington is a remarkable organization from top to bottom.

An equally voluminous collection of manuscripts resided at the Bancroft Library at the University of California in Berkeley which had absorbed the Magnes Collection, assembled separately to focus upon Jewish aspects of Sutro's life. A force of equal size and capability was available at Berkeley to match that at San Marino standing ready to document and detail Sutro's San Francisco life. No less than twenty library employees contributed to the mass of manuscript copies I acquired at Bancroft. Their supervisor was Susan Snyder who arranged access for me to an unprocessed collection of works by Oscar Lewis which I suspected contained valuable rarities about the war with the railroad kings. I thank Susan Snyder for eliminating the possibility. I also thank the dozens who labored on literally hundreds of manuscripts for me.

After seeing the size and quality of the Huntington and Bancroft manuscript collections, it became necessary to make many trips to the northern part of the region. I was able to scan holdings at all of the following: the State Libraries at Sacramento and (the Sutro Library) at San Francisco; the San Francisco Public Library History Room; the Mathewson-IGT Knowledge Center at University of Nevada-Reno; the Nevada Historical Society in Reno; the Green Library at Stanford University in Palo Alto; the Library of the Society of California Pioneers in San Francisco; and, by internet connection, the Beinecke Library at Yale University - New Haven. lt seemed there were impressive historical papers everywhere and experts to unravel their secrets as well.

Each of these remote facilities took days to examine and I owe a great many thanks to individuals whose efforts led to an impressive assemblage of manuscripts. Some of my productive contacts were made with Jacquelyn Sundstrand at University of Nevada-Reno, with Michael Maher and Arline Laferry at the Nevada Historical Society. Each collection I scanned seemed to feature a new aspect of Sutro's life yet the degrees of knowledge and expertise were surprisingly much higher than one would have suspected. Many of the librarian family had become 'Junkies", ardent followers of the subject, ready to let you in on a rare side story without being asked.

There was more. On my first visit to the Sutro Library, the collection was housed in a small building on Winston Drive adjacent to the campus of San Francisco State University and was not a part of the academic library system there. Later, the library was relocated to the two top floors of a brand new facility in the center of the campus. Needless to say, the entire folder numbering vs content system was changed. Martha Whitaker, who had been so very helpful earlier, had retired and Haleh Motiey had assumed the reins leading a much larger crew with expanded workload. Their assistance with the manuscripts was helpful beyond description. Still later, Dianne Kohnke unearthed manuscripts that had eluded the group searching. That was really helpful.

Moving libraries and changing personnel was always part of the complexity in an eight-year data research project. But individuals with top-notch skills saved me every time. I still extend many thanks to Susan Goldstein at the 6th Floor History Room of the San Francisco Public Library and to Francesco Spagnolo and Dr. Lara Michels of the Magnes Library. One very contemporary episode occurred causing our appointment with Patricia Keats to fall through when her airplane was grounded in Germany. My chance to see a rare biographical text at the Library of the Society of California Pioneers looked like it was doomed. However, she managed to reach an associate who covered the meeting perfectly. That time, two librarians saved the day.

The Acknowledgments Section of the *Chicago Manual of Style; 15th Edition* extended praise and thanks to 132 individuals who participated in the editing process leading to publication of that massive text. Most likely, this volume benefited from the efforts of Donald H. Harrison to a similar extent. The completeness and rigor of the text owe a great deal to him in a very significant way which the author values and appreciates.

Introduction

April 29, 2013, the 183rd anniversary of Adolph Sutro's birth was celebrated at City Hall, San Francisco, in a ceremony where a massive bronze bust of Sutro was unveiled. Mayor Ed Lee of that city addressed the audience which included Consuls General Andy David of Israel, Peter Rothen of Germany and Sergey Petrov of the Russian Federation. Other guests were Mrs. Cynthia Soyster of San Francisco, great-granddaughter of Sutro, and sculptor Jonah Hendrickson. Other direct descendants also attended. Sutro's birthday has been observed annually in San Francisco, usually at the Sutro Library branch of the California State Library where the remains of his great collection of books and ephemera are stored. However, this was a special occasion to honor San Francisco's first Jewish mayor albeit nearly 120 years after he took office. Annual birthday parties are also held for Sutro in Aachen, Germany (Aix-la-Chapelle, Prussia at the time), the city of his birth. In Virginia City, Nevada, a historical marker was placed in 2009 honoring three Jewish immigrants with engineering backgrounds for their "entrepreneurial spirit and creativity." Adolph Sutro was one of these.

It is appropriate that Sutro be remembered regularly for his many gifts, valued acts, and visionary entrepreneurial accomplishments during his life. This is not to say he was a perfect man – in fact, he was certainly flawed. But he had grandiose dreams for his community and for its populace and he struggled mightily to bring them to fruition. Other than his one term in the mayor's office, Sutro is probably best known for the tunnel that bears his name under the Comstock silver mines in Nevada. Planning, securing the means, and executing construction of that engineering marvel would have been a life's work for most men but not for Adolph Sutro. This book tells the story of Sutro's anxiety-filled existence as completion of the tunnel approached and was achieved and how he moved on to a new life of continuous accomplishments and great visions.

Born in Aachen, Prussia, on the border of Belgium, Adolph was the third child of Emanuel Sutro and the former Rosa Warendorff. Adolph had two older siblings: Emanuel (later known as Sali) and Juliana; and eight younger siblings, who in birth order, were Emil, Otto, Laura, Hugo, Ludwig, Elise, Emma, and Theodor. In 1850, when Adolph was 20, the family immigrated to Baltimore, but very soon afterwards Adolph decided to seek his gold rush fortune in California. Several of his brothers became involved in Adolph's business dealings.[1] His wife, from whom he separated but never divorced, was the former Leah Harris. Six of their seven children survived to adulthood; the third child, Gussie, died at the age of 5 in 1864. The others, in order of their birth, were Emma Laura (1856), Rosa Victoria (1858), Kate Elizabeth (1862), Charles Walter (1863), Edgar Emanuel (1865), and Carla Angelina (1867).

The journey from birth to the conclusion of his Comstock life is covered in great detail in the text *Adolph Sutro; a biography* (Berkeley, CA: Howell-North, 1962) by a husband and wife team of Robert E. Stewart, Jr. and Mary Frances Stewart. That book originated from a revised dissertation for Robert Stewart's doctoral degree at University of California, Berkeley in 1958. Their book dwells chiefly upon Sutro's early life and creation of the tunnel. All that followed received much less attention than it deserves. Unfortunately, a large number of the cited documentary sources in the Stewart book cannot be found so that many notational references in that text (and in the original dissertation) cannot be verified. A second biographical text, *Adolph Sutro – Pioneer: His Life and Times* by Pauline Jacobson and Carl Burgess Glasscock, (unpublished: San Francisco, n.d., ca.1938) bearing the imprint of the Alice Phelan Sullivan Library of the Society of California Pioneers, suffers from the same issues as the Stewart book. It is filled with quotes lacking reference as to who is quoted, to whom they were written or when. There are no notes citing source collections. One other book should be mentioned. Carl Burgess Glasscock wrote an earlier text, *The Big Bonanza,* (Portland, Oregon: Binfords & Mort, 1931) which is another story of the Sutro Tunnel and features a photo of Adolph Sutro on the frontispiece. Like the unpublished text, it contains no notes or references.

A number of other books and periodicals feature smaller biographical narratives about Sutro including: Dennis Drabelle's *Mile-High Fever; Silver Mines, Boom Towns, and High Living on the Comstock Lode* (New York: St. Martin's Press, 2009) which devoted some twenty pages to Sutro most of which cover his years at the tunnel project; Ava Kahn's *Jewish Voices of the California Gold Rush: A Documentary History, 1849-1880,* (Detroit, Michigan: Wayne State University Press, 2002) which included a short interview Sutro gave about his childhood; and superb articles in *Smithsonian* by Donald Dale Jackson and in *Wild West* by Doreen Chaky that present other capsule versions of his life with great emphasis upon the early tunnel years. No fleshed-out, properly-sourced narrative of Sutro's post-tunnel accomplishments exists. Further, and most importantly, there is almost nothing told about the character of the man other than his technical creativity and perseverance. There was a lot more than that to Adolph Sutro. When I found this situation, I was pleased with my decision to avoid re-telling the tunnel story and proceeded to concentrate upon the years following.

This book begins eighteen months before the Sutro Tunnel made connection with the Savage Mine and focuses upon the contentious events leading to Sutro's acrimonious withdrawal from the tunnel project, his entrepreneurial growth in the real estate and entertainment fields, his imprint upon the landscape of San Francisco, and his unhappy experience as mayor of that city. Of paramount importance, the text details his life as a husband, father, sibling, colleague, and friend, painting a radically different picture from the man in the earlier volumes. The last eighteen years of his life were Olympian and need recognition in detail.

When asked if they know who Adolph Sutro was, many people will confess they have heard the name, but not much about the man. Between 1880, when Sutro left the tunnel, and 1897, when his health began to fail, he promoted an endless string of exceptional accomplishments. He acquired and developed real properties covering one-twelfth of the city of San Francisco. He devised an ingenious method using ocean tides to fill land spaces leading to establishment of an aquarium that had a changing content every day for visitors who were admitted free of charge. He restored the Cliff House restaurant from a dingy hovel to the finest eating and social establishment in town and, after it burned down, rebuilt it better than before. By design, he accumulated the largest private book collection in the nation including hundreds of incunabula and other rare printed items from every corner of the world; he intended to build an appropriate library building for the collection which would be open to the public and, especially, for scholars – he never got to do that, but his collection did end up available to the public. He turned Sutro Heights, where he lived, into a magnificent park which was open for public use several days each week. He built the largest indoor swimming venue in the world which included seven separate pools with different water temperatures, 500 private dressing rooms, a grandstand seating more than 5,000, swimsuits for each customer, a museum of world-wide attractions and musical programs of every kind, swimming contests featuring Olympics-level performers and many water entertainments; as with his aquarium, the Sutro Baths were filled and emptied by tidal flows. Adjacent to the Sutro Baths, he built Merrie Way, an amusement park with a variant on a Ferris Wheel known as a Firth Wheel and many other rides and games; the Sutro Heights area thus being turned into the favored recreational destination for families in San Francisco. He imported and had more than one million trees planted including a forest in the northern portions of the community while each sale of his several thousand lots included at least one tree for the new landowner. He fought the railroad magnates to lower their fares, from the city to the beach and his entertainment center, from ten cents each way to a nickel each way; when they refused, he found ways to make them comply including building a competing rail line which charged only a nickel a ride, thus persuading them to reduce the fares. He campaigned successively for a law to protect sea lions that inhabited rocks off the coast below Sutro Heights which may have been the very first ecological law passed in the United States Congress. He led the successful opposition to a series of proposed Railroad Funding Bills which would have extended loan repayments by the Southern Pacific and Central Pacific by fifty or more years. He never campaigned for the position of mayor, other than by opposing the funding bill, but was swept into office. Everyone knew he could get things done and had the community's welfare in mind with every move he made.

Several interesting themes are woven into the narrative. The first, and most important, was Sutro's incredible entrepreneurial skill. From the time he first entered California until his passing he was successful in a variety of business ventures. Although his parents had been affluent in Prussia, he started his new life alone and with few financial resources. He built respected enterprises as a cigar merchant and as a mineral processor. He saw the benefits to be gained from the tunnel he planned, funded, and eventually constructed. When he left the Sutro Tunnel Company and re-located from the Comstock region of Nevada to San Francisco, he possessed considerable money which he used to purchase vast areas of land in the western section of the city. His real property holdings had been scoffed at by many in the city as being inferior for most uses but Sutro turned the land that no one wanted into one triumph after another. His forays into the restaurant and hospitality world included the finest eating establishment in the region. The world-famous "Pleasure Gardens" he constructed became the city's most desirable family destination for entertainment.

Adolph Sutro had received no formal education to prepare him for any of this, but his lack of technical training never stood in the way of a new venture. He relished books which he purchased in increasing numbers throughout his California years, providing all the source material he needed to make bold business decisions. He maintained himself current with advances in every science and he devised innovative solutions to a wide variety of thorny technical problems. There is no evidence of his having asked others for help although, after he had made up his mind how to solve complex issues, he was not averse to asking leading world authorities for confirmation. Sutro solicited input from Bernhard von Cotta and Baron Ferdinand Richthofen among others concerning mineralogy and from Thomas Edison regarding electricity. He insisted upon having the latest in technological equipment and he was inventive himself using ocean tides and waterfalls to obtain unique solutions for engineering challenges.

Another theme throughout the text concerns Sutro's selfish, self-serving life-style. While traveling cross country and over the Atlantic to seek funding for the tunnel, Sutro lived like a king eating the best food, drinking fine wines, and filling his wardrobe from London's finest Savile Row merchants. While he was staying at the best hotels in London, Paris, and Washington, DC, he borrowed heavily and virtually ignored his wife who was farming fruits and vegetables and raising chickens to feed the family back in Nevada. After he had spent most of the money he brought to California on real estate purchases, he found himself land-rich and cash-poor.

San Francisco grew dramatically during the years Adolph Sutro lived there and emerged from this expansion in a very ecumenical way. Except for Chinese immigrants, there were not the kinds of ghettos for various ethnic groups as existed in the larger eastern cities. That Sutro was a Jew failed to surface biases against him; he never made an issue of his religion. However, his origins led him into a lifetime of close contact with many Jews as colleagues, investors, and quasi-friends. When Sutro arrived in San Francisco, August Helbing had a large, well-organized chapter of the Eureka Benevolent Society which welcomed Prussian Jews who conducted their meetings in the German language. Sutro made substantial contacts with many society members that lasted almost fifty years and, despite his avowed secularism, being Jewish played a principal role in much of his success.

Adolph Sutro had his admirers and his detractors. He always believed he knew more about anything than everyone else. In contemporary terms, he always did his homework. Though he occasionally needed help from lawyers, there is no other evidence of his ever asking for advice. That alone made him a difficult person to like, but he was a fascinating personality.

One

THE SEARCH

They arrived separately. Three elderly, rumpled gentlemen exited their horse-drawn carriages and were admitted to the mansion where they were greeted warmly but joylessly by the young woman. They comprised a curious though impressive foursome: a noted attorney, a judge sitting upon the California Supreme Court, a former mayor of San Francisco, and a founder and leading physician of San Francisco's Children's Hospital. Their mission was simple. Looking for important documents, they were to open and examine the contents of the safe in the home of the doctor's father. The integrity of the group assembled to witness the process would speak for itself and could not be challenged.

It was February 8, 1898, just one day after Adolph Sutro had been judged insane and placed under guardianship of his eldest child, Dr. Emma Sutro Merritt. For several months, she had been providing his medical care at her home office after he suffered seizures rendering him far too ill to be treated at his residence on Sutro Heights. Now was the time to seek and find his will. Supreme Court Judge Elisha McKinstry took on the job of recording minutes of the search while former mayor Edward Pond and attorney Reuben Lloyd assisted Emma with removing and identifying the contents of the vault.

They agreed to proceed systematically, shelf by shelf and tray by tray, rather than grabbing anything that looked like paperwork first. The initial item was a document entitled "Articles of Agreement between A.

Sutro & Leah Sutro." The judge recorded this as item #1 but omitted the date. The nature of the agreement was not described on his list. The first seven items included more than seventeen letters, a checkbook and two copies of a deed identified as "Moore to Kluge." Next came a number of coins, some ancient and some specifically Roman, followed by a bag of cash. Several buckskin bags of engraved gemstones and many more ancient coins were found.

A number of documents were listed: several personal letters (no details regarding who had sent them or when); a catalog of the Hebrew and Arabic items in Sutro's library; an agreement of unspecified nature (also undated) among Sutro, Elliott Moore, William R.H. Van Alen,[2] and George Coulter; and two life insurance policies. Then they found the twenty-fourth item – just what they had been looking for – McKinstry recorded it as "Last will of Adolph Sutro" again omitting a date. Together with the will were three wax seals with Sutro's motto *Labor Omnia Vincit* ("Labor Conquers All") in his own handwriting, and a seal figure of a miner which Sutro had used on stock certificates.

There was much more: numerous gemstones (many engraved), books of autographs including famous people; gold coins; marriage certificates of Sutro's daughter Rosa to Pio Alberto Morbio and of his daughter Kate to Professor Moritz Nussbaum; two deeds from Sutro to Elliott J. Moore including rent receipts related thereto; a report to Sutro's personal attorney, Reuben Lloyd; a package of letters in German with German stamps on their envelopes; and a deed of trust from Sutro to Elliott J. Moore and W.R.H. Van Alen that was undated as were all the other document listings.

The final listed item, #41, was "tin box containing copy proceedings Leah S. v Adolph S.," also undated.

The safe contents raised many more questions than they answered, and the insufficiency of the list compounded the issues. The date of the will which McKinstry had failed to record was May 22, 1882, nearly sixteen years prior to the search. A decade later, there were lingering bones of contention over what was uncovered that day and what was not.[3]

PRELUDE

Two

FINANCING THE TUNNEL, EARLY

The struggle to pay for construction of the Sutro Tunnel consumed a major part of ten years in Adolph Sutro's life. Hardly a day went by without some danger to the fiscal integrity of the project; completion of the work was more like a miracle than a planned result. Along the way, three principal sources of financing were employed – government agencies, capital stock sales, and loans from banking houses. Certainly, others participated in the effort but when large infusions of funds were needed, these three were solicited one by one. Each had its own scenario and its own unique cast of characters requiring Sutro's interaction with literally hundreds of individuals – the famous and the obscure, the helpful and the interfering, those nearby and those half-way around the world – a mélange of personalities with intersecting lives and cross-currents of actions. Much of this story has been told before; much has been omitted in the telling. An earlier biography of Sutro presented a rather complete history of Sutro's struggles to obtain initial funding first from the Nevada territorial government, which had so much at stake in the silver mines, and later from the United States federal government whose congressional leaders understood their need for new revenues to pay down Civil War debts. Sutro obtained sufficient financing to begin the work fully confident that sales of stock would quickly add to the resources of the company. It wasn't that easy.[4]

The tunnel could not have been finished without the financial support provided by the London bank of brothers Robert and Hugh McCalmont and their partner William Johnson Newell doing business under the name McCalmont Brothers & Company. The McCalmonts were engaged in banking activities in America as early as 1838 and, by 1870, were the largest stockholders in the Philadelphia and Reading Railroad, a major carrier in the northeast.[5] They became interested in mining properties in the western United States and contemplated investing heavily in the North Star Gold Mining Company in Grass Valley, California. They took into the partnership Lewis Richard Price, an experienced investor and capitalist, who had spent many years in Mexico with varied interests in every aspect of gold mining and processing. The McCalmonts' cousin, George T. Coulter of San Francisco, who was also a member of the firm, had an option on the North Star mine and attempted to raise money in London. The entire Grass Valley area was a promising gold mining center and the Eureka Mine was considered the "best gold mine of modern times."[6] The McCalmonts and their associates held nearly three-fourths of the ownership of the Eureka Mine. They were serious and careful investors and had employed Henry Janin, a renowned California mining engineer, to conduct appropriate surveys before making decisions. He had never failed them. His inspection of the North Star Mine found the property exhausted and he recommended against the purchase. Investors in the North Star Mine had their money returned to them.[7]

But now, McCalmont and Price were still motivated to uncover promising mining properties in the West and responded to another of Coulter's "finds." This one was the Sierra Buttes Gold Mine near Downieville, California. Sierra Buttes had been a working mine for more than fifteen years but was felt to have more potential. Again, the syndicate turned to Henry Janin for a recommendation which they obtained. On the strength of his endorsement, the McCalmonts and Price invested £225,000, generated stock certificates, and sold half of them raising £120,000 working capital. Lewis Price was elected chairman of the board and was sent to California to arrange for local management through Cross & Co., agents for the McCalmonts in western America. Additionally, Price wanted to see the Sierra Mine for himself and to use

5

his own personal know-how to advantage in its evaluation, as well as to explore the entire region for new opportunities.

Traveling with Coulter, Price arrived in New York in the late spring of 1871 where he had the opportunity to meet with Joseph Seligman, a prominent banker. Seligman appeared enthusiastic about a project being promoted by Adolph Sutro who was looking for sources of financing; Price learned that Seligman had promised to "keep Sutro afloat until McCalmont or someone else could be got to take a share in the work..." Later that day, Sutro met with Price and explained details of his tunnel project. Sutro was well acquainted with Coulter, and one of Sutro's partners on the governing board of the tunnel company was Louis Janin, brother of Henry, who was so well regarded by Price. Apparently, nothing came of that initial meeting, but the contact had been made. Price and Coulter left for San Francisco with plans to visit the mining areas before returning to England. They conferred with Cross & Co. and with Henry Janin and were joined in their travels by Col. Charles W. Brush, a native of Baltimore, then residing in New York where he had performed legal services for the McCalmonts when needed. Brush was known to be "an old friend of Coulter's."

The threesome spent a week and a half traveling cross-country to San Francisco. Once there, Price lost no time in contacting Cross & Co. representatives and Henry Janin whom he had never met before personally. This led to meetings with interested and interesting people including John W. Gashwiler, superintendent of the Virginia City and Gold Hill water works company. As was common with most western businessmen, Gashwiler dealt in mine sales on the side. Conversations with Gashwiler preceded a meeting with John Wedderspoon, a Cross & Co. partner, who hosted the group at his impressive mansion in Oakland.

Price toured mining regions in California and Nevada accompanied by William Leets Oliver, Secretary of Cross & Co. Occasionally, Coulter, Brush, Janin, and Gashwiler arranged to meet with Price and Oliver for dinners and conversation about the properties they had seen. Price, Coulter, and Brush arrived in Downieville on a stagecoach and climbed the challenging hill to the Sierra Buttes Mine. Upon inspection, Price was impressed with the condition of the mine and the quality of the equipment and was prepared to generate enthusiastic approvals of the investment. After returning to San Francisco, Price toured other portions of the American Southwest, reveling in the beauties of the Petrified Forest and Lake Tahoe.

Price also visited Virginia City and met with Adolph Sutro again and was given a tour of the tunnel. Price recorded in his diary that "...when completed will be 7 miles long. It is a wonderful work and promises to develop the mineral resources of this district to an almost fabulous extent." [Actually, when completed, the tunnel was a little more than four miles long.] While there, quite providentially for Sutro, the United States Congressional Commission to evaluate the Sutro Tunnel was visiting the tunnel at the same time. Price met Professor Wesley Newcomb, the lone civilian member of the Commission, who "is wonderfully impressed with its advantages..." Sutro took Price to the Crown-Point Mine in which they descended to 1,100 feet below the surface. Price was astonished at the environmental conditions in the mine. "It was a grand sight [the ore vein], but the heat was so great we could only remain down about 10 minutes and the perspiration poured off us as though in a vapour bath, and in this atmosphere the poor miners have to work!!! They die in great numbers from miners' consumption, but all this will be changed & ventilation be perfect if the Sutro Tunnel be carried out." The next day, Sutro took him to see the hoisting works at the Savage and Hale & Norcross mines. Price recorded that, "In the former they spend $65,000 a year for fuel, consuming 15 cords of wood a day at $12 a cord. This will be saved by the Sutro Tunnel." It is difficult to imagine a better situation for Adolph Sutro than to be asking the McCalmonts for financial support.[8]

At summer's end, Price returned to England and the McCalmont organization began to exploit and enjoy the Sierra Buttes mine, which produced exceptional yields and rich dividends. Another mining investment, the Plumas Eureka in Mohawk Valley, also brought gratifying income to the participants who considered themselves to be, once again, "on a roll" in their American ventures. This led to purchase of another group of properties. Coulter arranged acquisition of three mines, Original Amador, Erie, and Pennsylvania, which he organized into a separate company structure under the name London & California Mining Company. Henry Janin had examined the properties and was enthusiastic about the prospects, saying "it was the most splendid combination ever offered to the English public." Reports from Cross & Co. substantiated Janin's comments as did those of William Ashburner, an American mining engineer with a significant reputation.[9]

Unfortunately, it turned out that Janin had falsified his report. In a conspiracy with Gashwiler and a third party named Bell, they had fooled Cross & Co. and collaborated in what Price considered to be a swindle. Further, Price suspected that Ashburner was either bribed or depended upon Janin's word and had issued his report without inspecting the properties. The three mines were not worthless but produced minimal returns leading to significant losses by all the partners, their relatives, and the general public. Furthermore, loss of confidence drove down the market price of shares in the Sierra Buttes and Plumas Eureka mines. That the McCalmonts looked for other kinds of investment opportunities was not surprising and Sutro clearly benefitted from that turn of events.[10]

At the end of April 1873, Sutro obtained approval of the Tunnel Company trustees to go to Europe and find a willing source of funds. A substantial block of stock was identified to be used as collateral – sufficient to give a controlling interest to the agency that provided enough cash to bore the tunnel to conclusion. Armed with a Power of Attorney outlining the limits of his authority, Sutro headed for London. The Seligmans had agreed to the plan and were reconciled to the eventual dilution of their share holdings, realizing that there were no better alternatives to funding the work. Their London office served as Sutro's headquarters during his search for money. He remained in London throughout May and until mid-June with the McCalmont Bank as his principal target. By the middle of May, he had negotiated successfully the acquisition of $8 million of 8 percent, 25-year bonds convertible into common shares of the Tunnel Company stock. This agreement needed ratification by the Tunnel Board of Trustees and would remain unsigned by the McCalmont brothers until William Newell returned from a lengthy trip and put his legal blessing upon it. That took two months of anxious waiting. In the interim, Joseph Seligman comforted Sutro with his endorsement of its many features including not having to award preferred shares to the bank, and offered congratulations for a job well done. That was high praise from a genuine authority.[11]

In early August 1873, Sutro Tunnel Company and McCalmont Brothers Company concluded three separate agreements for financing further work on the tunnel. The McCalmonts were represented in these negotiations by the firm of Freshfields & Williams, one of London's most prestigious legal houses. Freshfields' documentation over the ensuing two years made clear that Adolph Sutro had been a tenacious negotiator. They considered he had violated every principle of responsible business practice – he communicated with the wrong people; he was insistent about contractual demands which he surely knew could not be accepted; he withheld payments well beyond due dates; he sold shares before and during the process at severe discounts; and he tried to obfuscate the fact in the prospectus. That the bankers tolerated all of this and continued the process to completion was little short of amazing to the lawyers. The simple truth was that the McCalmonts believed they had an unrivaled opportunity for financial gains and suffered the indignities that Sutro heaped upon them in silence, expecting great results as their future reward.[12]

Over time, the relationship between McCalmonts Bank and the Tunnel Company was particularly rocky. More specifically, the relationship between the McCalmont brothers and Adolph Sutro was generally troubled. Sutro continued to promise significant rewards for their investment and the anticipated benefits never came. Not long before the financing agreements were signed, the Tunnel Board authorized an expansion of share content from twelve million to twenty million shares. This was the dilution which Seligman had understood would occur with the cash infusion. Coulter fired off a blistering letter to Sutro complaining that the share expansion devalued McCalmont holdings seriously and asking that they be issued an additional 200,000 shares free of charge to establish fairness. Sutro did not trust or care for Coulter and was in the middle of negotiations with the principals. Very likely, no answer was provided to Coulter directly. Progressively, everyone involved took sides in the disagreements between the groups. The McCalmonts were consistently backed by Brush, Coulter, Cross & Company, and Wedderspoon. Sutro could count upon investor Joseph Aron, the Seligmans, the Lazard Frères representatives (Alexander Weil and David Cahn) who served as treasurer for the Tunnel Company, and Judge Solomon Heydenfeldt, who was a top-notch legal advisor.

As the tunnel got closer to completion, relations between Sutro and Hugh McCalmont worsened almost to the breaking point. The McCalmont bank was firm in its stand to not provide any additional funds until they were able to see substantive returns in some form. Sutro had constantly predicted success in negotiations with the mine owners. Sutro had also assured the bank that a rich vein was certain to be intersected by the tunnel somewhere along its four-mile length which would provide a huge financial bonus. So far, these were just promises.

Three

THE ENEMIES LIST

Were he here today, Adolph Sutro would have enjoyed helping prepare his own biography. During his life, he took numerous opportunities to write about events he witnessed, or which were reported to him. He prepared lengthy descriptions of his travels at various ages from youth to his fifties. He sent reports of historical events to appropriate newspapers when he witnessed activities or when he was able to obtain first-hand accounts. He dictated extensive autobiographical information to hired associates for recording but, unfortunately, never completed them. And, his number one love in life was books which he accumulated passionately and was eager to share with the world around him. Consequently, a book about his life and times would have suited his ego as well as the need to express his philosophies more widely in the format he admired. He could certainly have provided answers to some of the questions which survived his days. His life started with one of those questions. Adolph Sutro's birth certificate identifies the child as Heinrich Adolph. Various texts tell us his name was Adolph Heinrich Joseph Sutro, but, in America, he was always known as Adolph Sutro. [13]

During his adult life, Sutro dealt with various opposing forces, each of which he assigned the status of arch enemy. The principal foes were The Bank Ring, the Bonanza Silver Kings, and the Railroad Monopoly "Big Four" (which he called "The Octopus"). His interface with each of these extended over many years and some of his nemeses opposed

11

Sutro's aims more than once. In order to gain the maximum understanding of events in the critical years, some recapitulation of Sutro's early encounters with these opponents follows.

William Chapman Ralston (1826-1875) was an important figure in the far Western United States - particularly in California and Nevada. After leaving Ohio as a young man, he went to the gold country to seek his fortune. Ralston had abdicated from an unsuccessful partnership with two friends and, armed with little knowledge of banking, formed the Bank of California. He realized that an established businessman had to be at the top of the bank's management and, wisely, he convinced Darius O. Mills, a prominent banker both in Sacramento and the East, to accept the position of president. Ralston took the position of cashier in which he was free to manage operations of the bank outside the glare of formal observation. He possessed two great gifts - intuition about banking needs and exceptional skill at judging people - which, in a short time, yielded considerable success in his new enterprise. The Bank of California became the major lending institution in the West.

When mining activities at the Comstock Lode in neighboring Nevada began to accelerate, Ralston wanted to establish a branch in Virginia City close to the mines. He selected as its manager William Sharon (1821-1885) a lawyer with real estate business background. It didn't take long for Sharon to become involved deeply in silver mining, including a painful experience with securities in which he was swindled out of most of his own money. However, Ralston had confidence in Sharon and stayed with him. Together, they grew the Bank of California to gigantic proportions and virtual ownership of the Comstock region. Their plan was simple; they loaned money to mining companies at bargain rates. When mines couldn't make payments, the bank foreclosed and took over the mines. They built mills of various kinds and lowered their prices until all the competition was driven out of business. Then they raised prices mercilessly. They made enough money to erect the Virginia & Truckee Railroad for transporting ores from mines to processors. The Bank of California was the principal monopoly in the Comstock and its leaders soon were known as the Bank Ring.

In the early years, the Bank of California and Ralston supported Sutro and his tunnel concept. Ralston had seen evidence of the difficulties that underground water could cause and the problems with insufficient ventilation in work areas. Ralston gave Sutro letters of introduction to financial houses in the East which Sutro took with him to secure financing for the tunnel. Eastern bankers were reluctant to invest until they could see an energetic participation on the part of West Coast financiers. Finally, Sutro obtained initial financing from the federal government after which the tunnel company tried to acquire the remainder through sales of stock. Meanwhile, the Bank of California's huge success and its assumption of control of the resources in the area had Ralston re-think his support for Sutro. The Bank of California was doing fine without the tunnel and had acquired new, modern machinery for removing water and for ventilation which convinced him to withdraw any encouragement for the Sutro Tunnel Company. Sutro saw them as an enemy and wrote lengthy diatribes against the Bank Ring which he had printed as booklets and distributed widely through the federal government. Ralston allied himself with western congressmen and senators to oppose Sutro. Nevada Senator Aaron Augustus Sargent, chairman of the Senate Committee on Mines and Mining, was close to Ralston and led Senate opposition to a bill which eventually funded the start of the Sutro Tunnel.

As the Comstock petered out, failures of the mines and excessive lending by the bank led to its demise. Ralston went for a swim in the ocean and his body was washed up on the beach. Whether he had died naturally or was a suicide was never determined conclusively. Sutro thought it was a suicide. Sharon quit the bank, owning considerable personal assets which he used to acquire major portions of Ralston's estate. He then ran successfully for the United States Senate seat vacated by William M. Stewart's resignation and served one term. Stewart had been the first president of the Sutro Tunnel Company. Sutro, in anger, attempted to mount a campaign to oppose Sharon but brought too little too late. At the next election in 1881, Sutro again prepared to oppose Sharon but stopped when Sharon withdrew his candidacy.[14]

The Bonanza Firm, or Silver Kings, was the partnership of four men: John William Mackay (1831-1902); James Graham Fair (1831-1894); James Clair Flood (1826-1888); and William Shoney O'Brien (1825 or 6-1878). All were from Irish stock; Mackay and Fair were born in Ireland, and Flood and O'Brien were the children of Irish immigrants. None had formal education of any significance, but they were all intelligent and brought different skills to the merger. Flood and O'Brien had met in San Francisco where they became partners in a lunch counter catering to stock brokers. Both had been in the area around the mines as shopkeepers or salesmen. The restaurant provided exposure to dependable information about securities investments. Success of the restaurant yielded discretionary funds to speculate in stocks. They did well enough to sell their business and open a brokerage of their own.

Mackay had gone to the gold mining areas with little to show for it. But, he continued working as a miner and then as a contractor and, with a partner, purchased the Kentuck mine thought to be worthless. On the contrary, it began to produce considerable profit and Mackay was getting rich. It was then he met Jim Fair. Fair had been working in the silver mines in a variety of capacities and, of the four, was the most experienced and knowledgeable about mining operations and the complex details of silver processing. For a time, he was superintendant of the Ophir Mine working for the Bank Ring; then he served as Assistant Superintendant of the Hale & Norcross Mine. Later, that mine appeared to stop producing and the stock price plunged from $2,900 per share to $41.50 over a six-month period. Fair and Mackay joined forces. Fair convinced Mackay that he could make the Hale & Norcross Mine worthwhile again and they began to acquire shares. In less than a year, they had 400

14

shares and obtained control of the Hale & Norcross at the board of directors meeting in March 1869. Fair was appointed Superintendant and turned the mine into a singular success.

At that point, Flood and O'Brien, now leading brokers at the San Francisco exchange, joined forces with Mackay and Fair. The combination of silver mining expertise and investment acumen made the group extremely powerful. The team acquired two additional mines adjacent to the Hale & Norcross - the Consolidated Virginia and the California. As in the earlier case, both were considered to have been played out, but Fair uncovered a narrow vein which he traced for a considerable way to a huge bonanza which was described thus: "No discovery which matches it has been made on this earth from the day when the first miner struck a ledge with his rude pick until the present." The partners were now incredibly wealthy and continued by organizing all of the parallel services into separate companies - the Pacific Mill and Mining Company, Pacific Wood, Lumber & Flume, and others. They were indeed kings of the silver world.

Adolph Sutro's tunnel was thought to be serious competition for control of the mines. The royalty attached to their future ore removal appeared onerous. Managers of the mining companies readily expressed their fear that Sutro would end up owning all the Comstock unless they were able to put an end to the tunnel. So, they tried. Mackay, by then the acknowledged leader of the mine entrepreneurs, pursued a path of obstruction to and non-cooperation with Sutro and the tunnel. On the surface, the relationship between Sutro and Mackay always appeared smooth and unruffled, but a variety of incidents and maneuvers was easily traceable to the Silver King and his mine-operator allies.[15]

Unlike the Bank Ring and the Silver Kings, Sutro did not have significantly contentious relations with the Railroad Barons until after the tunnel was completed and he had established himself in San Francisco. The group, known as the "Big Four," consisted of Collis P. Huntington (1821-1900), Charles Crocker (1822-1888), Leland Stanford (1824-1893), and Mark Hopkins (1813-1878). The principal accomplishments for which the Big Four are remembered were establishment of the Central Pacific Railroad Company, which connected with other rail systems to complete the first intercontinental railroad in America. Within the four, Huntington and Hopkins had been partners in a hardware and iron business in Sacramento; Stanford and Crocker were also successful as merchants and were convinced to join with Huntington and Hopkins as founders of the Central Pacific in 1861.

Stanford had been raised in a fairly prosperous family and obtained a law degree and admission to the bar in 1848. After a variety of unsuccessful business ventures and a fire which destroyed his law offices, he moved to San Francisco and joined with two of his brothers in a career as a merchant. He was active politically and helped to organize the Republican Party in California for its first convention in 1856. Five years later, just prior to formation of the Big Four, he was elected Governor of California. This new position dictated his selection as President of the Central Pacific. The subsequent parts of his career were equally remarkable including service in the United States Senate and establishment of Stanford University on property he purchased in Palo Alto.

During Crocker's youth, he farmed, worked in a sawmill, and learned the iron forge business. Eventually, he founded his own iron forge business. When he arrived in California, he opened a dry-goods business in Sacramento which turned into a very successful venture. He was reported to have $200,000 which Huntington considered the mark of a successful business man. When the Central Pacific organized, he became its construction supervisor and was apparently admired greatly by the working men on the railroad. His enthusiasm was transferred to the entire labor force.

The oldest of the four was Hopkins whose talents for financial administration were invaluable to the team. His reputation for thrift was widely recognized. Born in New York, his family had moved to Michigan in his teens, but he was also drawn to the lure of California gold in 1849. He and a friend established a grocery in Sacramento in 1850 but, five years later, he joined with Huntington in the hardware line. Hopkins functioned as the treasurer for the enterprise and the others depended upon him to validate financial decisions of every kind. Huntington was reported to have said, "I never thought anything finished until Hopkins looked at it." That was high praise from him.

Notwithstanding the organizational chart, leadership of the enterprise rested in the hands of Huntington. Collis Potter Huntington had left home as a youth and did odd jobs and saved every penny he could. He joined an older brother in a mercantile business, but when the gold rush began in 1849 he headed for California. During his travels, he spent three months in Panama during which he wasted no time and managed to earn more than $3,000 which he took with him to Sacramento. There he met Hopkins and they formed a partnership which turned out to be very successful - one of the wealthiest on the West Coast. Theodore Judah interested them in his dream of a transcontinental railroad system. They were smitten - Huntington and Hopkins began to search for partners and investors to form a railroad company to build the western portion of the cross-country line. The Central Pacific Railroad Company was formed in 1861 and the Golden Spike was driven into the ground at Promontory Summit, Utah Territory, in May 1869. During those years, Huntington had been the driving force for financing the construction. Years later, manipulation of finances became the issue of contention between Sutro and the Big Four and most particularly with Huntington.[16]

Sutro did not accumulate only enemies over the years – he also managed to acquire associates with whom he shared close personal relationships beyond their work connections. Sutro was not "warm and fuzzy" with colleagues or employees. He said of himself, "I am not [of] a social disposition. I am very much alone...I can spend more hours alone than any man you ever saw."[17] But he did reach out to some in a less rigid and formal way. The most important of these was Joseph Aron whose connection to Sutro is detailed later in this volume. There were others.

Natives of France, three of a family of five brothers started Lazard Frères & Co. in New Orleans in 1848 as dry goods merchants. Following destruction of the enterprise in a fire, one of the three, Simon, moved to San Francisco with the two brothers who were not in the original firm. Once there, they formed a company to exploit success of the California gold rush. Though the primary business was merchandising dry goods, a brisk program of exporting gold grew into various other financing activities. An older brother, Alexandre, also left New Orleans to establish a similar business in New York. Eventually, separate but related businesses functioned in the United States, France, and England with skillful family members in positions of responsibility everywhere. Lazard Frères survives to this day as one of the principal financial powerhouses in the world. Simon, Maurice, and Elie Lazard were members of the Eureka Benevolent Society in San Francisco along with their cousin Joseph Aron and Adolph Sutro. Those early social connections led to business partnerships and close working arrangements. Other Lazard relatives, including Alexander Weill and David Cahn, were sent from overseas locations to assume major roles in the San Francisco office. The Lazard enterprise served for some years as treasurer of the Sutro Tunnel Company with individual family members acting in behalf of the firm.[18]

One of the original directors of the Sutro Tunnel Company was Louis Janin (1837-1914) of New Orleans who, along with two brothers, pursued a career in the mining industry as an authoratative mineralogist. Janin had attended Yale before studying at the renowned Freiberg University in the city of Freiberg, Germany. Both Sutro and Janin had worked on extracting pure silver from its ore and were well acquainted with each other when the time came to bore the tunnel. Sutro was happy to lean on Janin's technical expertise and his connections with the many mining scientists at Freiberg. Janin had made arrangements to pay the $1,000 publication fee for Baron Ferdinand von Richthofen's treatise on the potential of the tunnel and had consulted for Sutro diligently in the early days of the tunnel albeit while moonlighting from his position with the Gould & Curry Silver Mine.[19]

Sutro had a remarkable ability to recognize genuine technical expertise. His own knowledge was broad, but he liked to seek out confirmation for issues at the very edge of contemporary science. He found outstanding engineering capability in two other men who had come to the Comstock. The first was Philipp Deidesheimer (1832-1916). As the width of its ore body increased, the Ophir silver mine encountered numerous cave-ins. Deidesheimer, who had also studied at Freiberg, was called in to devise a way to prevent the frequent collapses which made working conditions so dangerous. A long list of "experts" had already failed to find a solution but, after a month of study and trials, he developed the "square-set timbering" system which solved the problem. Large, reinforced rectangular assemblies of lumber beams were constructed in a pattern which successfully supported ceiling and wall sections of interior spaces in the mines. Without realizing it, Deidesheimer had saved the mining industry; soon, every mine was using this technique to overcome the structural problem. The Sutro Tunnel, built about the time of the first installation, also used square-sets throughout. The inventor neglected to patent his discovery which would very likely have made him a millionaire.[20]

The second engineering standout whom Sutro admired was Hermann Schüssler. It was he who devised and built the aqueduct system which delivered water over thirty miles from the Sierra Nevada range to the town of Virginia City in the Nevada Territory, without which development of the mining community would have been relatively impossible. Later, Schüssler worked for Sutro helping to locate the proper placement of vertical shafts between the tunnel and the surface on top of Mount Davidson. Sutro was impressed with that work but, still later in his career, Schüssler was Chief Engineer for the Spring Valley Water Company in San Francisco with which Sutro had intensely bitter disagreements. The two of them fought bitterly over water quality and price. Despite their confrontations, Sutro never lost his respect for Schüssler's intellect.[21]

There were other friends and foes as we shall learn as the story unfolds.

Four

ONE PROBLEM AFTER ANOTHER

The year 1876 had ended in a flurry of nagging issues. Sutro had been sick for several weeks with "catarrh," an excessive build up of mucus in the body. He repaired to the resort at Harbin [Hot] Springs Lake near Calistoga, California, to take mineral baths, which may have helped but he continued complaining about being sick for another month. He told his daughter Emma he would like to go somewhere warm for a week or so, but it was not to be. Notwithstanding his illness, Sutro sailed to London on December 6th. Between his departure and New Year's Day 1877, Assistant Superintendent R.S. Raw reported a series of problems at the tunnel including a rock fallout which killed two employees. Tunnel company attorney Elliott Moore told him about "foul play" at shaft #2. Moore was going to have detectives masquerade as miners to catch the troublemakers.[22]

As the new year unfolded, Raw reported yet another serious injury to a miner. There appeared no end to these incidents. But that wasn't Sutro's focus. He had crossed the ocean to continue discussions with principals of the McCalmont bank. He had telegraphed them, attempting to set up an appointment for Monday, December 18th. Lewis Price, McCalmonts' silent partner and president of the bank's mining interests, had responded enthusiastically and wanted to see him personally but not until after Christmas. Though Sutro was hardly content to wait; he hopped over to Paris and delivered a lecture, after which he enjoyed some plays and an opera before returning to London.[23]

Finally, Sutro was able to see the McCalmonts and concluded negotiations for a loan of $1,000,000, giving a mortgage on the tunnel in return. Under conditions of the agreement, the bank would send $24,000 per month to the Sutro Tunnel Company. Sutro was probably ecstatic about the loan but was disappointed to learn that Price's enthusiasm had waned. They met, providing an opportunity for Sutro to dissuade Price from selling 500 Sutro Tunnel Company shares he owned privately. Price agreed to think about it but shortly after they parted, Price sent a note to Sutro's hotel explaining why he would go through with the sale - he lacked confidence in the management. This was followed by a cold note from McCalmont's attorney, G. M. Clements, asking for a half-dozen copies of the Tunnel Company by-laws and repeating an order to communicate with another company lawyer. Unfazed by negative reactions from both the bank president and the company attorney, Sutro used previously-made reservations to return home - just days after the unsatisfying meeting with Price. The loan was the prize he had wanted.[24]

As soon as Sutro returned to New York he learned that Henry Foreman was about to be released from the hospital. Foreman had been Assistant Superintendant of the company and had been injured in an explosion in the tunnel. Sutro and Foreman had been close working associates and Sutro was genuinely concerned about his colleague's condition. This had not been the first accident involving blasting caps and Foreman had been in various stages of recuperation for nearly a year. Both Foreman and Sutro looked for someone to blame for the incident. Foreman consulted all members of Sutro's legal support team, including Elliott Moore, Peter Williams (of Freshfields and Williams, consulting attorneys for the Tunnel Company), and the Shellabarger & Wilson firm in Washington, D.C. Meanwhile, Sutro helped to defray the medical costs of a year's treatments. From all reports, Foreman's arm was much improved, but he was essentially sightless. They wanted to find someone to sue to keep Foreman from poverty in addition to blindness. The exploder manufacturer was a logical place to begin. Sutro had suggested as much to Foreman earlier but nothing had come of it. Sutro arranged for Foreman to receive payments from the Tunnel Company of $30 monthly for an undefined period. Both Sutro and Pelham W. Ames (the company secretary) received "thank you" notes from Foreman in which he expressed his hope that the payments would be "in perpetuity" which had not been stated. Neither of them could make that promise.[25]

Privately, Foreman's plight had bothered Sutro significantly and he was puzzled about the cause of the detonations. Almost concurrently with Foreman's release from the hospital, there was another exploder accident in the tunnel costing one of the men his left arm. Sutro began investigating the possible sources of ignition. He recalled walking around his home in bedroom slippers and creating a spark when he touched metal. He began to experiment at the tunnel. He placed an exploder in a remote enclosure and connected electrical wires to it at considerable distance - a safe distance. Wearing his slippers, he shuffled around the area and then touched the wires. The exploder was ignited and produced a loud burst. Sutro tested caps from several manufacturers and determined that some were more easily ignited but that all were certain to explode when sufficient static electricity was transmitted to them. Exploders from the Giant Powder Company blew up easily but those from Mowbrays, though harder to set off, created much larger detonations. Sutro pondered solutions for this problem and settled on one. He instructed Ames to order a large quantity of 3/8 inch-thick steel plate which was welded together to cover the floors of the powder, exploder storage, and processing areas. The plates thus were connected physically, and electrical wires were run from the plates to the stream of water flowing through and out of the tunnel. Effectively, the entire area became grounded. That was the end of exploder accidents at the tunnel. Unfortunately, it was too late to help Foreman. In mid-year, Sutro reported his findings to a scientific journal which published the article.[26]

The tunnel presented problems almost daily, or so it seemed from the reports he received from Raw, Col. Brush (a tunnel company trustee) and the Tunnel Company's secretary, Ames. Workers were injured, cave-ins occurred regularly, purchase order anomalies persisted, boiler repairs required repeated correction, visitors interfered – nothing serious but just enough to divert attention from the main task of intersecting the mineshafts at the far end. Over a period of several weeks, procurement of a huge lumber order was thorny – first Henry Yerington's price was too high, then, the delivered materials did not match the ordered quantities or specifications. Obtaining a competitive bid got the negotiations back on track. A visit from Sutro to Yerington's office in Carson City settled the overcharges. But, all these distractions intruded upon Sutro's focus and upset him.[27]

Meanwhile, in Washington, he and his personal secretary, Frank Young, directed a constant vigil over Congress, making certain that no new law or amendment be passed to reverse his tunnel authorization. When Congress adjourned in early March he expressed relief that there would be no more sessions until December.[28]

The *San Francisco Chronicle,* irreversibly tied to the fortunes of the mining interests, reported a non-existent "unpleasantness" between Jim Flood and Adolph Sutro purportedly intruding upon attempts to settle tunnel issues between the parties. Flood's denial was printed. Brush suspected the story was planted to drive the stock price down, so the mine owners could acquire large amounts. He alerted the London partners to quell their alarms at such stories.[29]

Sutro was indeed frustrated over the lack of success in negotiations with the mines. He had wanted to drive the talks to conclusion. The large lumber order was part of his plan which he finally shared with Aron. They would construct a gate to completely block the flow of water through the tunnel. The result would have water back up into the mineshafts all the way to Virginia City. The gate would be hinged and, therefore, easily removable once agreement was reached. But, with the gate, the tunnel could not be used by the mines to remove unwanted water in their shafts until Sutro permitted it and, moreover, the tunnel could not be flooded before work was completed.[30]

Reports accelerated each passing week about the ebb and flow of negotiations between Sutro and the mining hierarchy. Adolph's cousin, Gustav (head of the Sutro & Co. finance and banking organization), told Brush of meeting with "several very prominent brokers," friends of the Bonanza people, who were the "very best posted parties in this city" [San Francisco], who maintained that an agreement had actually been reached. Further, on the strength of that knowledge, friends of Flood and O'Brien were buying stock. Gustav concluded the Bonanza people had decided to accept the terms offered by Sutro. Brush did not believe it and cautioned Adolph that "a little game is being put up on somebody."[31]

In April, another situation reached the boiling point. More than three years earlier, Adolph had received a letter from Simon Ingersoll who had shared a train ride through Connecticut with Adolph's brother Hugo. Ingersoll was a farmer and inventor who lived in Stamford. He engaged Hugo in conversation which led to talk about the tunnel project. Hugo had spent a couple of years in Nevada with Adolph before returning to the East in the late 1850's so he knew much about Adolph's plans and the future glories of the tunnel project. Ingersoll was excited by the discussion and, in a letter, told Adolph he had invented a superior rock drill which he recommended be tried at the tunnel. He also had several improvements in the works, and he predicted it would be the best rock drill available in the world.[32]

At that time, Sutro was using rock drill equipment from the Burleigh Rock Drill Company, which also was located on the East Coast. He was pleased with the equipment and cooperated with Burleigh by having a model of the tunnel produced which Burleigh included in its display booth at the Philadelphia Centennial's mining exhibit the following year.[33] The Hoosac Tunnel in Massachusetts had created great demand for newer and more efficient mining equipment and the Burleigh drill had been one of the great advances that resulted. A United States government report advised that, "Burleigh's air-powered rock drill proved superior to every mechanical drilling contrivance tried at Hoosac…"[34]

But Sutro was eager to explore opportunities to use the newest and best. He ordered drilling equipment and drill bits from Ingersoll and utilized both companies' products concurrently for two or three years. The rival manufacturers sought contracts to service the entire project. In mid-1875, a competition was arranged to compare boring capabilities and repair experience of the two drill systems. The Sutro Tunnel Company people involved in directing the test were Jack Bluett, the tunnel supervisor, and R.S. Raw, formerly Chief Accountant, who served as Assistant Superintendent while Sutro was on the East Coast or in Europe. Finally, in December 1876, Sutro notified the Burleigh Rock Drill Company to "please not send any of your new drills, they will not answer our purpose."[35]

That looked like the conclusion of the issue until six weeks later when Sutro heard from L.C. Parke, a partner in the Parke & Lacy Company, sole agent for Burleigh in the West. Parke reminded Sutro of a conversation between them several months back in which Parke & Lacy suggested that Sutro Tunnel Co. employees had been bribed to favor the Ingersoll drills. In the new letter, Parke stated flatly that he had "all the facts in Black & White and more testimony that Bluett & Raw were both bribed."[36] Sutro was in Washington on his congressional vigil while his two key leaders at the tunnel were implicated. Any investigation was going to be difficult.

One week later, Raw heard from J.B. Reynolds, Pacific Coast representative for the Ingersoll Rock Drill Company, who advised that George Davis, an Ingersoll employee, "has commenced a blackmail suit against me" and was preparing an affidavit saying Reynolds had given cash to Bluett and Raw to influence results of the competition. Further, Davis was ready to leave for New Zealand immediately thereafter. It was imperative for Raw to come to San Francisco to refute these claims with his own deposition before Davis gets away.[37]

Raw was shocked to learn he was under siege. Both he and Bluett insisted they were innocent of the charges. As a ruse, the bribes had been referred to as "bets" which mystified him further as he had forbidden betting by tunnel employees and observed the restriction himself. He was aware that Davis owed a considerable amount of money that he had borrowed from several sources including Raw himself. Davis had told Raw that Reynolds would return the money he owed to Raw on his behalf. As for leaving the tunnel and going to San Francisco for a deposition, that was out of the question. There was too much work, pay day was "at hand," and Sutro was absent – he simply could not leave his post. A few days later, he told Reynolds of letters from H.B. Hanmore, a freelance newspaper writer, accusing Parke & Lacy of having purchased Davis's testimony. Raw stood fast refusing to leave the tunnel, but he said he would try to find a local notary and offer a deposition from there. He also suggested having nothing to do with Hanmore who "is in for making money out of the case."[38]

A few days later, Reynolds wrote to Sutro telling him that Davis had been fired, that Parke & Lacy exhibited strange behavior, that they were responsible for buying Davis's testimony, and were up to no good. About this time, Hanmore also wrote to Sutro on the subject. He told about his upcoming series of articles about the tunnel, which were to be published in the *San Francisco Chronicle*. He also reported that, in the interim, Raw had resigned.[39]

Notwithstanding the report of his resignation, Raw continued working at the tunnel and issued frequent reports to Sutro for nearly a month. Sutro returned to San Francisco in mid-March and spent eleven days there with the entire family. Now closer to the situation, he had a chance to assess the issues. When questioned about the truth of the accusations against Raw, he told an acquaintance that he was uncertain; information from a man named Davis may be unreliable. Reynolds told Sutro that Raw was being accused unjustifiably. He assured Sutro that he had given no bribes. He wanted both Raw and himself to get a fair deal. [40]

If Raw was innocent, he didn't get a fair deal and ended up leaving the company. He had appeared to be a loyal, hard-working, no-nonsense manager upon whom Sutro could depend and now he was gone – another distraction which Sutro hadn't needed. Meanwhile, negotiations between the Tunnel Company and the mining companies continued to churn daily. Rumors of attitudes and settlements were reported in newspapers throughout the state. The Humboldt County *Silver Slate* told its readers that "...efforts are being made by some mining managers to bring about a compromise with the Sutro Tunnel Company. They seem willing to pay liberally for the benefits the tunnel will confer but opposed to the royalty claimed by Sutro."[41]

By the end of 1876, the Silver Kings' Consolidated Virginia Mine had extracted more than $38 million worth of silver. An additional half-million had been removed from their California Mine. Both the State of Nevada and Storey County had imposed property taxes on the mines and succeeded in collecting them through 1875. Taxes were scaled to the value of bullion taken out of the mines. Consolidated Virginia and California had paid upwards of $550,000 to the county before 1876 taxes became due. This was approximately 87% of the total county taxation on Comstock mines. Although they had paid taxes all the years up until then, Mackay and Fair vocally opposed the imposition of flat rates for all property owners. They asserted that the silver mines deserved a lower rate than conventional properties. For them, a rate increase in 1876 was the last straw and Fair began a campaign to reduce or eliminate the taxes. Combined county taxes for the two mines during 1876 were scheduled to exceed $323,000. Fair and Mackay had been feuding with the Sharon and Ralston forces convinced that, through political connections, Sharon had arranged to obtain reduced rates. Following Ralston's death, all their anger was directed at Sharon. It appeared too coincidental that the rate increase for mines occurred at a time when the Mackay/Fair income was at a peak and the Sharon mining interests were flagging.

Actually, the rate structure was complex affecting various classes of businesses differently. The Virginia & Truckee Railroad, which had been built and operated by the Mackay/Fair organization, enjoyed reduced rates that provided a major benefit for them. They never mentioned this in their complaints. When they paid their first-quarter taxes in 1876, they advised the county and state that the payment was submitted under protest. They made no payments for the succeeding three quarters that year withholding more than $290,000 which the various governmental agencies needed desperately.

Over a period of several months, Fair and Mackay took turns lobbying the legislature in Carson City to reduce rates. They succeeded in having a Bullion Tax Compromise Bill written and submitted to the Nevada Legislature. It was passed in both chambers. Governor Lewis R. Bradley promptly vetoed the bill. But, Mackay and Fair still had hope. Earlier, they had brought suit "to enjoin the collector of taxes for Stor[e]y County, Nevada, from collecting a tax imposed .... upon the Consolidated Virginia Mining Company...." They had employed Hall McAlister, who had a national reputation and was considered one of the finest attorneys in the West, to press their case all the way to the Supreme Court of the United States. Storey County responded by hiring William Emory Fisk Deal, another renowned lawyer, to argue the case for them. The case, *Forbes vs. Gracey,* was settled in favor of the county in October 1876, adding to Mackay and Fair's disappointment.

Mackay and Fair ended up paying more than $300,000 in prior-year taxes during 1877. The strangest part of this entire affair was that it was never made public. When the *Forbes v. Gracey* case was first instituted, Sutro was convinced immediately that this was a plot against the tunnel. One of the primary issues raised in the suit was the difference between earnings of individuals or companies which owned property being mined, and earnings of individuals or companies which merely held claims on government-owned property from which they extracted ores with permission from the agency. That set off alarms in Sutro's head. He was convinced the aim had been to obtain a ruling against owners of claims including the Sutro Tunnel. He contacted Shellabarger & Wilson, his Washington law firm, and Judge Jeremiah Sullivan Black, his legal expert on everything, and told them of his fears. Both agreed it looked like the tunnel was the target. Sutro notified Col. Brush and told him to have Elliott Moore and Peter Williams prepare an appeal. Fortunately, the ruling in the case saw no distinction between the two forms of income insofar as tax liability was concerned. And, the appeal was denied. Consequently, the tunnel was not affected, and no appeal had been necessary.

Two days later, Sutro heard again from Shellabarger & Wilson advising that the decision had no adverse effect upon the tunnel and not to worry. Sutro told Brush, "I have but little doubt that this decision is the result of a long ago concocted scheme, carefully and shrewdly planned and intended to injure us. Even if it did, which I do not think to be the case, we have the power over the Comstock Companies so completely in our own hands, that I think we may dictate almost any terms." Despite all that bravado, Adolph Sutro probably had a more than a few sleepless nights unnecessarily.[42]

While the family was enjoying a ten-day stay in San Francisco, Sutro missed seeing a letter sent to him from England. On his last visit, he had made elaborate plans with Robert Warner, proprietor of Brooks Warehouse in London, who cleared space and prepared storage facilitation for large quantities of books which would be acquired throughout Europe and processed for shipment to America. Sutro had grand plans to create a library of world-class proportions. He had kept this to himself other than the arrangements with Warner and Karl Mayer, who would be his purchasing agent in Europe. Warner advised Sutro that the warehouse was ready to accept books.[43]

The San Francisco *Stock Reporter* published an interview with Sutro in which he explained that the tunnel header was now about 17,000 feet deep into Mt. Davidson. He had projected progress to average 300 feet per month and expected to intersect the Savage Mine in approximately ten months. He brushed off suggestions that the type of rock near the lode would prohibit keeping the tunnel open claiming "...the tunnel company had no fears on this score...they had already passed through material similar to, and quite as difficult as any met with in the main lode." And, most importantly, "As to rumors of a change in control of the stock of the company, Mr. Sutro answered emphatically that the management could never be wrested from him." The story was picked up and reprinted nationally and Sutro received a highly complimentary note from Griffith J. Griffith, mining correspondent for the *Alta California,* who "deemed it prudent to make mention of such a gigantic enterprise." [44]

Col. Brush notified Sutro that some stockholders wanted to list the company on the New York stock exchange without bothering to obtain approval of the trustees. Brush, now president of the Tunnel Company, was decidedly against such a move. Unquestionably, he was the hand-picked representative of the McCalmonts who were absolutely opposed to listing in New York. In a follow-up message, Brush reported having had a board meeting in which the trustees agreed to protest listing on the New York Exchange. He suggested the Seligmans had been behind the scheme.[45]

The Seligmans were having other problems at the time. Joseph Seligman, titular head of the American branch of the family, had arrived at the front desk of the Grand Union Hotel in Saratoga, New York, for a scheduled stay with his wife and children. The Seligmans had spent summers at the Grand Union throughout the prior ten years. The hotel manager at the front desk informed him that, "Mr. Hilton has given instructions that no Israelites shall be permitted in future to stop at this hotel." Mr. Hilton was Judge Henry Hilton who owned the hotel. Hilton had been a Tammany Hall member and an associate of Alexander Stewart, owner of the largest department store in the nation. During the early 1870s, Stewart and Seligman had been through a series of incidents leading to a hostile relationship between them. When Stewart died, Hilton was assigned as executor and took over management of his properties. Seligman questioned the clerk who explained that Jews would not be welcome at the hotel henceforth because the largely Christian guests "did not like their company" and were "beginning to shun the hotel."

Seligman was outraged. He returned to New York where he wrote an indignant letter to Hilton and began informing all his acquaintances of the episode. Two significant results came of this. Hilton responded with an incredibly anti-Semitic letter which gained wide circulation. Throughout the United States, Jews poured out messages of support and a boycott of the A.T. Stewart store in Philadelphia commenced which led to its failure and eventual sale to John Wanamaker. Author/historian Stephen Birmingham suggested that Seligman may have precipitated the "affair" intentionally either trying to embarrass the hotel management or testing whether he would be exempt from the new policy. In any event, effects of the episode escalated exponentially. A new wave of anti-Semitic feeling spread around the country. Many hotels followed the Grand Union in barring Jews. In response, a new collection of summer resort hotels sprang up in the Catskill Mountains to rival those in the Adirondacks which were no longer welcoming Jewish patronage. Birmingham attributes other anti-Semitic practices to fallout from the hotel issue – blackballing in bar associations, college and fraternity quotas, and similar restrictions in residential access. While that may overstate the impact upon the national scene, it appears to have had a serious effect upon Joseph Seligman and his relationships within the Comstock community including the tunnel.[46]

In San Francisco, the rumor mill was working overtime spreading stories about the suddenly excellent or suddenly terrible relations between Sutro and the Bonanza people. Brush was still convinced that Mackay, Fair, Flood, and O'Brien were responsible for stirring the pot to drive down stock prices, so they could swoop in and acquire at a low price. Newspapers in Sacramento and San Francisco discussed details of events that had never happened at actual negotiations between the parties. Jim Fair was interviewed by a newspaper reporter who suggested Fair was opposed to compromise with the tunnel company. Fair denied the claim, "On the contrary, I am strongly in favor of any arrangement that will be just to both parties." He followed additional questions by outlining his plan for paying the tunnel fees – basically defraying the cost of pumping water from the tunnel to the surface. This was hardly what Sutro had in mind as fair compensation.[47] He was waiting patiently for the right moment. Sitting at the hub of the incredible array of activities around him and his life, he had plans.

Adolph Sutro had spent nearly fifteen years promoting the concept of the tunnel and advancing the idea that a great deal of money was to be made in at least one of three different ways: (1) the process of digging the tunnel would unearth a major silver vein belonging to the Sutro Tunnel Company and the ore would yield millions in new revenue; (2) the mining companies would settle on Sutro Tunnel Company's terms and begin paying large monthly fees and royalties for use of the tunnel out into the future; or (3) Sutro Tunnel Company stock would rise significantly creating huge profits for the stockholders while small stock sales would fund ongoing costs of tunnel development. Whether Sutro really believed any of these in 1877 is uncertain. That he constantly trumpeted these predictions was known to everyone who came near him. In a letter to his daughter Emma, he indicated he attached some certainty to his own situation for one of the three possible reasons.

In 1870, Adolph Sutro's brother, Emil, had made several forays to Philadelphia and Boston to develop interest in Sutro Tunnel Company stock at brokerage houses in those cities. All Sutro's banking sources had ample presence in New York, and the company hoped to find a less volatile atmosphere for stock sales in the other cities. Emil had also canvassed the brokers in Baltimore where he lived and spoke in glowing terms about the reception his sales pitches had received. Emil's efforts never really bore fruit, but new contacts had been made. Adolph Sutro didn't forget about those.

Two weeks after his letter to Emma, Sutro communicated with Edward Dean Adams who had just been made a partner in Richardson, Hill & Company of Boston. A graduate of Norwich University, he had studied at Massachusetts Institute of Technology during its inaugural year where he honed his great interest in scientific subjects. Adams was fascinated by the Sutro Tunnel and the ingenuity of its technological approach to solving everyday problems in the mines. He expressed his interest in having his partnership invest in the project and was invited to visit and have a look before so doing. His partners did not join in Adams's enthusiasm but went along with having him go to Nevada to see the mines and the tunnel. By mid-November, Adams was in the San Francisco office of the Sutro Tunnel Company to scope a stock purchase. Sutro and Adams drew up an agreement for Richardson, Hill & Company to acquire at $5 per share 12,000 shares of Sutro Tunnel Company stock for $60,000 in two payments. Options were provided for an additional 12,000 shares two months later at the same price and 96,000 shares afterward for $480,000 in ten installments. They each agreed to seek approvals from their partners and to consummate the arrangement when done. Adams decided to return to Boston but, before leaving, he purchased lots in the town of Sutro, Nevada, for himself, and each of his partners, Spencer W. Richardson and William H. Hill, Jr.[48] He also arranged with Adolph Sutro to purchase 6,000 shares of tunnel stock for his own account at a discounted price of $4.75 per share.

Sutro did not believe that Adams's partners would approve the deal which required an installment payment on New Year's Day. But he was enthused over the discussions with Adams and the possibility that American investors would be drawn to the project with significant financial resources. He told Ames he would inform the McCalmonts about it and asked him to have the Department of the Interior General Land Office send the Sutro Tunnel model then on display in their Washington offices to Richardson, Hill & Co.[49]

Then, tragedy struck again. Sutro, H.H. Sheldon, Frank Young, and tunnel company physician, Dr. Abram C. Renninger, made the trip on horseback from the tunnel to the bank in Virginia City to pick up that week's payroll money which was a substantial sum consisting of gold coins. On the return trip through Six-Mile Canyon, Dr. Renninger's horse threw him, resulting in severe injuries. After being hospitalized, Renninger appeared to behave crazily, did not respond to medical assistance and, three days later, expired. The same day, in a separate incident, a mail delivery agent also was thrown from his horse in the same vicinity.[50]

That wasn't all. In those closing months of the year, in rapid succession, Sutro was peppered by a variety of events. Henry Yerington continued to present problems with every aspect of the lumber purchases

– the prices, the deliveries, the taxes. As a friend of the Bonanza interests, he was making things as difficult for Sutro as possible. In Washington, H.R. 1202 was introduced to prohibit acquisition of mining titles on land owned by the federal government. Sutro had seen that as another attempt to subvert tunnel company rights and had contacted Shellabarger & Wilson to look into the matter. They reported "no view of the within bill occurs to us which will hurt you." In a separate message they added, "We take the Cong.[ressional] Record and strive to do our best to watch your interests but to see something done in Congress (as you know) would require about all our time. Hence we would suggest whether the company should not have some sentinel on duty to keep us posted as to what we may not see." That was what they were being paid to do. Sutro was not pleased.[51]

George Coulter had sent a thirty-page personal history describing his relationship with Sutro, alleging he had been injured severely in their financial dealings. One by one, every irritant during the years of their acquaintance was agonizingly re-hashed. However, Coulter was willing to forgive Sutro for all his wrongs and wished him success with the tunnel – but he demanded 120,000 shares of tunnel stock for the McCalmonts and 100,000 shares for himself as compensation for all the times he was treated unconscionably. Sutro held a low opinion of Coulter and very likely ignored the letter. But just a month later, Tunnel Company investor Aron reported that Coulter had shown up (very likely in New York) and was trying to sell 120,000 shares of tunnel stock. Aron was checking hotels in Rhode Island and Massachusetts to see if Coulter was there. He later advised that Coulter's presence was doubtful and that he was returning to England. Very confusing indeed and no explanations followed, but the threat of a large stock sale had been avoided.

As 1877 ended, Aron—the cousin of the Lazard Frères principals-- continued to bother Sutro with advice and critical comments about everything: he had several negotiation ploys for dealing with Jim Fair; the tunnel company staff was not sufficiently careful handling stock certificates which were certain to have quantities altered on their faces; there were problems with the way the Richardson, Hill & Company agreement was written and he was trying to determine if the intrusion of the Seligmans had caused this; and more. Meanwhile, the rector of St. Matthews School reported two unpleasant episodes of conduct on the part of Sutro's son Edgar who seemed to care little about his school work.

Adolph Sutro took it all in stride. He had a plan. So, he took some time off, went home to see and hear his new Steinway grand piano, which the girls were trying to play, and he read through his advanced copy of Henry Drinker's *A Treatise on Explosive Compounds, Machine Rock Drills and Blasting.*

Five

ADOLPH SUTRO, FAMILY MAN

Emma was in her last semester at Vassar, looking forward to graduation in June 1877. Rosa (daughter number two) would have to be brought back from the boarding school in Baltimore to continue school nearer home. The other four children were getting along fine except Charley who seemed to march to his own drummer and would need more rigid control in his life than Sutro could provide while crossing the country and the ocean frequently. Then, Emma broached the subject of attending medical school. Sutro was proud of her scientific bent and her academic achievements but he wasn't so sure he would like her to pursue a medical career. He begged off more discussion saying it could wait until they were together. He wanted to attend the inauguration of President Rutherford B. Hayes and would come back from Washington and see her. Sutro recognized a lot of his own characteristics in Emma's dogged perseverance. He told Emma she ought to take courses in mineralogy and geology or perhaps take a trip somewhere. Meanwhile, he had asked a friend to get information about the medical college for women in Philadelphia, "not that I have any idea of letting you go there, but I like to be posted somewhat."[52] He certainly realized he was fooling himself. Emma was now a young woman past twenty years old and would not be put off when determined to follow a particular course.

Their relationship had undergone a serious transformation over the past few years. During the summer of 1872, both Emma and Rosa had spent their vacations at home in Sutro with the family. As will hap-

36

pen in families, disagreements arose with both girls. Rosa apparently raised her hand to strike Leah and was disrespectful to her father as well. There was an extended period of ill feelings between Rosa and both parents. That December, Rosa told "Dearest Papa" that "I feel so much happier since I have seen you [in Baltimore] for there seems to be a heavy load off of my mind & I hope never, as long as I live, to be so disrespectful to you again." She enclosed an embroidered handkerchief she had made for "Mamma" asking to forward it after seeing what she had done.[53] Apparently, Mama was not impressed greatly by the handkerchief or whatever note accompanied. Leah told Emma, "With regards to Rosy I feel very much discouraged and am only to[o] thankful that she is with Miss [M.] Reinhardt [at school]. I hope she will continue with her until she knows how to conduct herself with decency and propriety towards her parents. I never want to be disgraced by her again and the longer she is with Miss Reinhardt the more comfort I shall enjoy unless there is a great change in her conduct with regard to myself. I never intend to allow myself to be so grossly insulted by my children as long as I breathe the breath of life. I try not to speak of the past but whenever Rosy's name is mentioned that feeling that she struck her Mother is always present and if I do not feel the same love and affection for my children they have nobody to thank for it but themselves." But, little by little, Rosa worked her way out of the doghouse.[54]

Emma also incurred the wrath of Papa for some unspecified episode in which she showed a lack of respect. In late March, nine months later, Sutro wrote to Rosy, while on board a ship to Europe, saying, "I have not written to our Emma and do not mean to until she gives me the most unequivocal proofs of her truthful repentance for her conduct towards her parents last summer and you may to tell her." Rosy responded, "I am very sorry that Emma has not written to you but I think, she feels very sorry for what she has done for she often writes to me about it. I do not think that it is her fault, my dear Papa, that she does not write to you & tell you how she feels about it, for she is alone & has no one to tell her how wrong she was. I think it would be much better if you would write to her & tell her yourself how wrong she is & then she will feel all that she has done is wrong." However, shortly thereafter, Mama Sutro told Emma that Papa was still very angry with her, that her letters to him were not pleasing, and that he "…will have nothing to do with you that he will neither write to you or see you." Leah was seriously distraught and expressed her sadness over Emma's behavior.[55]

These emotional exchanges continued for several months. As the summer of 1873 approached, it had been decided to have both Emma and Rosa remain in the East rather than return home, as Papa was still in Europe and Leah had her hands full with the house and children who were with her in Nevada. Without checking with Adolph, Leah made the arrangements and told Rosa to stay with Miss Reinhardt in Deer Park, Maryland, for the summer. Then, she inquired into the possibility of Emma staying there as well. When that appeared to be workable, Leah got Adolph's approval for the arrangement. In passing the news on to Emma, she cautioned, "He [Papa] hopes that your conduct will be perfectly ladylike and that you will give Miss Reinhardt no trouble or annoyance. You are getting to be of an age now that any little indiscretion will be noticed and remarked on, and I hope that you will not give anyone an opportunity to pass any remarks on your conduct."[56]

One week later, Papa sat down and responded to a letter from Emma in which she had tendered her apologies. Adolph Sutro usually wrote on 5" x 8" sheets of paper. When at home, he used Tunnel Company stationery; on the road he wrote on hotel letter paper. Generally, his letters to Emma and Rosa would cover four pages except when he was in a great hurry and only one page would have to do. His letter to Emma, at least one year after their disagreement began, took him twelve handwritten pages.

"It has no doubt caused you a good deal of effort to write your letter of 7 Inst. [July 7] which duly reached me yesterday and on that very account I appreciate it all the more and will not fail to at once reply to it. I have no doubt that once you made up your mind to write to me you did so with candor and sincerity - two qualities of which I am satisfied you are possessed and on that account I am ready to forgive you for all that has transpired."

"I am quite willing and desirous of burying into oblivion all what brought about and caused me so much grief. But before doing so I want to allude once more and for <u>the last time</u> to the cause which compelled me to inflict a punishment upon you which was a greater infliction upon me than you, who received it, and which was the culmination of aggravations accumulating to such a degree that I was almost driven to frenzy."

This was followed by several pages of self-pity and guilt-inducing portraits of his difficulties. An example: "I fully recollect, though I am quite willing to forget, when arriving from my trip over the tunnel line day after day, exposed to a broiling sun for hours, enveloped in an irritating and stifling dust, aggravated by all sorts of incidents during the day concerning the work and the men employed, coming home exhausted, literally worn out in body and in mind, though hungry unable to eat because too tired, and men still disturbing me even at my meals. And what should I have expected from children to show I had made every sacrifice, and who for the first time had an opportunity to repay their parents for all they had done, by simply extending a little love, and kindness and devotion at the opportune moment? I should have expected that such opportunities would have been hailed and welcomed and clenched; but it was not and I will not continue on to draw the sad picture any further." But he did. He repeated his forgiveness but lectured her about her lack of social graces including his oft-repeated suggestion to take dancing lessons "...not that I believe in the stupid practice of hopping about to music, but it cultivates social habits..."[57]

It didn't end there. In November, Sutro still in London, unleashed another barrage at his daughter: "Your cool business[-]like letters give me but little pleasure. I used to think you had a good sense but I find more and more that you lack a very essential quality and that is a balance wheel to keep your thoughts and actions within their proper equilibrium. If you cared for your father who has been so uniformly kind to you until you broke out into open rebellion, and who even now is willing to quite forgive you, you would not write the style of letters you do. There is not one sparkle of affection or devotion or consideration in them. I asked you in one of my previous letters to let me know what you are doing. You can truly comply with my request, but you simply reply to me in the same style as if I was enquiring the price of butter from a grocery merchant. Your letter covers 2½ very small pages with not 20 lines on a page. If you keep up this sort of selfish conduct, for it is part that, part stubbornness, you will make me lose what little affection I may still have for you and you will be left in the world lonely indeed, for I know you will have no friend. Hoping you will again become the kind open hearted, affectionate girl you once were I am your loving father...."[58]

Of course, that had been four years earlier. Now and into the future, Emma was Sutro's favorite which he made very little effort to hide. But Sutro could be cruel, even to Emma. The other children competed vigorously for his attention and approval. Clearly, he loved them all in different ways but none of the others displayed the intellectual aptitude he admired in Emma and it showed. He had received letters from Rosa, Katy (including a poem she wrote for his birthday and an extremely cute drawing of a small band playing a variety of musical instruments), Carla, and Edgar but "Charley has not written to me for some time – when I get home he will be sent to some good school." Charley ended up at St. Augustine College in Benicia, a military school, and Edgar entered St. Matthew's Boarding School in San Mateo.[59]

Summer was about to roll around and Emma would graduate from Vassar College. Sutro sent carfare to Emma for her return trip and issued incredibly detailed instructions: don't take any side trips to the lakes, try to have Adèle Aron accompany you – if not come alone, on and on. The family didn't wait for her to return but took a vacation in San Francisco. Katy, Rosa, Leah. and the smaller children joined Papa at the Baldwin Hotel, his favorite dwelling in town.[60]

The Sutro family spent most of the summer of 1877 at vacation hotels around Yosemite and in San Francisco. Emma had graduated from

Vassar; no one from the family had been able to attend, but Sutro arranged for Tunnel company secretary, Pelham Ames and his wife to be there representing him and the family. When Emma returned home, she obtained a Nevada Public Grammar School Teacher's License and a position as teacher in the Sutro town school.[61]

While spending some time with the family in San Francisco, Sutro wrote to Emma, "I am sorry you could not be down here for it would be quite a pleasant change from the lonely life at Sutro [Nevada]; I fully realize how monotonous it is up there, but you have taken your own choice, for I never intended you should waste your life in that desert county teaching a lot of filthy urchins." But, he added, "Things will change however before long. I have struggled all these years to reach a success of the affairs I had started to carry out, and think that my hopes will be realized before long."[62]

Later, Sutro arranged for a family gathering in Oakland, near Mills Seminary (now Mills College) where Emma was taking classes, to discuss and celebrate the decision regarding medical school. Joseph Aron, true to form, expressed his disagreement with the decision; Emma will "loose (sic) her best years in a vocation hard for ladies." Emma and Aron's daughter Lucie had been friends during Emma's years on the East Coast and she had spent time with the Aron family during vacations. He thought Emma should visit the Philadelphia Exposition if she could come to the East.[63] Consistent with Sutro's affection for modern technology, Tunnel Company offices in San Francisco were having telephones installed and Ames, the company's secretary, was satisfied with the progress.[64]

FINANCING THE TUNNEL – LATER

Thanks to Edward Dean Adams' enthusiasm, Richardson, Hill & Company made the required installment payment, ahead of schedule, and Ames reported receiving the signed agreement for optional stock sales. In rapid succession, a number of steps were taken to cement the relationship. Ames began issuing weekly reports on tunnel progress to Adams. Sutro appeared particularly anxious to please Adams whom he described as having pushed his partners into the agreement with "personal exertions." Adams reported hearing of aggressive moves to sell tunnel shares on the open market in Boston. Roswell C. Downer Jr., son of Adams' partner Cutler Downer, visited the tunnel and was hosted by Sutro. After Downer's return to Boston, Adams delighted in telling Sutro how pleased Downer had been with what he saw in Nevada. Adams volunteered to invest in a supporting railroad at the tunnel if needed. All of this had taken place in slightly more than a month from the initial agreement. On top of all that, Adams reported getting Boston newspapers involved in publicity for the tunnel and its stock. And, best of all, Richardson, Hill & Company would like to make payments in advance sometimes. Would that be all right? At the beginning of 1878, Ames was directed to have Sutro Tunnel attorneys Elliott J. Moore and Peter Williams each respond.[65]

Throughout his life, Adolph Sutro exhibited a gift for associating with outstanding people. Consistently, he hired intelligent, dedicated employees for positions of responsibility. His choices of bankers, attorneys, and other professionals were invariably the best available. The same extended to household help, gardeners, and laborers on his properties. He sought and understood quality in human performance and was never satisfied with less. Edward D. Adams fit Sutro's needs in many ways. He was intelligent and educated and had a passion for the latest technology. His interest in the tunnel resulted in an endless string of queries and conversations. He understood the brokerage business and, best of all, worked outside of New York with its intensely inbred environment where everyone seemed to know everyone else's business, and nothing remained secret for very long. Sutro needed privacy in his dealings. Stealth. Adams would turn out to be perfect.[66]

Sutro had sued all the Bonanza mining companies for conducting mining operations in the portions of subsurface allocated to the Tunnel Company and that had to be settled in the courts.[67] Meanwhile, reputable mining men continued to predict that the tunnel would intersect rich ore veins, but it never seemed to happen. Col. Brush, representing the McCalmont interests, was worried about the conflicts that would arise over possession of the ore no matter who found it. This was heading for another serious court battle either way.[68]

The Sutro Tunnel Company filed suit in the United States Circuit Court in Carson City against every mining claim within 2,000 feet on each side of the tunnel. An earlier dispute with the Occidental Mine had been settled in favor of the mining company but was under appeal for more than a year. The initial complaints were sent to the General Land Office of the United States Department of the Interior, specifying each of the offending mine properties. The mining interests and their loyal newspaper following were outraged by the charges and there were dire predictions of intense legal battles. That Sutro expected to succeed in these claims is difficult to believe, but it was surely a useful ploy in the continuous jostling between the parties and partial revenge for H.R. 1202. Col. Brush reported having met with Coulter who told him that the Savage mine superintendent expected the tunnel digging to strike ore in their vicinity in a few days. Savage would take legal action to "enjoin" the Tunnel Company from taking any ore out of the excavation. Brush thought "we should be prepared to do the same by them, until the question is settled to whom it is to belong." He also had heard from the Savage superintendent, Col. Milton Gillett, that their men were working eight-hour shifts in 154-degree conditions. "Why should our men complain so much in a lower temperature?" Brush had obviously never been down where the work was being done. The McCalmonts insisted upon having Brush as President, so Sutro kept quiet.[69]

The political atmosphere within the Tunnel Company Board of Trustees promulgated considerable ferment. Sutro was determined to maintain maximum control through selection of loyal friends and business associates. With the financial leverage their loan provided, the McCalmonts were equally intent upon exercising their power. The contest of wills had hardened over time. Board member John Brooks Felton had passed away in early 1877. Felton had been mayor of Oakland and active in real estate dealings. Sutro had acquired a large piece of property from Felton who also had exchanged real properties with fellow Tunnel Company board members Michael Reese and Henry Barroilhet. Barroilhet was appointed co-executor of Felton's will alongside the widow. Sutro struggled to have a say in selecting the replacement and succeeded when Alexander Weil took the post at the annual meeting – a full year after Felton's death. Weil had married into the Lazard Frères family and, in later years, became head of the firm leading it into its most glorious days. Lazard Frères was established as the tunnel company treasurer and Weil was chosen to represent the firm in that capacity. Adams praised the choice. In the same message, Adams suggested there would be a major change in his own life and followed up with another letter advising Sutro he was leaving Richardson, Hill & Company, and moving to New York, where he would be a partner in the prestigious brokerage and bank of Winslow, Lanier & Co. He also expressed annoyance with the Seligmans, whom he blamed for interfering in the stock arrangements at Richardson, Hill & Company. None of this new information was good news to Sutro. Even the McCalmonts didn't want New York brokerage connections. And Sutro had plans which couldn't stand too much exposure. But, Adams was solid and continued to communicate almost daily despite the move and disruption in his life. At the Sutro Tunnel Company's annual Board of Trustees meeting, with Alexander Weil a key voting member, an amendment to the loan agreement with McCalmont Brothers was approved extending the time of payments and taking some of the pressure off Sutro.[70]

Joseph Aron, the Lazard Frères cousin, was also disturbed by the actions of the Seligmans in their activities with Richardson, Hill & Company – he referred to them as "games." In an aside, he passed along what he thought to be news that Adams was leaving Boston for New York. He also offered sympathy over a serious accident which Leah had suffered, and he had heard about. Their letters crossed in the mail, so that Sutro's response ignored everything in Aron's letter; he issued extensive details about preparation and modification of certain stock certificates and brought Aron up to date on the status of negotiations with the mining companies. He pointed out that the tunnel had not been draining water for several months and that it was unlikely this would happen soon since most of the active mines were already deeper into the mountain than the tunnel and were pumping their water to the surface when they were able. Sutro did not expect to provide drainage until they reached the Savage and the other large Comstock mines at that level. The bulkhead was almost ready; Isaac Requa (superintendent of the Chollar-Potosi Mine) had visited the tunnel and "was rather astonished" at how substantial it was. Sutro bragged, "As to closing it, that is a question to be left open, and I do not propose to vitiate any of our legal rights until I am driven to it, and if I should shut that bulkhead they will have to plank down several million dollars before it will be opened again." He went on to point out that the Bonanza grouping of Mackay, Fair, and Flood realized this and its members were anxious to settle with him. He went on and on with aggressive, optimistic forecasts of the settlements he would demand. He wanted a 99-year contract. Sutro mentioned a "certain operation" he planned to discuss with Alexander Weil which

Aron knew about and which would result from an agreement being struck with the mines. No details were provided. And, interestingly, Adams had told Sutro the Seligmans wanted to sell some of their stock through him. "That shows how anxious they are to get rid of some of it. Please be careful not to say anything about this." In a postscript, Sutro revealed his recent approval for daughter Emma to attend medical school in Europe.[71]

The rising tide of animosity towards the Seligmans from all corners was not really surprising. Apparently, there had been significant disagreement between members of the Seligman family regarding the Sutro Tunnel. Abraham Seligman was thought to be very supportive and lobbied to provide financing and other forms of help. Joseph, the titular head of the bank, was not so sure. As progress was made on the tunnel through Mt. Davidson, Joseph had been slowly converted to the positive side. Tunnel Company insiders were irritated that the Seligmans were now looking for ways to unburden themselves of the stock at a time when completion of the tunnel was imminent. Sales of large quantities of stock would surely devalue the remaining shares.[72]

The mining companies had not been resting through this period. Through 1873 and 1874, twenty-three of them had formed a coalition to reject the earlier agreement with Sutro including the detested royalty. Eleven of those companies actually filed suits, which had languished in the court system. In June 1878, Attorney George R. Wells told the lead litigator for the mining companies, C.J. Hillyer, that he had presented changes to the complaints to Thomas H. Williams, president of the Savage Mining Company. Williams, formerly Attorney General of California, had seen nothing to amend in the document. Boards of trustees of several mines were meeting soon to agree on how to press forward with the new suits. Ordinarily, this would have meant bad news for the Tunnel Company. Not this time. Sutro had been gaining inch by inch in negotiations with key elements of the mine leadership. The Savage Mine had indicated willingness to withdraw its suit and abide by the original agreement. Chollar-Potosi, Hale & Norcross and Gould & Curry were reported to be following close behind. Col. Brush expected the mines which had weak returns recently to all fall in line. Only the ones with significant production were going to continue fighting for a smaller royalty. Sutro had also discussed the plan with Williams and was insistent upon having only one agreement rather than separate ones with each mine or small groups. The McCalmonts were being solicited for their approval. Concurrently, Sutro was framing alternative royalty structures in the event agreement could not be reached with the rich mines on the proposed offer. He showed them to Brush knowing that the Mc-Calmonts would soon be told and their concurrence could be obtained in advance.[73] The Sutro Tunnel Company's legal team, Elliott Moore and Peter Williams, had pursued a number of issues including those resulting from movement of the case from state court to the U.S. Supreme Court, which reduced the number of items that could be discussed during a trial. There were also attempts to separate the Savage Mine case from the rest; the decision was pending. Apparently, everything was on hold which did not please Sutro. He allowed his annoyance to creep into a letter to Col. Brush who responded with a seriously apologetic message. Very likely, Brush did not feel guilty but did his best to mollify Sutro diplomatically.[74]

Negotiations continued, albeit often informally or roundabout. Sutro was able to present a settlement offer to Jim Fair through the Savage superintendent's office. G.S. Robel, Milton Gillett's assistant, relayed a response from Fair indicating "he appeared very much interested" and would be at the Palace Hotel in San Francisco on June 25th and available to talk with Sutro on the subject. Whether they actually met on that occasion is not known. However, 6,000 miles away in London, the absence of a negotiated settlement was becoming more irritating to the McCalmonts every day. They had heard Sutro's promises about how the tunnel was going to turn into a highly profitable venture for several years and were becoming very impatient. The ongoing expenses of tunnel activities now required a $30,000 check every month. Meanwhile, Sutro suggested endless improvements and embellishments to the tunnel, which would need additional funds. The McCalmonts gave their assent to preparing a tram road to the Carson River and extending cultivation of alfalfa and barley on the Sutro farm property. But it also specified, "This means that you will complete connections with the Savage & commence drifting laterally & that you will make the best bargains you can with the Comstock mines." They closed the message with "we adhere to existing terms of Mortgage due 1891." That last line was a warning they were tired of sending money. That letter was sent July 2, 1878, and probably arrived before July 8th, the day connection was made to the Savage Mine.[75]

A week later, Sutro advised the McCalmonts that recent digging had struck mineral-bearing quartz averaging about ten to twenty dollars per ton. While not exceptional, this was encouraging, and he wanted to raise their spirits with any opportunity. His relationship with the financiers had deteriorated as none of the promised benefits had yet matured. At the same time, he had suggested a variety of improvements and enhancements, all of which would require additional advancements of cash on their part which they made very clear was out of the question. Sutro relied upon his ability to convince people in personal exchanges – face to face – which led him to decide on another trip to London for a visit with the McCalmonts. He shared that with Col. Brush who was not enthused about it. "I hardly know what to say about your making another visit to London as the reasons for and against it seem to be about even ... if left to my decision I think I should say that it would be better policy to accomplish as much as possible first by correspondence ... that might be as conducive as to bring an invitation ... which would place you under much better auspices than if you went without it."

The decision was made for Sutro. The McCalmonts cabled Brush that Robert McCalmont was gravely ill, that banking operations were at a virtual standstill, and that they insisted upon the immediate curtailment of expenses to the barest minimum. They were not telling Robert about the connection to the Savage Mine for fear of exciting him. They added: "...our present purpose is to impress upon you that now the

great work is a 'fait accompli'; you must no longer look to us for sup-
plies; on the contrary, you will admit that we may now fairly look forward to reaping the rich harvest you have always promised us in return
for our outlay to long deferred hopes. We are much disappointed that
your telegrams announcing the connexion (sic) with Savage drift, & the
finding of a body of ore have not been followed up by some later & more
encouraging news of substantial results." These sentiments could have
originated from Hugh McCalmont, his attorney G.M. Clements, or
Lewis R. Price, the president of McCalmonts' mining interests. The only
genuine admirer of the tunnel was Robert McCalmont and he was, for
all practical purposes, gone. Sutro knew there was trouble ahead.[76]

In a separate letter, the McCalmonts told Brush, "…We are aware of
Mr. Sutro's ambitious views, necessitating enormous expenditures in
the future, such as draining the tunnel, leveling the floor, new lines of
rails, smoothing the sides of the tunnel, extensive drifts, prospecting,
locomotive power, or wire ropes, &c &c all of which however necessary
they may be, we can no longer provide. He ought at the point of progress
he has now reached to be in a position to make speedy & distinct arrangements with the Mining Companies, which shall insure to us relief
from all such future burdens…The 1st August is now very near, & at the
moment of writing, seeing that the header is now finished, we are quite
undecided as to whether to pay the usual installment, or any part of it, or
not….Any further advances beyond that date are entirely uncertain &
you must not rely on obtaining them from us." They went on to suggest
that, in the absence of a negotiated agreement with the mines, all work
should be suspended. They concluded with the same message about
their disappointment.[77]

Adolph Sutro must have been alarmed by this turn of events and
just a few days later learned that Robert McCalmont had passed away. A
series of telegraphic messages among Sutro, Brush, and the McCalmonts
records Sutro's efforts to keep them in the game telling them that withdrawal was tantamount to "suicide." Predictably, their response was an
insistence upon reducing expenses. The projected loss of cash flow from

London had serious implications upon the future of the tunnel. The timing was awful. But Sutro wasn't going to yield that easily. There was a contract and he was going to enforce it. Adolph Sutro made plans to return to London. He sailed on the S.S. *Russia* on September 11th, met with the McCalmonts' representatives and came away with assurances that the payment agreement would be upheld and that the negotiated extension of payment schedule would continue. Upon his return to America, the Tunnel Company board met and passed a resolution restating all these details and Ames, the company's secretary, was instructed to forward a copy to the McCalmonts.[78]

Back in September 1875, the Union Consolidated Mine had applied for a patent on its Comstock claim which had been issued by the Department of Interior's General Land Office. Some two years later, the Sierra Nevada Silver Mining Company, the oldest claimant on the Comstock, filed suit asking that the patent issued to Union Consolidated be "recalled and canceled" due to a dispute over claim areas. In August 1878, the General Land Office issued its ruling in favor of Sierra Nevada and directed the surrender of Union Consolidated Mine's patent. The Sutro Tunnel Company had also issued counter-claims to numerous patent requests where claims were adjacent to the ground ceded to the tunnel by Congress, and tunnel attorneys Shellabarger & Wilson had been on "automatic notice" for both patent applications and decisions. They had been waiting for years for news about Sutro's claim against the Occidental Mine. While encouraging, the Sierra decision was merely enticing to Sutro when he heard about it. But, just a few days later, the Occidental case was settled in favor of the tunnel claim. A dozen or more still awaited resolution.[79]

Material and labor costs for the drain and the two drift excavations began to surge exceedingly. Sutro let Brush know he expected to need $100,000 they did not have by early June and was trying every way possible to acquire it. Once he mentioned the possibility of a loan, Brush jumped upon him, pointing out what a negative effect public disclosure would have upon the stock. There must be another way. Meanwhile, the

McCalmonts wrote a congratulatory message cheering the settlement with the mining companies but reminding Sutro that "we cannot deviate from our fixed determination of not advancing more money." Sutro responded with an offer to modify the existing mortgage to a new eight percent, $2 million bonded mortgage in which Sutro would participate in a small share of several hundred thousand dollars. Their telegraphic rejection was swift and blunt, "Superintendent proposes reduction of option; inform him McCalmont Brothers & Co. absolutely decline. He can sell his free shares." Sutro had hoped to extend the schedule of payments on the current loan to free up cash for ongoing expenses. Now, a loan was the only way to continue the work. Cahn and Weil at Lazard Frères had opened the door to the possibility of a loan and Sutro entered. Terms of a $150,000 loan were negotiated under which Sutro would put up 50,000 shares of his own tunnel stock as collateral. The loan, finally concluded in mid-June, was to be paid back with interest in mid-October by which time cash flows from the mining companies would be sufficient to continue the work. Interestingly, the loan appears to have been made by David Cahn himself rather than the Lazard bank. In the interim, while all these financial issues were being settled, two hundred miners and seventy-five carpenters had been laid off from the tunnel crew. The Tunnel Company's secretary Ames had tried without success to cancel orders for some very expensive structural items and Lazard cousin Aron had delivered another message of exasperation. Sutro explained that he "did not deserve to be put in such an akward (sic) position" and expressed his "hope I will never have to go through again what I did the last 2 month (sic) – if I would I really believe it would make me 25 years older." He said he was leaving for a vacation at Capon Springs, West Virginia, taking his wife and daughter Emma with him.[80]

Back in San Francisco, news of the Lazard Frères loan had gone full circle. Aron had telegraphed instructions from New York to Alex Weil laying out a schedule of payments against the Tunnel Company overdraft. Weil was having difficulty getting Aron to understand the connection between the money and the 50,000 shares of stock suddenly dropped in his lap. Weil had sent several return messages patiently outlining the conditions under which they could be sold and trying to lower Aron's anxiety over that transaction and the transfer of stocks from the McCalmonts to Kidder, Peabody & Company. Obviously distraught over the turns of events, Aron told Weil "I shall make a full report of all I had to do for Sutro Tunnel Co. in order to raise the money I have; they may hereafter employ somebody else to attend to Sutro Tunnel Co. matters." Weil invited messages from Sutro to confirm details of the financial arrangements. He sent out a list of new cipher codes for use in telegrams including the name "Lesseps" for Adolph Sutro and "Tempest" for Joseph Aron. The choices were meaningful; both the flattery and the irony were clear. But most importantly, the pressure of finding cash to pay ongoing expenses for the immediate future was suddenly relieved. The same day, Sutro told Ames excitedly that the water wheel they had built at the tunnel exit was working perfectly and was driving a belt system connected to the machine shop. He also wrote to Aron that everything was going great, that the work force was down to 150 men, and that Aron should go sell some of his stock to cover more of the debts. Sutro was exultant.[81]

Around him, things were not so smooth. A seriously negative communication from the McCalmonts alarmed Sutro. They expressed once more their disappointment over the lack of financial benefits following connection with the mines and signing of the agreements. "We certainly had grounds for expecting more hopeful prospects after all the effort & after successfully reaching the Comstock when such glowing results were predicted & assured, but it would appear now that the difficulties to be surmounted are greater than ever, & the U. States public can have little confidence in the eventual success of the undertaking inasmuch as they shew (sic) themselves entirely indifferent about taking any pecuniary interest in it, as evidenced by the slowness of sales of shares in New York." They went on: "The only financial propositions which your letter [Aug 9, 1879] makes appear limited to: our reducing the limit on our

52

stock, which you have always insisted upon was so valuable; to water our mortgage, for which we have paid out of pocket hard dollars; or, to advance more money; all of which propositions are out of the question." Sutro had offered to visit again which they rejected as useless. They closed saying there would not be any more financial help from them. Sutro didn't get around to responding for more than a month. He had other problems. Money was just pouring out of the treasury to cover construction expenses and he had to find another source. He went to New York but, just prior to his arrival, a block of 100,000 shares of company-held stock was sold. This provided cash to make the periodic payment on the Lazard Frères loan. He was quick to tell McCalmonts of the sale to blunt some of their criticism over the weakness of the market for shares. He planned to sell some of his own shares to develop cash when needs exceeded what was in the treasury. He asked that they send the 350,000 shares of his, which individual members of their firm hold in trust, to Kidder, Peabody & Company in New York in the event they are needed. He also explained that "…the reason we have no more income as yet is that during the 3 or 4 years that mining co[mpanie]s held back, developments were so retarded as to reduce the production far below any known heretofore."[82]

$\mathcal{S}$even

THE MINE CONNECTION IS COMPLETED

The Savage miners and the Sutro Tunnel workers had been hearing each other's diggings and explosions for some time getting progressively louder and it was clear the connection was imminent. Several newspaper accounts tell of the historic juncture being completed. On July 8, 1878, a small drill hole had penetrated from one cavity to the other. A significant rush of hot air blew from the tunnel side into the mine cavity and out the vertical shaft to the outside. Many had wondered which way the draft would develop when the two were no longer separated. Sutro had told people over and over that the tunnel would provide ventilation to the mines; he had been correct. The flow of air was extremely noisy and the excited conversations between men on both sides could only be carried on by shouting. Sutro was notified and wired Savage Mine Superintendent Milton Gillett, "Should your men succeed in knocking a drill hole through let them stop and not enlarge it until I am fully notified. There should be ample time given for your men and ours to retire, for I am afraid a column of several thousand feet in length of hot, foul air, suddenly set in motion, might prove fatal to the men." This was followed by another dispatch, "The men report a drill hole knocked through near the north side. Put in your blast and let your men retire to the incline. Will be at the header at 11 o'clock."

Sutro arrived close to eleven o'clock and the charge was ignited blowing a five-foot-square opening between the two tunnels. Despite the massive flow of hot, foul air roaring through the hole, workers on both sides proceeded to enlarge the opening. Accompanied by his two sons, Charles and Edgar, Adolph Sutro climbed through the opening and greeted Gillett and his party of well-wishers. Beer had been ordered and the Savage miners went to the surface in the elevator cages to enjoy fresh air along with their drinks. Adolph Sutro and the boys returned to the town of Sutro through the tunnel.[83]

The next few days were spent celebrating the accomplishment. Cannon firing and bonfires were all around. A visiting party from the town of Sutro made the trip through the tunnel all the way to Virginia City. The group included Adolph, Kate, Charles, Edgar, and Carla Sutro, Joseph Aron, Sutro Tunnel Supervisor Jack Bluett, Peter Savage, the new company doctor C.B. Brierly, Sutro's personal secretary Frank S. Young, *Sutro Independent* editor Frank Mercer, and Aaron A. Sargent, U.S. Senator from California, Chairman U.S. Senate Committee on Mine and Mining, superintendent of the Comstock Mine in Virginia City.[84] The group traveled in ore cars probably pulled by mules. The air was still hot and foul, and one report told of having sent clothing ahead to change upon arrival. Prior to making the trip, Sutro had wired Gillett to let him know the party of ladies and gentlemen would be arriving. Gillett responded that he would solicit permission from the head office in San Francisco but when the Sutro party arrived at the Savage, they were told permission would not be forthcoming. Sutro led his group into the Savage mine and up the shaft to Virginia City streets above. The issue of refusal would be dealt with later. By the following day, the tunnel air had cooled significantly, and the ventilation was pleasant – but only in the mines directly connected to the tunnel.[85]

That day, all the miners and townspeople gathered at Sutro's home where he made a speech "thanking them for their kindness" and speaking of the "hardships and dangers miners have to pass through in order to earn their days' (sic) wages." He contrasted their situation with "the comforts and elegance enjoyed by those in power in the mines." He was quick to point out he would not censure those who enjoyed comforts "so long as the miners were fully paid for their labor, and [were] allowed all the possible benefits of fresh air to breathe while they were laboring" and had "the means to escape in case of a catastrophe." His speech evoked three hearty cheers for Adolph Sutro. The shift of tunnel miners was given the day off and Sutro arranged for drinks to be provided at all the bars in the town of Sutro. The report that "there was not a drunk, nor a fight, or a brawl of any kind" was probably inaccurate.[86]

Accolades for Sutro's accomplishment came from far and wide but he must have been most gratified by the words of the *Gold Hill News* which had so long opposed and scorned the tunnel.

"There is only one Adolph Sutro in the world. There is only one man in the world possessed of his persistent, obstinate, dogmatic concentration of will and purpose…" and "…he has had more to contend with than any other man ever did under similar circumstances." Continuing, "His franchise and his contract were repudiated and opposed by the ablest legal talent, even in the halls of Congress, and throughout the country he was held up to scorn and popular derision as an unprincipled adventurer, using the people's money for his own benefit…" It went on ending with "All hail, Sutro, the only Sutro; King of the indomitables." This was great praise indeed from what had been the principal organ of the enemy.[87]

That month, The Sutro Tunnel Company and the Julia Consolidated Mining Company came to terms regarding use of the tunnel for removal of water, transportation of ores for processing and access fees for employees of the mine traveling to the Julia work areas. By the terms of an earlier agreement, Sutro was required to complete a branch connection from the main tunnel to the Julia mine. For the first time, The Sutro Tunnel Company could anticipate collecting fees for functional uses of the tunnel. It was not really ready for that, but this was a necessary and very satisfying first step.[88]

All of these uplifting events put a new light on the value of the tunnel company stock. A special Board of Trustees meeting was arranged and a new board lineup with new company officers was arranged. The new president was to be Elliott Moore, Sutro's attorney and confidant, elbowing Brush out of the top role. Of course, Brush and Thomas Wedderspoon, the Cross & Company partner and McCalmont associate, remained on the board. Others included Edward M. Hooper, J.J. Williams, F.F. Low and Adolph's cousin Gustav Sutro of the financial firm. Adolph Sutro retained his position as Superintendent of the Company. After the election, resolutions were passed establishing limits of borrowing, confirming the extension of loan repayments to McCalmonts and "empowering you [Adolph Sutro] to list the shares of the company at the New York Stock Exchange." This last item was a radical departure from policy that had been enforced previously by the McCalmonts. At long distance, using a combination of telegraphy and United States mail, Sutro and the corporate secretary Ames worked arduously to have new, elegant certificates prepared appropriate for use on the New York Exchange. Signatures of the appropriate officers and a seal of the Company were required for proper registry. Election of a Registrar of the company was filled by Lazard Frères who would receive the munificent sum of $50 per month for its efforts. By mid-November, the New York Stock Exchange had accepted the application pending receipt of new certificates. Almost immediately thereafter, the market in mining stocks was hit by a "panic" [sudden drop in prices] for which the source could not be determined. Ames reported that Gustav Sutro was on top of the problem; he believed "the bad look of the mines to be the cause." Others were laying the blame on Mr. Flood, but no one really knew. In New York, Sutro felt helpless and waited for Gustav to come up with answers. [89]

The trouble, which had national implications, had originated in Virginia City. A prominent local figure, John Skae, had co-managed the Utah Mine with Jim Fair for a dozen years and made considerable money. He had gained some fame from a party he tendered in late August for about 150 of his friends and associates which Alfred Doten described as "the best entertainment ever known on the Pacific Coast." Editor Doten wrote a feature article in the *Gold Hill News* the day following the event and was generous in praise. Just weeks later, Skae was feuding with Jim Flood over ownership issues relative to the Sierra Mine. Skae, also a long-time member of the Virginia City Water Company board, had been in New York on water company business while a sudden surge in the stock price tempted Flood to invest heavily – so heavily in fact that he assumed control of the company from Skae. When Skae returned, the stock went through several iterations of rising and falling price and Skae lost $100 per share in one day. Other mining stocks followed but in far less violent fashion. Skae was nearly ruined financially and only recovered by staying with the water company until it produced substantial earnings. The mining panic ended in a short time but, as Jim Flood was reported to have said, "There are not quite so many millionaires on the street as there were yesterday."[90]

Brush and Ames worked feverishly to prepare the new certificates for the New York Stock Exchange. Problems with sealing the package and a late delivery by Wells Fargo caused further delays in getting the materials back to the Wells Fargo shipping office. The following morning, Brush took a boat from San Francisco to Sacramento to catch the overland mail.

During the same week as the stock panic, Virginia City was visited by Thomas A. Edison. Following a tour Edison was given of the Consolidated Virginia Mine, Alfred Doten recorded having been introduced to the great electrical inventor. Sutro had been trying to establish contact with Edison to arrange for lighting in the tunnel. When the connection was made with the Savage mine, the resulting draft extinguished a large number of torchlights and this became a repeated problem. Electric lights would provide a solution. Later in the year, Sutro tried again only to learn that Edison was too busy until after December 15. Sutro put it on the back burner. There were too many higher priority issues in front of him.[91]

Tops on his list was obtaining sufficient cash to cover ongoing tunnel costs including loan repayments, salaries, and commissions to brokers on stock sales and purchases. Sutro kept demanding that the trustees pass a resolution giving him the authority to sell the company-held shares of stock plus $25,000 cash outright for commissions and the expenses he ran up himself in travel and living and family needs. There was great resistance from London over this which ended up influencing Brush and Wedderspoon against the idea. However, the trustees did vote to send 108,000 of "old" shares to Lazard Frères in New York giving Sutro the option to use them at $5 per share. Sutro cabled Brush to have the trustees reduce the option price to $4 ½ per share which was more consistent with the then current price. He went on, "Liberal disbursements needed at once. Telegraph through the Sec[retery] that it is done. No expense is too great to insure success. I am satisfied with McCalmont now." But not for long – just two days later Sutro cabled again reporting having sold 3,100 shares of stock in New York and added, "I am prepared to act independently now; McCalmont repudiates further payment of installment £3000." Of almost equal importance were the payments from the Julia Consolidated Mining Company, which were absolutely essential for tunnel operations to continue. Although Ames was worried that the money was a few days late, the current payment was made.[92]

Another serious situation arose when Isaac Requa, superintendent of the Chollar-Potosi Mine, gave notice they would begin pumping water into the tunnel by the end of the first week in January some twenty-five days hence. The tunnel was not ready for that. Sutro instructed Brush to have the lawyers respond and to advise the Chollar-Norcross-Savage interests that they would be notified when the tunnel could accept water. This was all part of the negotiation process – putting pressure on the opposition to gain advantage in the financial dispute. Sutro was good at that and did not flinch from taking up the gauntlet. He was always careful to use all the professional help on his team – Elliott Moore, Shellabarger & Williams, Judge Solomon Heydenfeldt, and Judge Jeremiah Black. He generally knew as much about a given subject as any of his advisors, but made certain to obtain their assent on proposed steps to be taken. At this point, he judged it to be a war of words and he thought there was little prospect it would escalate beyond that.[93]

The constant need to shore up the McCalmonts had placed great demands upon him physically, as he crossed America and the Atlantic to talk with them. Keeping Aron happy with the stock program was challenging especially when Sutro needed to invade his own holdings to produce cash. All this interfered significantly with Sutro's personal life. He hadn't been home in months and his family life was surely far below the level they would have considered acceptable. His wife Leah needed cash from time to time and he was hard pressed to find it without a dependable draw on a cash account which he lacked. Ames' six year-old son, Worthington, was seriously sick with pneumonia, and so the company secretary was absent from the office for large periods of every day. Tunnel progress, though impressive, had not produced the financial results he had predicted – there was precious little silver in tunnel scraps. Even the Julia mine assays were extremely disappointing after their great efforts and congenial relationship. Lawsuits were stalled. Negotiations with the mining companies were at a standstill despite one agreement and the rumors in newspapers. Even the connection of the tunnel to the combination shaft, despite the hoopla attending the event, produced nothing genuinely positive for Adolph Sutro or the Tunnel Company. After a series of successes, the company stock dropped from $5 per share and languished somewhere between $4 and $4.50 per share. The tunnel was not ready to receive large quantities of water from the mines, but the mining companies were threatening to deliver water for disposal almost immediately. Sutro's plans for disposing of stock were not going smoothly. At a time when he should have been on top of the world, enjoying the fruits of many years of incredible difficulties, he was still wrestling with problems in many quarters. However, if there was one characteristic in Sutro's makeup that would stand out it was perseverance. When he saw a goal, he went after it – nothing stopped him.

Eight

HARD TIMES

It is not then absurd to surmise that in addition to the known lines of quartz deposits there may be some unknown ones the faint outcroppings of which are concealed by the shingle and decomposition of the surface. The determination of this and similar possible facts in this district cannot be made until the Sutro Tunnel section receives proper study... ... In any event, the known lines of ore deposition and the number of comparatively small quartz seams running in various directions, should teach us to regard this whole district as one which may in future support very widely extended mining operations, and perhaps a metallurgical industry of much greater scope and complexity than it does at present.

John Adams Church, Professor of Mining
The Ohio State University, 1879

As 1879 dawned, Adolph Sutro learned, with relief and pleasure, that young Worthington Ames had survived his deathly illness and was "out of danger and doing well." Not so Tunnel Company trustee Edward M. Hooper who passed away on New Year's Day. Now, there would be a new election for a replacement trustee but very likely not before the annual meeting on March 1st. Other changes were equally ominous.[95]

In late December 1878, Kidder, Peabody & Company had notified Sutro that 215,000 shares of Sutro Tunnel Company stock belonging to the McCalmont brothers had been transferred to the New York office of the brokerage and were being held in trust subject to Sutro's decision to acquire them for "$5 United States gold coin per share."[96] Obviously surprised by this turn of events, Sutro, in New York during early January, questioned the authority for the transfer and received a cold, blunt repetition from Kidder, Peabody & Company.[97] He fired off a letter to the McCalmonts including his suspicion that they contemplated selling their shares which he considered a mistake. He went into extensive detail about how completion of the tunnel was imminent and that all the rewards they had waited for were coming their way soon and that they should remain involved for their own good.[98] It is unlikely that Sutro really expected wonderful things to happen soon; he was probably doing what he considered necessary to keep the financiers in the game.

However, the following day must have brought him further news on the subject and he sent an angry letter to the London firm suggesting very strongly that it appeared they were about to back out of their arrangement with the Tunnel company.[99] In that event, Sutro would have been destroyed financially. Concurrently, Ames was telling the mining companies that the tunnel was nearly ready to accept water flow from their shafts; unfortunately, some of them thought it was already able and that Sutro was stalling intentionally to bias discussions about the royalty. Ames spoke directly with Albion Harmon, president of the Chollar Potosi Mine, who pleaded that Requa, the mine's superintendent, really believed the tunnel was ready to accept water when he wrote the letter demanding flow access. Harmon requested an approximate date which Ames could not give him; wisely, Ames told him that he would pass the question to his superiors.[100]

Aron continued issuing his obsessive warnings about the consequences awaiting any sale of stock by Sutro. "You must bind yourself as demanded, and others will do same – What confidence can people have if you alone retain right to sell." Dealing with Aron was becoming painful.[101]

Likewise, the McCalmont Brothers & Company: A new letter from London expressed their lack of surprise that tunnel stock sales were slow in New York, but they had no expectations of anything better in that area. They bore down upon the necessity to enter negotiations with the mining companies immediately and settle on a program for the future. Further, they didn't believe that Adolph Sutro should be involved in those negotiations – that a third party "might pave the way.... Failing arrangements with the mining companies we see nothing but to suspend the works until the various interests can come to an understanding." The letter concluded with a contentious paragraph quibbling over details of what they did or did not say prior to Sutro's last visit. "You must admit that we have been mainly instrumental in bringing the work to what we were always led to believe was its goal – the Comstock Lode. The enterprise must now stand on its own merits & we have no doubt of a fair success if only conciliatory & sensible views are adopted by all parties interested." They did not have to add that they considered Sutro to be non-conciliatory and not sensible; it fairly leaped off the page and he didn't like it. A similar letter with the same sentiments expressed in almost the same words was addressed to Brush; it concluded ominously with "we shall never consent that the company should run into debt" and "If the worst comes to the worst the work [meaning the tunnel] will have to be utilised (sic) as a drain & revenue obtained from the various Mining Companies benefitting from it."[102]

A few days later, John Kiernan, who owned a newspaper watchdog service, sent Sutro an article having wide circulation that announced the first flow of water from mineshafts into the tunnel. Isaac Requa's letter had not been an idle threat. In the newspapers, this was interpreted as "war has been declared between the mines and the tunnel company."[103] If that wasn't enough, the attorneys for the Savage Mine warned Sutro against blocking the drainage and threatened legal consequences. An injunction was obtained restraining the Tunnel Company from installing a bulkhead or other restriction to the flow of water from the mine. When Sheriff Charles Williamson went to the tunnel to serve the injunction, he found eighteen miners at work constructing a bulkhead and all of them were arrested and jailed. Sutro's Assistant Superintendant, H.H. Sheldon, was also held briefly. The miners remained in jail over the weekend, but were released on bail the following Monday morning.

The next day, February 4th, newspapers reported conclusion of a compromise between the Tunnel Company and the mining companies in which Sutro agreed to accept a $1 royalty on ores yielding less than $40 of silver content per ton. The $2 per ton royalty on richer ores would be maintained. Apparently, though not yet signed, an agreement had been reached and the water could flow.[104]

The report proved to be premature. Once again, negotiations stalled, and the new agreement was not signed. Two weeks went by without incident until late afternoon on February 16th when pumps of the Hale and Norcross mine sent hot water through the tunnel without warning. Miners and mules were driven from the tunnel in panic causing numerous injuries. The pumping continued for two days endangering structural integrity of the tunnel and preventing any work. The 120 tunnel employees were forced into idleness. Sutro furiously accused the mining companies of a "bluff game to force him to accede to their demands." He reported sixty inches of water at 130 degrees Fahrenheit flowing through the tunnel.[105]

Sutro had returned to the West Coast in late January and spent a week with most of the family at the Baldwin Hotel in San Francisco. His wife Leah enjoyed a whole month there with little Carla. While in the East, he had tried to get daughter Emma back west so that she could join them, but he was overtaken by events – too many things were happening at one time and he told her to stay in New York instead. She would have an opportunity to come home at the end of the school year in time to attend her sister Rosa's graduation.[106]

In mid-March, Lloyd Tevis, president of Wells, Fargo & Co., finally succeeded in arbitrating an agreement between the Tunnel Company and the mines exactly as Sutro had framed it back in early February. Both sides compensated Tevis for his efforts; the Sutro Tunnel Company paid him 1,000 shares of stock.[107] Of course, that didn't end the pressure from the mining companies to begin utilizing the tunnel for drainage. In early April, Col. Brush reported to Sutro that the Julia Mine was pumping hot water into the tunnel and suggested they be forced to stop. He had conversed with John Livingston of Julia Mine who pleaded they had no alternative and had not been able to convince Sutro to install a small runoff they could use until the major drain was completed. They were threatening to sue. Brush was ready to knuckle under to the mine's pressure suggesting that Sutro install a temporary relief for them. Instead, Sutro sent a response telling Julia Mine that no more water would be received after noon on April 15th. He promised completion of the drainage system in ten weeks by a "force of over 700 men being engaged thereupon by day and by night."[108]

About then, Sutro received a letter from Aron telling about Ignatz Steinhart having bad-mouthed the tunnel and causing a sale of tunnel stock by Steinhart's brother who was a partner of Aron's in Weil & Company. A long-time member of the Eureka Benevolent Society, Ignatz Steinhart was an influential banker in San Francisco who had been a member of the Sutro Tunnel Board of Trustees for several years. This was a damaging turn of events. Coupled with the apparent collapse of the McCalmonts' confidence, Adolph Sutro concluded he must make plans to get out; it might not become necessary, but he had to be prepared for the eventuality. And, it had to be done very carefully.[109]

Two weeks later, Theodore Sutro reported having sold 900 shares of brother Adolph's Tunnel stock at 4 3/8 less commission of 1/8. The check was enclosed for which Theo requested a receipt. Theo, now thirty-four years old, still single and living with their mother, split his time between working for Adolph, working for the Tunnel Company, and practicing law on his own in New York. As Theo was the "baby" in the family, Adolph had a habit of treating him more like a son than a brother and Theo responded by following Adolph's directions precisely. In the same letter, Theo expressed admiration for Joseph Aron's efforts to promote investor interest in the stock and, thereby, "pump up" the price. Additionally, he had spent ten or twelve days in Washington in the early part of the year as a Congress-watcher for Adolph. This letter included a second request for payment of some minor expenses he incurred on the trip. Despite these traces of immaturity, Adolph hoped he could be counted upon for discretion about the stock sale. For Adolph Sutro, this was perhaps the beginning of the end of his Sutro Tunnel life.[110]

Aron's next letter included a scolding – Theodore had shown him Adolph's telegram instructing the sale of an additional 6,000 shares of stock. Aron expressed "astonishment" at this turn of events and went on to detail all the efforts he had taken to keep the price of the stock up and the risks he had taken by issuing interest payments before he had the cash to back them up. "Why you should want just at this time to raise money on your shares passes my comprehension." He pleaded that he had not sold any of his and would have to buy up shares that were sold anywhere to maintain the price. He went on and on about who was selling shares and the problems it caused for him. Aron also chided Sutro for not having issued enthusiastic messages to the national press describing progress toward completion of the tunnel and the imminent availability of the drain. He had asked him to do so previously without success.[111]

Shortly thereafter, Sutro's personal secretary, Frank Young, sent a letter in Sutro's name to James Simonton of the Associated Press outlining construction of the drain, growth of the town of Sutro, opening of the Sutro Opera House. and the concert performed there by Mrs. Murtha Porteous, "the new prima donna." The forecasted date for accepting water flow was July 4th. "Millions of tons of low grade ore, passed by in former times, will be made available and it is expected that one thousand additional stamps [ore crushers] at the mouth of the Sutro Tunnel may be kept going for half a century to come."[112] Frank Young's message to the Associated Press really didn't tell the whole story about the town of Sutro. The expanding possibilities from use of the tunnel promoted growth in a number of ways. John Mackay and Jim Fair, two of Sutro's long-time antagonists, visited the town and returned to Virginia City using the tunnel and access through the Savage mine. Local newspapers reported they "expressed themselves highly pleased with what they saw, and marveled at the magnitude and extent of the work itself." The report went on to say "the town of Sutro is building up, and presents a scene of much activity. The place is thronged with people, town lots are in demand and buildings are going up in every direction." They concluded that "eventually, this will be the largest town in the State." William Hewlett, a local real estate trader, leased his sixteenth piece of property in town. Edward Adams inquired of Adolph Sutro what kind of business was needed in town; he had plans to build a brick building upon his lot and wanted to design it appropriately. The Sutro Tunnel Company offices were being surveyed for installation of telephones and, in May, the project commenced. Another newspaper reported that Silver City was almost depopulated; Sutro was now the major town in Lyon County. All of this was happening before the tunnel drain was completed; ore tailings had not yet become the major source of mining operations.[113]

Sutro had to mollify Aron. Keeping the share price up was certainly going to be worthwhile. But, how many times had he told Aron that the sales were necessary to get cash to cover interest payments? The nature of their personal attachment underwent wide variations during the tunnel project but never more extreme than they were about to see.[114]

The month or so between mid-May and mid-June found Sutro performing like the proverbial juggler with nine balls in the air at one time. A great deal happened within his world, much of which was affected by geographic separations and the attendant delays in communication and messages crossing each other on the same subject. Rosa was about to graduate from Mills Seminary in northern California. Sutro had hoped Emma could come west and that the whole family, himself included, could attend. Events prevented any of that from happening as planned. Emma was forced to remain in New York at Madame Olea Da Silva's Finishing School for Young Ladies. Sutro became wrapped up in negotiations on three fronts at once making his attendance impossible. Colonel Brush stood in for the family at Mills.[115]

Aron had purchased the 6,000 shares Theodore offered for sale in Adolph's name. While doing that, he learned that "a great many shares [were] sold here in P.W. Ames name as Trustee. Whose were they?" His letters were shrill; he seemed to be on the verge of exploding with anger and frustration. Sutro contacted Ames and asked whose shares he was selling. Ames was offended – he had already received a nasty telegraph message from Aron on the subject. Ames explained that the only shares he had ever sold were 5,000 of Sutro's, 125 as administrator of the estate of deceased Tunnel board member Edward Hooper, 250 for an employee of the tunnel and ten shares of his "little boy's." He insisted that Sutro tell Aron the same.[116]

Another distraction for Sutro in the same period was the law suit that Henry Foreman had brought against the Giant Powder Company concerning his injuries from detonation of the exploder cap many months earlier. Foreman, now virtually blind, was convinced that he had an iron-clad case which the manufacturer would want to settle rather than permit a jury to decide. He was wrong. Sutro had a vested interest in seeing the case settled as the tunnel company was providing substantial portions of Foreman's subsistence. So, Sutro attempted to intercede with Julius Bandmann, the local representative of Giant Powder and a principal of the company, to arrange a payoff to Foreman. This was done through Ames who had day-to-day contact with Bandmann and enjoyed a good relationship with him. Ames was less than enthusiastic about the possibility. Earlier, Bandmann had told Ames, "he would not be likely to arrange the matter....it was a matter of principle not to compromise any suits but to let them go to trial and fight them out as otherwise they [Giant Powder Co.] would be liable to no end of trouble from parties who thought they could be squeezed." Bandmann didn't budge.[117]

Sutro's estimate of the time to complete the drain system had been accurate and Elliott Moore passed the word to Sutro that they would be ready to accept water from mines on July 1st. Moore and Brush suggested that some test be devised to assure success of the drain at least a couple of days before the contractual start. Moore also raised the possibility of sending notices to the mines about the go-ahead date but offered his opinion that this was probably unnecessary. Sutro thought otherwise and wired "Let Mr. Moore forward notices to mining companies at once." Regional newspapers carried copies of the notice inviting mines to test the drain in advance and to be ready for full utilization at 6:00 a.m. on June 30th. Water from the Savage Mine and the Julia Mine was sent through the system successfully and several others released their flows on the appointed day. The drain capability of the tunnel was a success. Water level in one of the flooded mines was lowered one hundred feet in eight hours. As water poured out of the tunnel and cascaded through the boxes arranged on the streets of the town and continued downhill into the Carson River, residents migrated toward Sutro's mansion where he and his family and the key employees watched the spectacle. Sutro obliged with a lengthy speech concluding by saying that the engineering part of the tunnel surpassed all expectations. Bonfires and beer were found in abundance. As usual, Sutro paid for the beer.[118]

The crushing events of the past months – scrambling for money, endless negotiations on various issues, personality conflicts, almost continual travel cross-country and overseas – could be put aside for a while. It was time for Sutro to enjoy the fruits of his labors even if for only a brief moment. But, it was not to be. Over the more than ten years he had been working to get the tunnel designed, approved, funded and built, Sutro had spent long segments of time away from home. One period, from late 1872 until the end of 1873, he was away from the West Coast more than an entire year. Though she mentioned it, Leah Sutro never complained about that in letters to Emma and Rosa. Further, she never hinted at suspicions about Adolph Sutro's faithfulness. But, it surely must have crossed her mind. Successful men always attracted women and being thousands of miles from home while living in first-class hotels provided opportunities to lead an adventurous and risqué life stealthily. When traveling, Sutro always used the services of an amanuensis so the numerous breakfasts for two at New York, Washington, London and Paris hotels were easy to explain. Very likely, Leah never saw those bills anyway.[119]

In the spring of 1878, Gilbert and Sullivan's newest operetta *H.M.S. Pinafore* had its first performance and became the rage of London. It didn't take long before traveling casts were formed by the D'Oyly Carte Opera Company and launched to the corners of the English-speaking world including, of all places, Virginia City, Nevada. Adolph and Leah Sutro and some of their children traveled from their home in Sutro and registered at the International Hotel in Virginia City to see a performance of the show. Earlier that week, a Mrs. George Allen had come from Washington, D.C. and was staying at the same hotel. Actually, the name, "Mrs. Allen" was a pseudonym for her real name – Miss Hattie Trundle. Within a short time, the lady had become a local curiosity owing to her elaborate black dresses and over-abundant jewelry. She acquired the nickname of "the $90,000 diamond widow." A bizarre episode occurred at the hotel; the plethora of newspaper accounts diverge significantly.

It should be noted that newspapers of the period often reflected views of a single individual. They were politically and socially biased to favor friends or condemn enemies of the publishers. Adolph Sutro did not have many allies in the publishing world of Nevada; the only newspaper he could count upon for encouraging or positive accounts was his own *Sutro Independent*. What actually happened on the night of July 3, 1879 isn't clear. One account had Adolph and the attractive lady caught by Leah in "improper relations;" a second report indicated they had merely dined together in her room on quail and champagne – that Sutro maintained they had just been introduced; others claimed he had "long been intimate with the woman, their relations having been established in the East" while they made a show of just meeting; that Sutro had told his wife he no longer cared for her and wanted to live away from her. What was described fairly consistently was the fact that Leah Sutro broke into the room where Adolph and Mrs. Allen were together and attempted to attack the lady with a champagne bottle. Fortunately, she was stopped, but she persisted in verbal abuse of Mrs. Allen and accused her husband of infidelity.

Most of the community rallied around Leah Sutro or, to be more accurate, against Adolph Sutro as published accounts of the incident seldom suggested he was innocent. Unquestionably, Leah Sutro saw something she didn't like and reacted violently. However, it is difficult to imagine that a man of Adolph Sutro's intelligence would run the risk of exposure with his wife and some of his children that close by. Despite the likelihood that so much written reportage was inaccurate, the connubial relationship of Adolph and Leah Sutro ended. As we shall see, the marriage survived but they never lived together again. Equally interesting is the fact that Adolph Sutro spent the remainder of his life denying that anything romantic had taken place between Miss Trundle and himself. Attempting to quell rumors and suspicions within his circle of colleagues, he told the Lazards that he had "…not seen Madam since I came [to New York] and simply wished to acquaint her with general facts showing she is entirely unjustified [in believing he had an affair with Miss Trundle and demanding half of his assets]. No arbitration can be had until grounds of demands are specifically stated, which he (sic) refuses, and I do not think any exist. If legal arbitration is paramount to a law suit and things have come to a pass that I now prefer the latter."[120]

Sutro must have been prepared for this eventuality; he launched into the necessary actions as if he had a plan all established. He made a quick trip to San Francisco very likely scouting for real estate; by September 22, he had completed the purchase of property at Hayes and Fillmore Streets upon which a gracious home was later built for Leah and the children. His business life continued almost without missing a beat. The Savage Mine counter-proposed a modified royalty and, within two weeks, the Sutro Tunnel Company was receiving royalty payments

71

from two of the mining companies although Mackay and Fair feigned ignorance of the agreement. Sutro resumed correspondence with Thomas Edison about lighting the tunnel and power distribution in the Comstock region. Edison claimed the ability to provide Virginia City with 65% of its power requirements using water flow in the tunnel to run his "dynamo machine." Sutro wanted Edison to build a prototype 30-horsepower system, to conduct trials upon it, and to then go on to a 200-horsepower unit. He asked his brother Theodore for information about patent applications and the legal implications. Adolph Sutro went on with his life and work as if nothing had happened.[121]

Around him, things were not so smooth. That week, Sutro also came to agree with repeated Shellabarger & Wilson's suggestion that a "Congress watcher" be stationed in Washington to see that new laws not have riders affecting the Sutro Tunnel Company adversely. This surveillance had to be constant; there was no limit to the mischief the mining companies could muster through their congressional representatives or through the Interior Department General Land Office. Sutro concluded that Shellabarger & Wilson were the ideal parties to deal with this assignment and arranged to hire them for the purpose at $50 per month. He proposed to McCalmonts that they pay for this service. He also had been including costs for publication of the *Sutro Independent* newspaper in monthly billings to the McCalmonts. Col. Brush let him know in a very blunt letter that neither of those charges could be passed on to London.[122]

Relations between Sutro and Joseph Aron began a rapid downhill path. Aron had continued to pursue his anxious opposition to stock sales for any reason. He made a number of inquiries of Ames and Brush about Sutro's share balance and other financial issues. To mollify Aron, an internal audit was conducted by Ames who was sending a copy to Aron. David Cahn of Lazard Frères had reviewed the work prior to completion and was satisfied. However, Brush sat with Ames for two days going back over the same material and another communication was sent to Aron. The major benefit to Sutro was confirmation of his holdings;

there was no longer any question about how many shares he owned. Sutro was in New York from where he had planned to go to London if necessary. He no longer thought that would be useful. Aron had not only fussed over the stock issue but continued to urge more frequent public relations releases to Whitelaw Reid of the *New York Tribune* or J. W. Simonton of the New York Associated Press. Sutro had his personal secretary Frank Young send follow-up dispatches to Simonton and send copies to Aron. Young also wrote a lengthy letter to Aron pointing out that the Tunnel Company would eventually control and own the entire Comstock – it was inevitable. Day after day, Ames sent copies of upbeat reports and news of progress to Aron. Everyone was doing everything possible to quell his anxieties and get him to leave Sutro alone. It wasn't working.[123]

In desperation, Adolph Sutro wrote an emotionally charged letter to Adelaide Aron virtually pleading with her to arrange a meeting between Sutro and her husband at which she would be present. He told her: "It seems that Mr. Aron has worked himself into a state of mind which makes him feel concerned that a great wrong is being done him, and the more the subject is being argued with him alone, the more his own excitability prevents him from looking at matters as they truly exist." Sutro had begged Aron "over and over" to have a discussion in her presence but Aron had refused. Sutro offered to meet anywhere convenient to her – her hotel, the Gilroy House, or other venue. He would invite his brother Theodore and his daughter Emma or whoever Mrs. Aron desired to have present. Most of all, he explained that "the unfortunate misunderstanding in numerous matters, which exists between Mr. Aron and myself, after so many years of friendship, no one regrets more deeply than myself." There is no record of any reply.[124]

Things were not going smoothly in the separation of Adolph and Leah. They had agreed upon the size of periodic payments he would make. From New York, Adolph instructed Ames to pay Leah the $600 due her and to deposit the remainder of the wired funds into his account. Ten days later, Ames wired that Leah had refused the payment –

"says she will sell furniture unless paid $750." Ames wanted to get out of the way of this disagreement and suggested Sutro "remit by telegraph direct to Mrs. Sutro."[125] Leah had been involved in a series of exciting events at the Nevada mansion. A lengthy letter to Emma explained much of it. With Sutro away, H.H. Sheldon, the Tunnel Company's assistant superintendent, had visited her to say that the former President of the United States, General Ulysses S. Grant, was expected to arrive in a few days for a breakfast and tunnel tour to which he and a large coterie of officials had been invited. Sutro had instructed Sheldon to play host which Sheldon confessed readily he had no ability to do, so Leah took over. Leah "…escorted the General to breakfast he sitting to my right and the Governor of Nevada to my left and all the lesser lights in rotation. They all seemed much pleased to have me present. The Governor and Jim Fair seemed to try in every way to make themselves agreeable to me… after breakfast the General was cheered by the crowd that thronged outside the mansion. Then the Governor after[ward asked for] three long and loud cheers for Mrs. Sutro which greatly surprised me. And what surprised me still more [was] not hearing the least sign of a cheer for the projector of the Sutro tunnel."

There was more. "After the party left, a whole delegation of women from Sutro called to wish me goodbye. I never was so much effected (sic) in my life. They said how pained they were at my leaving and all the years that they had known me both here and in Dayton [Nevada] that I was always the friend of the poor and if their prayers and blessings could help me that I would never have a days (sic) sorrow. After that you would have thought there was an irish (sic) wake for there was one prolonged fit of crying." Following this session, Leah left for San Francisco immediately never to return to the town of Sutro. Her letter went on to complain about "Pa" not leaving the money he promised for the gardener, the water, and the gas. She believed the $150 shortage on the payment through Ames was due to Sutro having given Emma her allowance directly. But, since she had no notification, she had refused the lower amount. The new house was beautiful in concept but had serious drawbacks not the least of which was the hill she had to climb to get there. She wanted a horse and carriage. "If you hear any news dear Emma, I wish you would let me know. I hear nothing of your father any more than from the dead. Mr. Brush or Ames never come near us. They are afraid of their Master."[126]

Twenty-four years of marriage were over. In those twenty-four years, Leah Sutro had worked tirelessly to support Adolph's efforts. In the earliest days, she had been the proprietress of rooming houses, sometimes two at once. In later years, with the large family growing, she had been a farmer raising food crops, pigs, and other barnyard animals, butchering what she bred and preserving considerable prepared food. She told of growing "Water melons, mush Do [melons], cucumbers, squash, onions, radishes, peas, beans, potatoes, cabages (sic) spinach and celery and various other things too numerous to mention. I have raised over one hundred chickens and ducks also two turkeys." While that was going on, Adolph Sutro was living in the finest hotels and apartments that London, Paris, New York, and Washington, D.C. had to offer, eating sumptuous meals, drinking copious amounts of claret, and finishing every evening with a serving of strawberries and heavy cream.[127]

Still in New York and armed with accurate information about his Tunnel Company holdings, Sutro made use of his brother's proximity to begin selling small amounts of his stock. Credits to his accounts at Lazard Frères and J & W Seligman began to mount up. In San Francisco, Ames continued the program of creating new stock certificates which, with Sutro's urging, were being shipped to New York almost before the ink was dry. Aron was certainly aware of these transactions and ended all contact with Sutro. But the stock sales accomplished what Sutro had desired; they could pay the running costs of the Lazard loan and would keep tunnel construction going at an acceptable rate until mine payments accelerated sufficiently. Once again, Sutro was the juggler.

There were other problems. In the last week of October, the town of Sutro had experienced the worst fire in its short history. Among the losses was a pair of two-story buildings belonging to William Hewlett, whose real estate dealings had been particularly annoying to Ames and Frank Young. Hewlett, who had leases on sixteen lots with homes, wasn't exactly dishonest but he needed to be watched all the time. His deed documents were always in a semi-disruptive state, he was consistently late with rental payments, and there was great uncertainty whether he was keeping up with insurance premiums. Some months back, he had proposed purchasing the leased lots from the company. In a very confusing conversation with Ames, following having been kicked in the head by a horse, Hewlett offered to provide security for the purchases by acquiring insurance policies but confessed he would need the company to be "lenient" about installment payment collection. Ames was very busy at the time and Hewlett rambled on somewhat less than coherently. Ames promised to transmit the offer to Sutro, but it appeared he just wanted to get Hewlett out of the office, so he could work. Ames wrote at length to Sutro describing the visit and begging Sutro to get the details of what Hewlett was offering because Ames did not want to depend upon Hewlett's explanation to understand it. Apparently, nothing came of the proposals. After the fire, Young learned that Hewlett had permitted insurance coverage on the two burned houses to lapse prior to the fire representing a total loss to the Tunnel Company.[128]

However, Sutro's interests now lay elsewhere. Having shed his wife and his closest associate, he pursued his plan to withdraw from tunnel activities if it became necessary. Over the past several months, messages from the McCalmonts were constantly negative stressing the differences between what Sutro had forecasted about the future financial rewards and the meager returns that the completed tunnel was producing. Truthfully, Sutro had to be wondering himself whether there really was a bonanza to be had from the tunnel. No great vein had been hit during construction of the tunnel and, recently, assays of ore samples from both the north and south drifts being cut were virtually free of silver content. The promise of a huge ore tailings industry looked less and less likely. There was no clamor from the mine operators to pay for water removal or ventilation. Perhaps it was time to cash in.[129]

Sutro pushed Ames to finish converting all the stock certificates to small denominations. He had made arrangements to put the Tunnel Company funds in the Farmers and Merchants Bank long ago after all the contentious dealings with Bank of California. Farmers and Merchants Bank was headquartered in Los Angeles with a branch in San Francisco. This was another element in Sutro's scheme to minimize local awareness of his activities. But, he was not yet willing to abandon his stake in directing the Tunnel Company without a fight. The McCalmonts had made it clear they were not pleased with his leadership and he expected they would attempt to establish a greater role in the management for themselves. If they could not, they would leave. He had to be ready to take whatever steps were necessary to maximize his share before they made that impossible. At the upcoming meeting next March 1st, a struggle for positions on the Board of Trustees was inevitable. Sutro expected Aron to align himself with Brush and the other allies of McCalmonts; he had to tread lightly around all of them. He notified Brush that he had developed sufficient funds to satisfy repayment requirements on the $150,000 Lazard Frères loan. Brush termed it "very gratifying" and delivered a lengthy explanation of tunnel modifications which could be considered to accommodate a potential mine contract he had been tendered. He also offered encouragement about having the Tunnel Company trustees agree to pay Shellabarger & Wilson for Congress-watching if the McCalmonts would not. If Sutro had wanted his messages to deflect Brush's suspicions about Sutro's future, he had actually succeeded.[130]

While still in New York, he accepted an invitation from the New York City Bullion Club, a group of specialists within the American Institute of Mining Engineers, to address their membership with a detailed account of the tunnel story. His speech was a masterpiece of personal promotion and self-adulation which had to have taken close to ninety minutes to deliver. Sutro was elected to membership of the club following the meeting. Then he met with Edward Adams and his associate, Ernest Kempton, to plan details of his financial withdrawal from the Sutro Tunnel Company. Cipher codes were established for telegraphic messages. Stock certificate and cash deposit locations were identified. Last, but certainly not least, Adams and Kempton were advised there was no longer any connection with Joseph Aron and he was not to be included in communications. Ames was also made aware of this – "I have no further relations with Mr. Aron" and "There are many objections to telegraphing everything to Mr. Aron."[131]

In an interesting diversion, Sutro requested and was happily accommodated with a tour through the Steinway piano factory in Astoria, Long Island. Theodore Steinway, brother of the company's leader and plant manager of the grand piano factory, conducted the tour.[132]

Still sensitive about Leah's rejection of his last payment, Sutro tried to calm her down. He sent a telegram promising a check before the first of the month [December] which would include funds for an extra two months of expenses. As promised, he followed up a week later with a check in the amount of $880. He detailed each and every item showing how the total had been calculated as if he were dealing with the local butcher. In his usual warm and gracious manner, he closed the letter to his wife of twenty-four years with "very truly yours, Adolph Sutro." Leah had understood the status of their relationship long before this "tender" note; she was busily engaged in filling the new house with furniture, equipment and supplies and charging them to Adolph. [133]

In the Sutro family, Adolph was certainly the most prominent person at least at this time. He had a national reputation and was known far and wide for the tunnel project and his many contacts within the federal government, the Congress, and the world of business and finance. Two times during the year, he would receive greetings from many of his far-flung relatives – on his birthday in April, and as New Year's Day approached. He had begun to issue allowances and year-end gifts, a practice he continued throughout the rest of his life. So, it was not unusual for him to receive a letter and check from his brother Louis near the end of November. The check purported to be the return of funds from a long-forgotten business transaction that Sutro vigorously denied re-

membering. He responded by rejecting any claim to the funds and outlined a distribution to their mother; sisters Juliana, Emma, and Elise;
fourteen months of payments to Henry Foreman; and the remaining
amount for a gift to Louis's son. Less than a month later, another letter
went to his brother Hugo with money for painting and repairs on some
of the houses Hugo tended for him. An additional $100 was included
for Christmas and New Year's gifts for the children in the family with
instructions to give books when possible but that toys, candies. and nuts
were acceptable.[134]

In December, Sutro inched closer to breaking away from the
tunnel. He outlined final instructions for how Adams was to sell
Sutro's personal shares of tunnel stock now that many were re-issued
on small-denomination certificates. His brother Theodore had been
busy since the first week of the month and had sold 19,025 shares
which netted Adolph almost $75,000. Adams followed shortly with
the sale of 25,000 more shares yielding more than $91,000. In the
future, the annual gifts and the family allowances were not going to
be a problem. Sutro wound up his affairs in New York; pressed Ames
to send as many more small certificates as he could lay his hands on
immediately; arranged to meet Rosa and Emma for a meal before
leaving; agreed to stop in Reno, Nevada, on the way home to see
Sutro Independent editor Frank Mercer; and headed back to the West
Coast. The plans for his trip to the West Coast were apparently fre-
netic. Sutro went from New York to Baltimore; visited with the family including daughters Emma and Rosa; and telegraphed Ames that
he was leaving for California the next day. However, he didn't leave.
On the following day, he told Ames he was leaving the next day and
to not send any more letters to him in the East. He also found time to
write lengthily to his brother Theodore detailing his agreement to
the purchase of a house in the upper Manhattan neighborhood of Inwood, with various exceptions and conditions, and suggestions about
how to gather the funds to complete the deal. The house would serve
as a home for his mother. Finally, he instructed Theodore to send a

telegram to every train stop on his trip home, awaiting his arrival, which will include up-to-date stock price information and progress in sales. If there was upward movement in the stock, he was willing to sell all 150,000 shares then in Theo's hands. [135]

Just before New Year, he telegraphed the McCalmonts: "Rumor unfounded that I have sold all the STC stock; hold more than 300,000 shares; will stand by STC."[136]

Maybe.

Nine

ESCAPE FROM THE TUNNEL

Sutro attended Christmas 1879 dinner at the home of the Tunnel's assistant superintendent H.H. Sheldon's family, along with a large assemblage of local celebrities, after which he spent the New Year's week cleaning up affairs in isolation. He offered his brother, Theodore, suggestions to help blast victim Foreman's lawsuit. In the same message, he rejected the idea of committing to purchase the Inwood property for his mother until the current owner, Ella Beck Childs,[137] was able to certify ownership. And, above all, "hurry up all certificates particularly San Francisco 1000."[138]

That same Sunday, he wired broker Ernest Kempton at Winslow, Lanier & Co. to reduce the Sutro Tunnel Company stock selling price minimum to $3.50 per share and to send his bonds, New York certificates, and daily market reports to the San Francisco house.[139]

Finally, he prepared a long and complex letter to the McCalmont firm covering many aspects of tunnel business in excruciating detail. Primarily, he wanted to dispel their notion, however correct, that he intended to dispose of his stock. He covered many other topics: (1) following removal of their shares from the tunnel company's San Francisco office, he expected the McCalmonts to sell their stock; (2) he had heard from other sources that the McCalmonts expected him to join some other partnership – which he denied; (3) that holding the majority of the stock, McCalmonts controlled the election process and no one could interfere including the Bonanza people who appeared to be leaving the Comstock; (4) that Sutro's withdrawal of shares and subsequent sales were necessary to cover loan obligations to Lazard Frères and Aron; (5) that Aron and Coulter had conspired to avoid paying claims which Sutro had against them; (6) he had sold only enough stock to "place my family beyond want" and still had 350,000 shares "locked up" which would only be touched if needed for expenses unless the Mc-Calmonts' interest should "fall into other hands" in which case he would feel free to dispose of his whole investment; (7) he would be sorry to see the management changed at this time but the Nevada climate has been a problem for him – however he would sustain any personal sacrifice to see the concern come out fully as well as he had always predicted; and, finally, (8) this year, many good things will happen and you will like them. He closed with several earnest paragraphs:

"I have in the above given you candidly and fairly my views on the situation, and I wish in conclusion to repeat, that I never for a moment entertained the idea of withdrawing from the concern or doing anything whatsoever which might be detrimental to the final success of our undertaking to which I have been devoted the best years of my life."

"I have my satisfaction of knowing that I have managed the affairs of the Company to the best of my ability and with the strictest of integrity."

"I shall be glad to continue in the service of the Company, if you so desire it, and shall cooperate with you and guard your interests and those of the Company, as I have done from the beginning – I have steered the course through all sorts of difficulties and complications, and if you will leave me alone you will come out ahead much better than you anticipate –"

"It is, of course, of importance for one to know what is going to be done at the election on the first Monday in March. If you intend to let the present board of trustees and general management remain please indicate it by cabling me the word "<u>management</u>" within a few days after receipt of this letter. If I do not receive such a message I shall construe it to mean that you intend to make a change —"[140]

Of course, Sutro had already commenced liquidating his interest well beyond family needs and had a detailed plan to complete that. If it appeared to be highly beneficial personally, he could still reverse course but was convinced that he needed to withdraw from the Sutro Tunnel Company. Sutro repeatedly told the McCalmont management that he considered Coulter to be working against him and that Aron was now a co-conspirator with Coulter in these actions. Two days later he wrote to London again. He had read defamatory items about himself in local newspapers which he attributed to Aron and Coulter. He repeated some of the prior message about how loyal he had been to the company and what he was prepared to do for it and them so long as they stayed "interested" [financially connected to the enterprise]. He recommended dis-incorporating in California and re-incorporating in New York. In closing he emphasized if they were satisfied with the current management that would be fine with him. If not, as owners of the company, do what you want, select who you would like. "I will also serve for another year if that be your desire."[141]

However, a short time later, Sutro penned a lengthy message to Adams including all his plans for withdrawal from the Tunnel Company and the accompanying rationale:

"I am almost convinced that an attempt will commence tomorrow [February 2] to get up a deal in the stock, and I believe the plan is to sell out McC[almonts] 850,000 shares during February, which stand on the books of the Farmers Loan & Trust Co. in the name of Harry Debrot, and which they can vote at the election thus securing a board of trustees of their own choosing. -- Not having any longer a share interest in the concern they may manage affairs so, that the stock will much depreciate and I have no desire to have any share interest left in the company under such circumstances – You will therefore understand my desire to sell out…"

"I stated in my last letter, it will not be good policy on our part to show our hand too soon, but rather to let them proceed and get the stock up pretty well before throwing much into the market. – They, no doubt, think that we will not be able to sell, not having any stock in 100 [share] certificates, but they will find their mistake…you have been able to borrow at least 100,000 shares to begin with – should your borrowed stock give out you may then commence to sell either 10, 20, or 30 as the case might seem to require. In fact, with my personal surmises, should they prove correct, I should be desirous of selling out my whole remaining interest of 300,000 shares, provided that quantity can be sold at fair prices."

There was more; Sutro laid out a plan for gathering proxies from the shareholders prior to sale. Adams was to forward these to the Sutro Tunnel Company attorney, Elliott Moore "without making a stir about it." He did not expect to control the election of the board but hoped to get two or three seats on the seven-man panel which would be "protection to some extent against unjust measures." Earlier, Sutro had specified converting the sales into 4% coupon bonds due in 1907. He warned of the possibility he might prefer to have the money transferred to pay for an unspecified piece of property he was negotiating to purchase. The letter closed with an extensive list of changes and additions to the cipher book they were using.[142]

Theodore had posed questions about Adolph's message regarding the Inwood property lawsuit. The older brother scolded Theo saying he [the lawyer] should be the one answering the questions he had passed on about the subject. Then, Adolph confessed, "I have lately sold a few shares through another party in New York. Why it was impossible to do it through you, and why I had to employ this other party I shall before long explain to you. Do not in any wise let on that you know anything about this."

He added: "Coulter has no doubt written a pack of lies to McCalmont as concocted between him and Aron. In consequence, McCalmont has discharged all their stock from the San Francisco office to

84

Kidder, Peabody & Company." Sutro thought that McCalmont and Coulter were forming a combine to take control and feared they could succeed.

Lastly, "Family matters – are moving pretty smoothly and am splendidly fixed in the new house and everything moves along harmoniously so far. I have hopes that things will continue that way for Mrs. S[utro] was the [illegible] of her course and does not propose to interfere with me any longer or regulate my private affairs."[143]

Sutro may have thought family matters were moving pretty smoothly, but they were not. Both older girls were in the East, 3,000 miles from parents and siblings and not living with each other. Emma was housed temporarily with the Sutro family in Baltimore while Rosa was nearby at Mrs. Reinhardt's. Papa sent Rosa money to pay Mrs. Reinhardt for board; she had been there as a visitor, but Adolph insisted that "a visit cannot be extended indefinitely." Meanwhile, Leah confided in Emma about the family situation. She had seen letters from the family to Papa telling him that Emma was "quite gay and goes a great deal into society." That news pleased her but the flow of letters from the family to Adolph did not. "How people will cater to a rich man's vanity." Moreover, "…I suppose it would interest you to know how your father behaves. All I can tell you is that I am afraid there is no chance for his reform unless he should loose (sic) his money or become sick. I let him go his way unmolested and make no remarks on his conduct. In fact it does not grieve me as much as it did. He comes when he likes and goes where he pleases. He has his own apartment and I have mine….I know nothing of his business – no more than the greatest stranger. It does not do for me to think about his conduct." And, "If I could only get him to settle something on me as long as I live I should not bother myself about him or his doings but I do not think I shall ever get a cent of him unless I should have to force him to do so." In closing, "I receive letters quite often from dear Rosy. She seems to be having a nice time at Miss R[einhardt's]. Your Father seems very anxious to have her remain with her and not return home. I think he would be happy if he could get the children to desert their Mother." That hardly qualified as "running pretty smoothly."[144]

The exchanges between Adolph and Theo continued regularly through the month of February. Adolph bore down on the need to secure proxies for the trustee election on March 1st. He sent updated lists of stockholders on the books of the Farmers Loan & Trust Company of New York urging Theo to "control" those he could or to have associates intercede as needed. "Coulter may have a majority of the stock after all; that makes no difference – all I can tell you is that I look upon it as of the <u>highest importance</u> to get as many proxies as it is possible to get even with the [help] of a few hundred dollars... If Coulter party gets absolute control I shall look upon it as <u>very</u> damaging to the concern and shall likely manage to sell out." As time went by, Adolph's letters and telegrams became more demanding and his tone more arrogant. "For Aron and Coulter have made their plans to get control of the board of trustees and then go for me. All they will make out of that they can just put in their eye – I think I can show the Co[mpany] <u>owes me</u> over 150,000 shares." Adolph sent six cipher telegrams in nine days which were nothing but nasty expediting. Theodore claimed to be working as hard as he could to obtain the proxies his brother wanted. He reported situations with individual stockholders and with various agents of the Seligman financial empire and rebuked Adolph for his late and overly cautious start which permitted the "other side" to gain a substantial advantage. Then he unleashed his anger over the sales of stock through Adams. "I am afraid there is after all some truth in what they say of you that you 'go back' on your friends and (in the maxim of your old friend Steinbach) are inclined to use people like lemons throwing them away when they have served your ends. Your continued sales both during the latter part of your stay here and also now and lately of the flood of "few shares" (as you term them) certainly give me reason to speak so. Yes! I feel hurt about it and think that I ought to. They must be overpowering reasons indeed which prompt you to give to any penny broker what every obligation of duty should have told you of right and justice belonged to me, not to speak of your own interest to which you sometimes through some perverseness appear to be wholly blind for no one surely could have done worse or sold at more miserable prices than your present representative." More angry words followed but, strangely enough, Theodore went right on gathering proxies which totaled more than 150,000 shares near the end of February. In a follow-up letter, Theo explained, "Mr. Aron is very much exasperated at me that I should have secured so many proxies for you; they have been making a tremendous effort and have, I fear, even paid for proxies. No doubt they would have paid me most any price for the proxies which I managed to control. The only thanks which I received from you was that you went behind my back and sold your shares through another broker." There were other irritants; concurrently, the purchase and overhaul of the Inwood house in which their mother would live continued.[145]

The complexities and complications of a life in the wake of Adolph Sutro were even more vexing for Leah. Part time, she and Adolph continued to share facilities in the new home on Hayes and Fillmore in spite of their contentious marital status. Leah told Emma: "We have a French man and his wife. She is a splendid cook and he is an excellent waiter. We never have been so well pleased. Pa is in extacies (sic) about them. We live splendidly and I never had less care which is a great comfort. The pictures have arrived also the books. I expect the house will be in perfect order in about two weeks. We will be comfortably settled and then I shall try to take some care of myself." She also told Emma of Adolph's plans to go to New York and then to Europe to be gone for five years and inquired whether Emma ever saw Mr. and Mrs. Aron. Leah expressed her shock that a lawsuit was pending between these old friends. Who would have ever thought of so much animosity taking place between two such friends? "It seems to me that your father must have a perfect mania for making enemies of his best friends." The next time she is in New York, they [the Arons] will be her first visit.

Leah described the attention Adolph's Baltimore family was lavishing upon him since he appeared to be getting very rich. She abhorred how they fawned over him as well as how completely they ignored her. Then she came to the point of her message. "After I get all my affairs settled here I may possibly pay you a visit but not for some time yet. I am very anxious to know my posision (sic). As yet your father has come to no understanding with me which places me in an unpleasant situation. It will not be long before we will have to come to some permanent arrangement with regards to my future."[146]

Adolph responded to Theodore's rant: "Proxies reached. Thanks. My reasons will be self-evident and conclusive when explained. Why compelled to employ certain parties. Will telegraph as soon as advised of election of trustees tomorrow."[147]

Between January 28th and March 6th, Sutro sent more than 20 letters and telegrams to either Adams or Kempton with instructions about sales of his shares in the Sutro Tunnel Company which resulted in having $920,700 converted to 4% coupon bonds. In his communications, he repeatedly stressed details about what kind of stock certificates were needed and whose signature would be valid. Almost daily, he urged them to obtain proxies for the upcoming trustee election but to avoid contact with the Seligman organization on that subject. Adams was advised to take power of attorney to sell a block of 50,000 shares during February in advance of the books closing. Sutro believed that Coulter had formed a combine to "get up a deal in our stock as soon as the books close." He suggested letting Coulter's group get the price up to $5 or $6 or even higher and then sell as fast as they could. Sutro had another 200,000 shares "all cut up in 1,000 [share] certificates ready to be forwarded as soon as the books open."[148]

March 1, 1880, arrived, and the annual trustees meeting of the Sutro Tunnel Company took place. The subdued newspaper coverage could never do justice to the contest of wills which took place there; neither could the bland, technical content of the published annual report tell stockholders the true story about the proxy war leading up to the event. When it was over, the McCalmont interests had retained control with four of the seven seats – C.W. Brush, F.F. Low (representing Seligman), William Irvine, and W.H. Tillinghast. Adolph Sutro was returned to the board as were Elliott J. Moore and David Cahn (who replaced his partner Alex Weil) in the seat held by Lazard Frères. Most importantly, the board voted to accept the resignation of Adolph Sutro as Superintendent which had been tendered previously. Sutro's relocation to San Francisco was reported in newspaper accounts.[149]

The plain truth was that, over an extended period, Sutro had been fully engaged in feathering his own nest while telling the McCalmonts that he was loyal and willing to work for their interests. Similarly, Sutro had all but abandoned his wife of twenty-four years, putting her on an allowance instead of a share of his fortune which she had preserved with her labors. Further, he managed to dissolve the only genuine friendship he had developed in his adult life and ruptured the relationship with his youngest brother who had served him in numerous ways during the years approaching these events. With all of this, he was content and, as we shall see, pleased with his situation, and defensive about accusations from those he had deceived or tossed away.

Following the trustees meeting, Sutro pursued accumulation of safe financial instruments. His bonds were secured in the Coleman, Benedict & Co. vault in New York and the register/transfer agent in Washington was instructed to send interest checks to Elliott Moore at the Montgomery Block offices in San Francisco. Sutro brought Adams up to date with an extensive report about the election and its implications emphasizing the conclusion of his relationship with Aron. A history of their financial connection and its recent deterioration was spelled out in some detail. Of course, it was a one-sided view which may have been colored by Sutro's emotional excesses. Sutro conceded that Aron "had rendered me good service in the early stages of the enterprise in which I was engaged so many years" but Aron's claims to have acted as a friend turned into speculation; further, "…friendship for which payment is demanded can hardly be counted as such." Sutro complimented

Adams on how well he had managed the stock program and outlined the next steps in his plan to divest himself of all of it. He was amused at Brush's discomfort at having to sign 2,000 of the new, low-denomination certificates.[150]

However, Sutro derived little amusement from other communications he received shortly thereafter. One letter from his nemesis, George Coulter, informed that Sutro's intention to sue Coulter to recover funds from a promissory note would be defended vigorously. Coulter claimed he was "not in any respect indebted to you and I repeat, that I am supremely glad to learn you are about to test the question....I hope you will lose no time in bringing your action." Brother Theodore Sutro followed with three messages. In the first, Theo detailed his efforts to repair the Inwood house where a number of estimates for work varied widely in price; how much did Adolph want to spend? Did Adolph want him to continue working the details or did he want to do it himself? He closed with a double-barreled blast: "You are silent as a tomb since the election; I am not surprised at this however; it is in conformity with what I stated in my last letters [that] I might expect...We celebrated Mother's 77th birthday last Sunday at Sightman's [Restaurant]. Every member of the family was either present himself or sent his congratulations except yourself."[151] In his next letters over a period of months, Theo refused to provide a bill for his legal work and other efforts in Adolph's behalf going into much detail about what he did and didn't do and how what he did was great work but simple and what he didn't do was work he deserved to get from Adolph but was given to someone else who did a poor job of it. Theo lambasted his brother for consistently underrating the work he did for him. He "would infinitely prefer to let also these matters go into the long list of unsettled and long-forgotten scores." He had offered to work for a regular salary which Adolph had rejected. Theo had a full plate; he re-located his offices in New York City and arranged to obtain a desk at the Shellabarger & Wilson office in Washington where he could share the Congress-watching duties. Repairs of the Inwood house stretched out many weeks beyond their expected finish forcing him and his mother to take temporary shelter in a boarding house in the city. Beyond that, the disagreements between Theodore and Adolph were not settled. Adolph continued to press him to send a bill. Theo persisted in refusing; "You insist on getting final statement of all claims. The latter word falls to the ground after what I have written to you…I leave the matter entirely to you; what more do you wish, or have you a right to 'insist' on?" A full page of angry words followed.[152]

While all of this was distressing for Adolph Sutro, he could not take his eyes off the central issue – converting his tunnel stock to cash and getting out of the arrangement with the McCalmonts. The only one he could consistently and genuinely depend upon was Adams whose ability and loyalty were nothing short of outstanding. Sutro filled in all the missing information for Adams – the saga of Aron's apparent defection from Sutro's "team" after so many years of close personal working collegiality; the breakdown of mutual confidence between Sutro and Mc-Calmont; and the in-fighting and warring over proxies leading to the election result. Sutro summed up the situation; "All the advantage Mc-Calmonts gain by their course is that there is no longer a Captain to guide the ship, and the management has fallen into incompetent hands…." He was content in his belief that, despite the apparent representation of the board members, his interests were completely protected. Sales of Sutro's stock strung out until the end of the year.[153]

Sutro had been toying with the idea of a trip to Europe, including taking some of the older children with him. Though unstated in any of his correspondence, Leah's suspicions about his desire to separate her from the girls may have been at least partially true. But, by late spring, he realized that it was not going to be possible or convenient. He had too much going on concerning his withdrawal from the Tunnel Company and by the time he could go east and thence overseas it would be summer with the uncomfortable heat he disliked. He was irritated further by another issue. Leah had apparently told Emma about wanting a "settlement" from Papa rather than monthly allowances. Emma, in turn, took it upon herself to bring up the subject with him. He responded angrily:

91

"In regards to family affairs, it is entirely useless for you or any one else to keep harping on the same proposition of a settlement on your mother that will not be done. A very liberal monthly allowance will be made for her here to keep house, or a liberal sum if she chooses to go abroad, say $1000 per month, for herself and such children as wish to go with her. I have very fully explained my position verbally and if you suppose that arguments or threats will change it, you will find you're mistaken, and at the same time you may charge yourself with having aggravated matters to a very considerable extent. The sooner this matter is dropped the better for all." He closed with, "Affectionately your father."[154]

Family issues never seemed to end. Theo opined: "No doubt you think that I have written you some pretty disagreeable letters and that I am an ugly customer to deal with. But if you had been and were exactly in my position under all the existing circumstances, though you might not write them, your thoughts would not be much different from mine. It would surely be to my gain to join in the ranks of your flatterers but that goes against my grain." He went on to express admiration for Adolph's kindnesses to other family members, especially their mother, which he contrasted with "injustices" towards himself. He went on about the beauty and value of the Inwood property and homestead fairly fawning over Adolph's choices and decisions. He invited his brother to come for a visit in the summer as he would be sharing the home with their mother. He had negotiated and supervised installation of a lengthy sewer line from the home to the Hudson River which would result in increasing the value of the property significantly. Please sign the papers sealing the agreement with the neighbors for access. Theo concluded with several paragraphs summarizing some minor costs for which he needed reimbursement but excluding the large bills for legal fees Adolph had demanded.[155]

On top of his stock-selling activities, election campaigning and travel planning, Sutro was busily engaged in acquiring property with his sudden wealth. In addition to the new "mansion" at Hayes and Fillmore (in San Francisco) and the Inwood house (in New York City) for mother, he bought a substantial piece of property in downtown San Francisco from the estate of the deceased one-time Sutro Tunnel Company trustee Michael Reese for $240,000. This was followed by purchasing 46 acres of the so-called "Byfield Tract" on the western side of the city for $46,294 followed by 1350 acres of the San Miguel Rancho property adjoining the Byfield spread for another $240,000. These real estate transactions took place over a period of less than six weeks. In the calendar year 1880, Adolph Sutro acquired and recorded forty separate pieces of real estate.[156]

In July, Adolph and Leah concluded a separation agreement. This was followed the next month by a complex arrangement for maintaining Leah and the children in the house at 701 Fillmore Street. Under its terms, Sutro's two associates, Elliott Moore and William Van Alen, were appointed trustees of various rental properties in the heart of downtown San Francisco to be managed for the benefit of Leah and the children. These had been part of the Reese property purchased only one month earlier. Leah was to receive $500 per month for herself, $100 for "suitable maintenance" of Carla, $200 each for Emma, Rosa, and Katy, and $150 each for Charles and Edgar. Provisions were made for age progression of the children and the demise of any participants. Likewise, replacement of trustees was provided if necessary. So, indeed, Leah was not going to receive a "settlement" or anything approaching her fair share of Adolph's fortune. The agreement was kept under wraps for some eight years.[157]

As the year rolled on to its inevitable conclusion, the McCalmonts and Coulter exerted considerable effort beating the drum for potential fortunes in the Comstock which were now there for the taking with access through the tunnel; Adams and Kempton continued their relentless program of stock sales in behalf of the tunnel's visionary developer. *The Sutro Independent* ceased publication permanently. Adolph Sutro sent New Year's gifts for all of his East Coast relatives to his brother Louis in Baltimore asking that they be distributed.[158]

FUGUE

Ten

NEW BEGINNINGS

In his own words, Adolph Sutro had "the most exalted ideas regarding the future of California" and the West Coast. He expected it to expand in population and commerce and to "grow in civilization and arts and sciences until we will rank first among our countries…" He attributed much of this to the invigorating climate which would produce a "magnificent man and woman of bright mind and liberal in their views and go-ahead spirit, who would foster and encourage the development of all the better traits of nature." He foresaw a thickly-populated region from San Diego to the Straits of Fuca between the Pacific Ocean and the Sierra Nevada Mountains supporting as many as 30,000,000 people. He predicted that products of California, especially of fruits and grapes would find a wide market – the former being dried and canned, while the grapes would be made into wine and find a market throughout the whole world. Within that grandiose vision, he emphasized he "had particularly in mind the city of San Francisco, which contains almost one-third of the population of the state (at that time)."[159]

Consistent with that forecast, Sutro had a plan for exploiting the coming growth in his community. His land acquisitions added up to nearly three-quarters of a million dollars, most of it in areas that other investors did not want; further, entrepreneurs in the real property world wondered why he made such a huge investment in useless, barren country which offered little opportunity for income-producing activities. They thought that land he bought was too loosely compacted, too hilly, and too remote from the city and its business centers. However, Sutro envisioned growth of the city to cover the entire peninsula. He contemplated gradually developing the land he had purchased and selling lots to yield approximately $100,000 per year. He would retain the remainder year after year. The residual areas would increase in value progressively and he would always have plenty of lots to sell. Meanwhile, he would plant various grasses and trees to strengthen the soil and retain moisture in the ground he was developing. However, he was in no hurry; there was no huge demand for his land yet and he was willing to wait until it became choice property. All of this was ongoing at the turn of the year and he had made enough progress to once again consider his planned trip around the world.

However, there was a new reason to defer the trip -- the campaign for United States Senator in Nevada. Years earlier, Adolph Sutro's name had been entered on the Independent Party ticket (in 1874) opposing the candidacy of his business adversary William Sharon, the Republican Party choice. A third candidate, General Thomas H. Williams, ran on the Democratic ticket. Sutro was determined to prevent the Bank of California and the mining companies from having their own Senator who wanted to "cripple the tunnel enterprise." All three candidates opened their purses and hired orators to address political party gatherings in their behalf. In describing the election, historians Thomas Thompson and Albert West referred to the "Battle of the Money Bags." Sutro's efforts were in vain. Sharon won easily and served as one of Nevada's United States Senators from March 1875 to March 1881. When his term concluded, Sharon wanted to run again. However, after William Ralston had died, Sharon inherited many of his assets, most of which were in San Francisco, making him suddenly extremely prosperous. He had also acquired a mistress who claimed to be his wife "by contract." The combination of this new attachment to California and the breath of scandal weakened Sharon's political muscle and he dropped out of the race. Before his withdrawal, Sutro's name was contemplated as an Independent Party candidate. Instead of Sharon, Jim Fair, another of

Sutro's "Silver King" enemies, ran as a Republican. Sutro never actually participated in the election campaigning. He and some of his daughters showed up at the Ormsby House hotel in Carson City. He "merely sat in the room, talked pleasantly with all comers, and had very little to say of a political nature." Sutro was waiting for some indication that Fair's support was weakening but it never happened. Fair won election handily. Adolph Sutro had contested for a seat in the United States Senate (albeit weakly) in every election between 1872 and 1881 without receiving one vote from Nevada's state legislators who, prior to the 17th Constitutional Amendment in 1914, were authorized to elect United States Senators. Meanwhile, the process had been one more diversion from his new life after separating from the Sutro Tunnel Company.[160]

While continuing to plan his trip around the world, he never stopped looking for business opportunities. One he could not resist was the Cliff House. The Cliff House had been operating at the extreme northwest corner of the peninsula since 1863 attracting a combination of San Francisco millionaires and high-level politicians to its excellent restaurant and spectacular views. Remote from town, it was difficult to reach without one's own adequate means of transportation. After a few years, the high-society patrons moved on and it became a meeting place for a "fast crowd" of gamblers, playboys (and playgirls), and couples trying to avoid being recognized by spouses. Sutro had acquired a significant amount of property in the vicinity and his interest was aroused. In May 1881, newspapers reported that "Mr. Sutro has purchased a part interest in the Cliff House property; indeed, it is rumored he has purchased it all." In fact, between March and November, Sutro bought thirteen separate parcels of land in the Cliff House Ranch area including the Cliff House structure. By January, the real estate community recognized that "a movement has been going on along the Cliff House road, and in the vicinity of Ocean Beach, that cannot fail at an early day to greatly enhance the value of property in that vicinity. Adolph Sutro has been particularly prominent in this matter, having purchased largely on both sides of the road." There was further talk of reclaiming the sand dunes and opening the tract for buildings. Once again, Sutro had been at the forefront of an entrepreneurial venture.[161]

His daughter Emma had completed her medical studies and was taking some time off prior to beginning graduate work in the East. She and Papa went for a Sunday morning ride to the Cliff House area in their horse-drawn carriage. Sutro pointed out an elevated location he had never seen and suggested riding up there. The horses had a difficult time negotiating the sandy soil but finally made it to the crest of the hill where they found a "beautiful rose garden and a little old-fashioned four-room cottage with a beautiful view of the ocean." The property was surrounded by a high fence but as they approached they met a very tall man that Sutro knew. This was Samuel Tetlow, the owner, from whom the Cliff House had been purchased. After a short, pleasant visit, Sutro asked if Tetlow would sell the place; surprisingly, he agreed. The next day, Sutro completed arrangements to acquire the home, the property and the contents of the house.[162]

Meanwhile, Leah Sutro had sued for divorce from Adolph. He did what was necessary to protect himself by hiring private detective J. J. Robbins who visited Virginia City to find witnesses and others with knowledge about events leading up to the fracas at the International Hotel. Robbins continued working through the summer. A court date was set for August 30th which was continued until September 5th. Late in September, newspapers reported Leah's abandonment of an amicable separation and her new demands for half of Adolph's property. But, less than two weeks later, Robbins issued a final claim for fees from Sutro which specified that "said suit had been settled, dismissed and ended."[163]

Adolph Sutro went on with his life as if nothing had happened. He reported his address as 701 Fillmore which he allegedly shared with Leah. In reality, he lived at the Baldwin Hotel which offered all the creature comforts he sought and enjoyed wherever he traveled. He ate the finest foods, drank the best wines and smoked Havana "segars." Answering the census taker, he identified himself as a "retired miner," an amusing twist of the truth.

Sutro outlined his general plans for the Cliff House to Moore, the Sutro Tunnel Company attorney, and William R. H. Adamson, whom he had retained to attend to details of his finances. Sutro initiated various refurbishing projects; and finally left for his oft-delayed trip around the entire world which he had been anticipating with great pleasure. Moore, the attorney, and Adamson, the financial expert, were given detailed instructions concerning when and how to communicate with Sutro and he trusted them to follow orders completely. Further, they were very well paid and could be counted upon to handle even the most delicate matters without his involvement. However, he demanded complete reporting of everything... more, indeed, than less talented and less capable employees would have tolerated. Sutro simply could not stand any level of incompetence and required assurances at every step along the way.

During final preparations for the journey, Sutro received a letter from his mother which distressed him greatly. Mother asked why Adolph owed Theodore a large sum of money and had not paid him. He had no time to deal with the problem and shared his concerns with his brother Louis. Adolph was furious; he told Louis that "...I owe him nothing; he has been amply and liberally paid for all he has done for me and besides earned as commissions sums of $12 or 15000 within 60 days, more money than he ever handled in his life. --- Now it is a disgusting outrage that he should embitter our dear old mother's life through misrepresentation."

He went on and on about the difficulties he had endured trying to establish equity in his unsuccessful dealings with Theodore. He concluded it was possible that he owed Theodore for helping to secure some (Sutro Tunnel Company) proxies --- "his services thus rendered would be well paid for with $200 – considering that his time is no more valuable than any other agents who would undertake such work. – But I enclose a check for $1000 – to your order, which you may pay him providing he gives you a receipt..." In addition, Theodore would be required to certify that this covered all demands against Adolph whatsoever to the current date. In the event Theodore refused the money, please arrange to give it to Adolph's sons Charles and Edgar. In closing, he asked Louis to refrain from mentioning this to mother other than saying Adolph had written to him on the subject.[164]

Adolph got to New York by train and shipped out to Europe, arriving in Paris in early February, 1882. His travel plans included eventually meeting in Paris with daughters Emma, Rosa, and Kate, along with his brother Hugo who would accompany them. They would have some time together there and the young ladies would go to other major western European cities while he went on his own. But first, Sutro went to Jerusalem arriving around April 1st. Upon arrival, he found a letter jointly penned by his daughter Emma and her now very close friend and traveling companion George Merritt. They had brought him up to date with issues at home in California and told him about much they had seen while traveling around the southern and eastern states prior to Emma's heading for Europe and further medical studies. Sutro was resting after a whirlwind five- day tour around the Holy City and wrote an extensive response covering a variety of subjects. He reported having sent an agent to London with instructions to make abundant book purchases at various stores and auctions. Of course, at the appropriate time, Sutro would accompany him at these events so both could offer judgments and Sutro could provide final approval. His plan was to build a comprehensive collection relating to "history, the arts, mechanics, science, geography, travels, biography and literature. My idea is to have a library in which everything relating to these subjects can be found from the beginning of printing. So if for instance you would wish to write a <u>history</u> of medicine, all the material be on hand and so with all these other subjects." This was the first written confirmation showing the grand scope of Sutro's library collection; everyone knew he was gathering books but none could have imagined it would reach the size and intellectual content he achieved.

Sutro's library acquisitions had actually begun in the mid-1870's and by the early 1880's he had accumulated some 35,000 volumes. Between 1882 and 1884, as he moved from London to the European mainland and the Middle East, he made major purchases at large, important book auctions. The Sunderland Library sale extended more than a year and a half during which Sutro bought significant quantities at every session. By the close of the Sunderland sales, he had more than 50,000 books plus thousands of pamphlets, maps and broadsides.[165]

During the middle part of the 19th Century, Prussia was the scene of the so-called "Kulturkampf" political revolution in which secular agencies wrested power from the Catholic Church. In the process, "Landtag Laws" were passed in 1875 under which they confiscated all the church's valuable property, including books from monasteries, and turned them over to lay trustees. The books were consolidated in the hands of noblemen and, around 1883, Sutro bought major portions of these collections during auctions at the Buxheim Library and the library of the Duke of Dalberg. He continued this buying spree at the Royal State Library of Bavaria in Munich where he acquired some 6,500 volumes. Very likely, he then possessed upwards of 80-90,000 books including approximately one out every seven incunabula in the world. By 1888, his library was thought to contain 110,000 texts.[166]

Continuing his response to Emma and her companion, George Merritt, he summarized his incredibly negative feelings about the symbols and practices of formal religion all around him. "I have now been five days in Jerusalem and I think if any intelligent being comes here with religious ideas, he will surely have them sadly shaken. In Rome they say 'Roma viduta, fida perduta' (*sic*), but that applies more strongly to this place." Later, "The curious part of it is the Muslims, the Christians, catholics both Roman and Greek, the Jews, the different shades of protestants, all come here to worship pretty much the same thing and are ready to kill one another on account of slight differences of opinion … a company of Turkish soldiers is stationed to keep the pilgrims from fighting."

His plans for the upcoming weeks included trips to Bethlehem, the Dead Sea, Jericho, Beirut, Damascus, Baalbeck, Smyrna, Athens, Constantinople, Varna, Vienna, Münich, Paris and London. If this sounded ambitious, he admitted having to forego going around the Black Sea, the Caucuses and the Caspian Sea; those would have to wait for another trip in the future. The reason: he had to return to California as soon as possible, maybe in June. He had asked his cousin, Gustav, to obtain a franchise for a road north of Point Lobos Avenue to the seashore and he must look after it at once for things were not being managed to suit him at all. "I shall soon straighten things out when I get there." Even though he was half way around the world, Adolph Sutro personified the multi-tasking, hands-on manager; he may have been the prototype.[167]

Emma, Rosa, and Kate obtained passports and prepared for their trip to Europe in early April. Of course, as they floated across the Atlantic, their father was returning to California to oversee constructing a railroad line to the ocean. The original travel itinerary included having the three girls and son Charley accompany their father whenever it was possible to do so. That would have to wait. Arriving in San Francisco, Sutro learned that his brother Theo had refused the $1,000 check which once again raised his ire. "If he tries to cause any black mail games on me he will not succeed; no one ever did yet." Once more he asked Louis to find out what would satisfy Theodore. "I have only the kindest feelings towards him, but he must not embitter me like others have to their sorrow attempted to do."[168]

In late May, with things once again under control at the railroad construction, Sutro sailed to Japan beginning a five-month, east to west journey through Asia including Malaysia and China and ending in Paris after stops in Geneva and Vienna. Throughout this travel, Sutro continued to receive reports from Moore and Adamson about real property, construction projects, and finances which brought responses from him every time he reached a port. From Geneva, he had complained to Moore that every two weeks was too long between letters and to write weekly. Moore agreed obediently. Adamson had been assigned responsibility to provide accounting reports at short intervals but Sutro was never satisfied with anyone else's accuracy. He instructed Adamson:

"Now as to <u>your</u> and John's [Adamson's assistant John Gavin] examination of the accounts, I expected, and desire, that <u>you</u> should examine every item and <u>nothing whatever</u> should escape your scrutiny. – You might as well not examine the accounts <u>at all</u> as to learn part of them incorrect. – If transactions pass between Adamson and Sutro & Co. or others you should be cognizant of <u>every item</u>. – I shall be very particular about this and must request you to examine and be able to understand and approve of or not, of every item appearing in the accounts from beginning to end." Sutro was never too far away or so detached that he would neglect business issues. He heard from Robert Warner, owner of the London warehouse in which his book purchases were being stored. Warner had received the initial monthly payment from Adamson but had been notified by Karl Mayer, Sutro's book buyer, that twice the contracted space was going to be required. He assumed Sutro would be solicited for approval of this change. He also asked for additional payment for the increased management and administrative costs connected with this change and the plans which Mayer had outlined to him. Once again, Sutro had his hands full while thousands of miles away.[169]

Then Sutro got word that Emma and young Merritt had become attached seriously. His next letter to Moore was marked "Confidential." He wrote, "There is a young man in San Francisco who lately graduated at the Medical School and who studied together with my daughter Emma to whom she has for some time had a good deal of partiality, and he for her. They have been corresponding together and she has suggested to me to give him the means of finishing his medical education in Paris, to which I have consented, and I hereby enclose a check on Sutro & Co. for $1500 which you may collect, deposit in some other bank and take a certificate of deposit then for in the gentleman's name, which is Dr. George Merritt, residing at 809 Montgomery Avenue San Francisco." A sealed letter to Merritt was enclosed. Moore was instructed to call upon Merritt, give him the letter, and inform him that the money was available to him as soon as he designated the most desirable form in which to have it. Further, tell him "you are my confidential friend" and this sum is intended to defray the costs of one year at school and travel both ways. You may suggest others have been assisted in the same way. And by all means, do not make "the slightest allusion to any knowledge you may have that my daughter has any special regard for him...now, please go to work and find out all about this young man in a most quiet, and secret manner and promptly report to me his reputation for sobriety, industry, etc etc." Then, "If things turn out favorably and I like the young man as far as character is concerned, I believe a match may result, for the one party most concerned, appears favorably inclined." Sutro went on with details of how to do every part of the assignment, how much to help with travel plans, schedules, why he chose to not have anyone in the family involved, what to find out about Merritt's family, and more. The letter was a classical example of outrageous interference in the lives of others easily rationalized as a good deed. In addition, it was micro-management at its zenith. He wasn't through yet. In a later paragraph, he noted that, "Young Pierson (sic) called on us a few days ago. Why wouldn't he make a good partner for one of the girls (Sutro had two other daughters, didn't he?). He is now gone up the Nile. Supposing you give him a little hint on your own account; we shall probably meet him at Rome after his return. Tell me something in detail about him; his character, etc etc all, of course, in strict confidence."[170]   Sutro's reference was to Charles William Pearson, a missionary to Africa who later in his life became the vicar of Walton, England.

Sutro's next letter had an anxious tone. Merritt had received an appointment to an internship at the San Francisco County Hospital. Before leaving for Europe, Emma had advised him to apply. Sutro urged Moore: "...you might suggest on your own account, that he had better go to Europe now, as the advantages he gets, as an interne at the hospital, do not compare to those he will have in the large hospitals of Europe." "Do not breathe a word about this to anyone, as it would give mortal offence to Emma."

In the same letter, for transparent reasons, Sutro unburdened himself to Moore about his problems with Theodore. "I have, for a long time, had my suspicions that the actions of my brother Theodore were not straightforward; he lost his money in stock operations, and has become pretty desperate on account of it. He blames me for selling out and not telling him about it and makes claims against me of the wildest nature, and I shall not be astonished if he will bring a suit against me. I am told he puts his claims at $130,000; I do not owe him a penny. He has been liberally paid for all he ever did for me and the Sutro Tunnel Co." Sutro continued, telling about how his mother had become involved and insisting that Moore "not say anything to anyone about it"; he closed suggesting that Theodore was trying to get possession of the Inwood house. Of course, Moore was the attorney who would represent Sutro were any of those issues to become legal matters.[171]

Two months later, Sutro again wrote to "Friend Moore" thanking him for the prompt and official manner with which he attended to the private matter. Merritt was already in Paris, had already proposed marriage to Emma, and Sutro was convinced he was an exemplary young man and would make a very good husband for his daughter. "I do not know how brilliant he is, but I think a man of not too positive opinions would get along better with Emma than one of too firm a mind."

His travel plans included stops in Palermo, Catania, Syracuse, Messina, Malta, Tunis, Algiers, Gibraltar, Cadiz, Lisbon, and Madrid, ending in France. He expected to be in Paris by early April in order to attend the wedding. He added a caution about keeping the marriage plans secret as "Emma does not wish to create any talk about her intentions."[172]

The next two months involved a blur of events in Adolph Sutro's life. He embarked upon his Mediterranean travels without knowing that brother Theodore had arranged a gala 80th birthday party for their mother at Pinard's Restaurant in Manhattan. At the time of the party, Rosa Warendorff Sutro had fifty-one descendants and thirty-six of them attended the festivities. Of course, Adolph and his family were missing as they were all in Europe or in California. Had he known, this would have reinforced his suspicion about Theodore wanting to acquire the Inwood house through Mama's largesse although Adolph owned it. Adolph surely read about the party in newspaper accounts. But, he was too en-grossed in the upcoming wedding which, for some reason, took place in late March in London rather than early April in Paris. The marriage was performed by the local Registrar in the offices of the United States Con-sul General on March 27, 1883, with Adolph Sutro in attendance. Leah was not there.[173]

Still in London two months after the wedding, Sutro engaged in lengthy letters of instruction on every possible subject to Moore and Adamson. One exchange, regarding the caretaker at Sutro's Arcadia, California, ranch, included this segment from Sutro: "When grass gets short, California cattle become peculiarly desperate, and will go through most anything; there was a bull about Sutro, Nevada, against whom no fence was proof until we got the barbed wire ones. If he found he could not jump a fence, he would take the lead and throw his side against a fence with such force that it had to give way and all the cows, after care-fully watching his proceedings, followed in his wake, and we often found in the morning, a vegetable garden and young trees almost destroyed. This bull had learned this trick and played it on all the farmers in the neighborhood, who had filled his hide with buckshot; but he did not mind that any more than so much hail. I have given you this chapter on bulls, so you will be on the lookout, and not come into the plantation some morning, and find half the trees eaten up or trampled under foot. You may not think that cows eat pine trees; but when they are ravenous they will eat most anything." The breadth of Sutro's knowledge was truly remarkable and he used it to maintain absolute control over his employ-ees. This little lesson was followed by a request for a full list of all the tenants on San Miguel Ranch and other outside lands, with a detailed description of how many acres each had, how much they pay, and vari-ous other data. This assignment probably kept Adamson busy for days on end.[174]

Sutro traveled through the Scandinavian countries which he en-joyed greatly. He was enchanted by his proximity to the pole and made mention of the absence of lights in his bedroom in Trondheim, Norway, where there was sufficient illumination all night to write without candles. After a time in Stockholm, Sweden, he moved on to Moscow which he also found fascinating. The abundance of trees and other foliage in the areas in and around the city inspired him. He told Moore and Adamson, "I propose to plant over a large portion of the San Miguel with trees, and we may as well prepare to put out about 200,000 certain of half that number, each season…we must complete planting the Byfield mountain and surrounding areas; next the Felton blocks, at least the southerly ones. After that, I shall probably give instructions to plant a good portion of Point Lobos and all around the signal station and Lands end." Surely, this was the beginning of what became the Sutro Forest over the ensuing ten years.[175]

The pleasures of his journey were brought to an abrupt stop when he arrived in Warsaw to find letters there informing him of his mother's passing a week earlier. Telegraph messages had been sent to Paris, but did not catch up with him for the intervening two weeks. "The death of my dearest mother has thrown the whole family into the deepest mourning and I hardly feel able to write to you today." Three pages of detailed business issues followed immediately including instructions to make no more payments from his mother's accounts…and also to collect rents of the Stockton Street property which had been owned by his mother.[176]

After a stop in Baden Baden, Sutro moved on to Carlsbad, Bohemia (now Karlovy Vary, Czech Republic) where he wrote at length about Moore and Adamson's inept reporting. "Your letter of August 22 lacked a single line of news." He listed the roads, properties for sale, construction projects item by item pointing out exactly what he wanted to learn about in every one of their reports. Additionally, they were to use better envelopes for accounting reports as they arrive "torn to shreds."[177]

From Münich came a twenty-four-page hand-written letter containing a startling message. "This brings me to the state of my finances. I know quite well they have reached a low ebb and as I do not think I can suitably dispose of any property just yet, there is but one thing left, (which I do most reluctantly) and that is to borrow." Sutro went into a detailed analysis of his desire to borrow [actually acquire a line of cred-it for] $100,000 but to only pay interest on that portion of the total that he actually receives. From time to time, he would take more and pay additional interest. He felt confident that such an arrangement could be made with Sutro & Co. owing to the relationship he had with Gus-tav. The loan would be for a period of two years with his intention to pay it back in one year after selling some of the Felton Tract. He certain-ly did not expect to pay more than 6% interest. It is difficult to imagine that someone would go on a multi-year trip around the world lacking the financial resources to pay for it, but Adolph Sutro expected the world to accede to his needs because, though cash-poor, he was land-rich and could turn land into cash when he really needed it. It is equally difficult to understand why he spelled out all of this to Moore and Ad-amson. He did ask them to give that portion of the letter to Gustav, but he could just as easily have written to his cousin separately. Ten other pages of the letter were devoted to criticism of the Cliff House overhaul plans. Among other things, there were not enough water closets or uri-nals. He quibbled over the name – didn't like "Cliff House Gardens" but preferred "Cliff House Terrace." He complained about many struc-tural and safety issues and he wanted to see cost input information "speedily." He wanted to block off a portion of the beach near the Cliff House: "I should not like to have a lot of hoodlums get around the little branch and disturb the beautiful sea anemones and such fish which ex-ist on the other side of the great flat rock nearest to the beach the west side of which can be reached at each low tide." He also told Adamson that he wanted reports from him twice per week; Moore was only re-quired to write weekly "whether there be anything of importance to communicate or not."[178]

Two letters from Emma and George reached Sutro in München mo-tivating him to continue explaining the plans and progress for his library. He pointed out that, contrary to their presumptions, very little of his collection would be in the German language notwithstanding his efforts in this city which were ongoing but so far unsuccessful. He had been at the Royal library for the past three weeks and was sorry to say though he had identified more than "... 1000 incunabula (printed before 1500 [AD]) and many other works on art, mechanics, sciences etc I shall fail to make an arrangement, as they have raised the price on me twice and will not be depended upon." Despite this setback, he planned to collect the finest library in the United States. He lectured them on the extent of bibliographic information available forming the basis of his searches for early works. He also confessed that he could not undertake this effort alone and that he would employ a staff of librarians after he got home. The next two weeks would take him to Stuttgart, Frankfort, Bonn, Cologne and Aix-la-Chapelle before returning to Paris where he would see them. He also had his mind on the other children in his family. Sutro wrote to Thomas Edison asking for a position for his son, Edgar, emphasizing he would accept any position where he could learn about electricity. The response from Samuel Insull, Edison's administrative manager, explained that there were no openings at present but to keep checking back from time to time. That was not what he had hoped, and he would deal with it when he got home but, for the time being, Sutro was in no hurry to get back.[179]

Sutro's next two messages to Adamson and Moore from Madrid and Biarritz sounded particularly abrasive – Moore came in for criticism having failed to include information about the Central Pacific Railroad and for being two days late reporting; Adamson's handwriting drew complaints as his "S" was often not clear resulting in misfiling of letters at the post office; to preclude further problems of this kind, Adamson was instructed to have pre-printed self-addressed envelopes prepared; several leases bothered Sutro and he was not going to extend one of them for more than a year at the current rate; on the Reese Block, a clause needed to be inserted into every lease stating that "we do not undertake to keep the roofs or cellars in order, and that damages caused by overflow etc is not at our risk"; and finally, "... As regards Theodore Sutro, you must make no payments to him, as the security is not <u>sufficient</u> to pay the mortgage ..."[180]

The pattern of communication back and forth between Sutro and his pair of subordinates continued unabated throughout the months of his travels. The duo tried their best to keep Sutro up to date on the many details at home but every letter to them contained criticism of some kind: the Cliff House had been advertised for rent from late October until mid-January of 1884 when it was leased to Hugh McCrum and George Sheldon who operated it as a hotel but, despite the $1,000 per month income, the deal angered Sutro who "did not suppose that the place would be let furnished and renovated inside and out.....I should not like, ordinarily, to have any considerable sum of money expended without being first consulted, especially as telegrams can so easily reach me." In that same period, Sutro visited Aix-la-Chapelle and reported: "I am here in my native town, the spot selected by the great emperor Charlemagne as his nostrum; streets, hills and valleys awaken in me recollections of my boyhood days but I have not seen much yet as I want to reply first to accumulated letters. Most of the people I used to know are dead, bringing it to my mind most firmly that our earthly career is but a passing event." This poignant lapse was inserted into a fourteen-page letter filled with crabby complaints. While in Seville, Spain, Sutro learned the terms he had been given on the loan from Sutro & Company and he was hot under the collar. The line of credit he had sought was not in the contract; the very favorable 4% interest had to be applied to the entire $100,000 up front. "But I did not, and do not propose to run in debt for such a large sum, when the money is not required - ....unfortunately I did not keep a copy of the power of att[orney]; I am afraid it is recorded so that a loan of not less than $100,000 can only be made. If that is so a new one must be sent to me for correction, containing the words 'or any part thereof'..." From Cairo, he registered his disapproval with Moore, who had written two letters thirteen days apart, which Sutro pointed out "does not quite come up to the promised two letters per week." Then he launched into a scolding about expenditures which "rather frightened" him. "I wish here to say once more distinctly and particularly that I wish no further expenditures of any sums whatever, which are not included in the general routine of business (such as water rates, insurance, absolutely necessary repairs &ca &ca) except specifically authorized by me, and this injunction is meant as much for Mr. Moore as for you Mr. Adamson." There was more. Sutro repeated his complaints about the Cliff House – "I must candidly say that this Cliff House business is all wrong." He conceded having agreed to a $1,000 per month rental but "... I never expected that I should foot the bills for the purchase of carpeting, curtains and I know not what all else." Additionally, his instructions, months earlier, to have a sidewalk built immediately had not been completed and he was receiving inquiries about blasting issues which should not have been considered for a temporary walkway. The possibility of blasting would have potential consequences for the railroad construction that Gustav was arranging on top of Sutro Heights and Adolph was very displeased about that. He announced his intention to return to San Francisco during the summer to get things all straightened out. Unfortunately, this was only March.[181]

In late April, Moore went to great lengths explaining the issues Sutro had critiqued and how much he and Adamson had consulted Sutro's cousins during the process of completing their tasks. Everything was fine and they were confident he would have made the same decisions. And, by the way, you may have heard about the flimsy bridge that was built by the contractor on your Cliff House property which people started using and which then broke due to overcrowding and fell down injuring several visitors who had panicked. One law suit has been filed against you; there will probably be others. Sutro arrived back in Paris in May after an extensive Middle East and Mediterranean tour including stops at Jerusalem, Jaffa, Beirut, Damascus, Baalbec, Athens, Constantinople, Pest, Vienna, and Münich. Although his communication seemed to project a better mood, he was still annoyed at his cousin Gustav but conceded he may have "done him wrong" and will be "the first to acknowledge any wrong if it proves to be so." He also thought "Mr. Van Alen did wrong in reducing the rent on Reese Block ... he is a very poor agent always in favor of reducing rents and spending money for repairs." Sutro offered a veiled apology to Adamson; he "did not mean to convey the idea that I hold you responsible" for the unauthorized expenditures at the Cliff House but that he only meant they should have had his "special permission." However, when he received the next accounting report, Sutro scolded Adamson again with "...why you are two months behind in your accounts I do not quite understand." He expected to reach San Francisco early in July when he could decide things "on the spot."[182]

Before returning to America, Sutro accelerated his book acquisition program in several ways. Right after his return to Paris to see the girls, he had immediately traveled to London to find a storage facility for his books and he settled upon Brooks Wharf along the Thames River. Professionally run by its owner, Robert Warner, this was a combination warehouse and import/export packing and shipping facility. Clerical help was assigned to coordinate with Sutro's librarian on the accuracy and completeness of shipments in and out of storage. Sutro hired a second librarian, Mr. E. Hofstädtler, who joined him in London. Unfortunately, he spoke no English and the book purchasing agent, Mayer, would have to help him with that. The firm of Langstaff, Ehrenberg & Pollak had been engaged to search out books Sutro might want to purchase and a lively correspondence followed with many offers. Seven separate insurance policies were acquired through Robert Warner's staff in order to spread the risks of coverage for books stored or processed in the warehouse.[183]

Sutro's travels had invigorated him – actually elevated his energy level—and he launched into a variety of projects and issues any one of which would have kept the average manager incredibly busy. There were extensive plans for new structures at Sutro Heights including a conservatory building. Architectural renderings showing the general form of the building had been sent to him while he was still in Paris. He had uncovered rare historical documents in church archives at Seville which he had arranged to photocopy using camera equipment. He launched a campaign advertising these acquisitions to key members of the local historical society emphasizing the importance of the find to California's status in national intellectual circles. Manuel Maria Peralta, Sutro's acquaintance and Minister Plenipotentiary of Costa Rica in the United States, had told him there was little chance of finding anything new and worthwhile because Hubert Howe Bancroft had "left you and everyone else in California quite behind." Beating Bancroft to the punch would have been particularly pleasing to Sutro. He was also working feverishly to construct roads and train tracks from the residential parts of town to the Cliff House and the area surrounding the heights so that an immense entertainment center could be established that all citizens of the city could access easily and economically. His real estate business had multiple issues, among them, defining and selling lots, building structures for rental, managing rental properties, and the manipulation of funds, loans, and other fiduciary documents. There were law suits of all kinds including some he initiated and some against him. His program of forest creation on the vast hillside spaces of his property was proceeding including the use of Chinese laborers which Sutro had foresworn all his years while constructing the tunnel. Of course, the library and its books were being pursued passionately. In each of these efforts, Sutro had competent help but never let the details out of his sight for one moment.[184]

Eleven

JOSEPH ARON

One of the early contacts Sutro made through the Eureka Benevolent Society was Joseph Aron with whom Adolph Sutro had an incredibly close and beneficial relationship over more than twenty years. Aron, born in 1836 in Phalsbourg, France, married Adelaide Adèle Cahn, a member of the Lazard family. Aron was also a first cousin to the five Lazard banking brothers, to Alex Weil and David Cahn, all of whom spent the major portion of their working lives at Lazard Frères. Late in his life, Aron recalled how he had become interested in the tunnel project. He told of being approached by Adolph Sutro who came to Aron's office and described the tunnel he had in mind and the number of high-level people he had gathered at its organizational birth. Aron expressed disinterest. Though Sutro had been involved with Weil & Co. in his cigar business days, all that had been before Aron joined the tobacco importing firm, and he claimed to have not really known Sutro that well. But Sutro was persistent; he "came to me day after day" and continued to solicit Aron for a small investment in the project. Finally, "tired of Sutro's insistence," Aron subscribed $1,000 for what was described as one share – the equivalent of $50,000 worth of the tunnel stock. Months later, at a chance meeting, Sutro lectured Aron on the technical issues and bragged about the endorsement of Baron Ferdinand von Richthofen who was an acknowledged international authority on both geology and mining. Aron was sold. His enthusiasm ran away with itself and he gave Sutro a needed $3,000 in cash to support a trip to Washington D.C. where he intended to obtain government financing. Their relationship grew from there.[185]

As soon as Sutro had sufficient money to start work on the tunnel, the Sutro Tunnel Company was incorporated in San Francisco and a new Board of Trustees was elected including Joseph Aron. In the months leading up to that event, Aron had handed over hundreds of dollars in response to almost weekly appeals from Sutro who had been unable to develop any significant source of funds to carry the work forward. Through several of those early years, Aron was an active partner in Weil & Company. By early 1870, Aron made his residence in San Francisco and sorely tested the patience of his New York partners by his absence and his failure to produce revenue for the company. But Aron was fascinated by the tunnel challenge and completely under the spell of Sutro's dreams. Sutro spent much of the next two years searching for substantial financing in Washington, D.C. and in Europe. Beginning in August, 1871, Aron wrote numerous letters to Sutro throughout the ensuing two years – more than one each week – containing information about progress in the tunnel, political situations within the board, attacks from their enemies at the Bank of California and the mining companies, and more. The extent of his loyalty, patience, and good intentions went far beyond what any employee could ever have been asked.[186]

In 1873, another turnover in trustees took place during which Aron became President of the Sutro Tunnel Company. Concurrently, the Mc-Calmonts had invested heavily making direct loans with company stock as collateral for which they also held two seats on the board. These were filled by Col. Charles W. Brush and Thomas C. Wedderspoon. Aron's communications with Sutro continued at a merry pace through the tough years of the tunnel construction. After Aron was replaced as President, he returned to New York and continued to write regularly to Sutro no matter where Sutro happened to be at the time, but principally to Washington where opponents of the tunnel repeatedly proposed changes to the Sutro Tunnel Law in Congress requiring Adolph Sutro to be lobbying constantly. Aron received reports from J.A. Benjamin, the acting tunnel Superintendent (in Sutro's absence), which he filtered and passed on to Sutro with suggestions, criticisms, recommendations, and considerable editorial comment. There was simply no end to his involvement or his dedication to the cause.

Most importantly, his principal issue was accounting the shares of company stock – how many there were, who held them, what they had cost originally and what they were worth in the current market. The major stockholders discussed potential offers and sales constantly and, somehow, Aron was always knowledgeable about these. He appeared to know everything that went on at great distance from the source and reported all of it to Sutro. In summary, the relationship was bizarre with the rich man who had no credentials totally subservient to an uncrowned boss with empty pockets.

In May 1874, Aron and his family moved back to France where both he and his wife had been born. He went primarily to obtain treatments for rheumatism from a renowned doctor. Before he left, Aron wrote to Sutro summarizing the contributions he had made in both personal involvement and in money. "Being very near my departure for Europe and possibly some unforeseen accident may happen to me I think it a duty I owe to my family to make a demand I am justly entitled to... you know that for five years at least I have given most of my time and not only my time but also my money... I consider the Co. owes me justly at least from 50 to seventy thousand dollars... you have told me often it will be made all right one day... if I should die shortly I will leave my wife in not as comfortable a position as I should... I rely on you my dear Adolph and feel satisfied you will cause to be done what is right and just..." He went on in this vein for another page.[187]

Once Aron arrived in France, the flow of letters to Sutro continued except that Aron was not receiving any responses. Some of his letters were childish, full of inane questions and expressions of annoyance at being ignored. He admitted knowing that Sutro was extremely busy but literally begged for a short letter. A year later, Aron began getting responses again. Sutro needed money badly and asked for cash loans. Aron still had a small drawing account from Weil & Company which he began giving to Sutro - $250 every month. Without being asked, Aron plunged himself into the relationship between Sutro and the Mc-Calmont brothers. He visited the McCalmont London offices and continued for three consecutive days embroiled in conversations with both Robert and Hugh McCalmont about the value of the tunnel, the value of their investment and personal issues of what seemed to be deteriorating relationships. Sutro's antipathy towards Brush, Coulter, Wedderspoon, and the Cross organization surfaced, and Aron reported a considerable amount of information which Sutro never would have obtained personally otherwise. The Arons returned to the United States and were living in New York. He continued to send suggestions about plots and plans to defeat the Bank of California and to bolster the tunnel stock. In the summer of 1876, the Aron and Lazard families vacationed at Glen House Resort in the White Mountains of Vermont. Emma Sutro joined them as a companion for Aron's daughter Lucie and remained at their home until school started again at Vassar in the fall. Despite minimal personal contact among the four parents, in the entire duration of the Sutro marriage this was certainly the closest thing they had to an intimate social relationship.[188]

When the Seligman bank group began lobbying to have the tunnel company stock put on the New York Exchange, Aron anguished over the concept. He fired off a lengthy dissertation to Sutro that criticized the idea while soliciting "friend Adolph's" opinion. Aron's paranoia over stock issues never failed to arouse his passion and drove him to seek the security of Sutro's concurrence. On the other hand, there are virtually no examples of Sutro seeking opinions from anyone on any subject; he always believed he knew more about everything than those around him. However, he was careful to avoid saying this – especially to Aron upon whom he depended for cash over long periods of time.[189]

In November 1878, another re-organization took place and Aron was no longer president of the company or a member of the board of trustees – in fact he had no connection with the Sutro Tunnel Company at all. Brush and Wedderspoon retained their posts and Sutro's loyal legal right hand, Elliott J. Moore, took over the presidency. Somehow, Aron could not get over the fact that he held no position of responsibility in the company. His attachment to Sutro and the extended continuity of his financial and other commercial connections to the company drove him to behave as if he were still an officer and a trustee. At the same time, the insiders of the company considered him a valuable resource for his dedicated adherence to rigid financial constraints, confidentiality, and encyclopedic familiarity with the company stock and stockholders. He had sufficient income from outside sources that he pursued his tunnel connection as a *pro bono* activity. Very few major corporate entities could count upon a volunteer like Joseph Aron. Consequently, Aron stayed in close touch with the key players at the Tunnel Company as they did with him. He always knew what was going on and when there were problems of construction progress, loan payments, or radical fluctuations in stock price or vendor costs. Notwithstanding his lack of authority, his counsel was sought by Pelham Ames (the company secretary) and Theodore Sutro (Adolph's brother) and, very likely, Brush and the other trustees. Everyone assumed he had Sutro's confidence and his ear and were willing to make him a partner in the information flow to stay on his best side.[190]

That situation began to erode, but it was not obvious to outsiders. Sutro was becoming irritated over Aron's paranoia about the stock. Aron was becoming more aggravated daily over Sutro's aggressive stock manipulations and potentially dangerous loan pursuit. As the negotiations between the Tunnel Company and the mining companies became more intense, threats of tunnel blockage, water release, and law suits flew back and forth testing the ingenuity of the tunnel hierarchy. Aron launched himself into the middle of the fray and issued a stream of coded telegrams to Sutro with one outrageous suggestion after another about negotiations with the mines. He urged Sutro to close the bulkhead effectively shutting down the tunnel so that mines could not use it. He also expressed his disagreement with the idea of Sutro's daughter, Emma, studying medicine where she might "loose (sic) her best years in a vocation hard for ladies." When the agreement with the mines was looking more likely, thoughts of blocking the tunnel evaporated; Sutro had already advised Aron he approved Emma's medical school plan. Conclusion of the negotiations with the mining companies and connection to the Savage Mine stimulated another flow of messages from Aron with dire warnings about stock issues. In May 1879, Sutro's sale of some stock to raise cash infuriated Aron. "Really my dear Adolph if I expected to have competition from any body in the offering of shares it was not from you. I am perfectly amazed at it and only hope it will not occur again till I have the money all raised for the Company."[191]

Eventually, Sutro's stock sales through Edward Adams drove an irreversible wedge through the relationship. Sutro tried to calm the waters by drawing Adelaide Aron into the situation without success and their friendship was over. Sutro left the tunnel company and withdrew to San Francisco. Aron, in New York as representative for Lazard Frères, maintained his ties to the tunnel company and particularly with Theodore Sutro who also continued to labor in pursuit of tunnel profit growth. At the annual meeting in 1881, Aron was returned to the Board of Trustees of the tunnel Company.[192]

In 1886, the McCalmont Bank sued the Sutro Tunnel Company when interest payments were not made on their loan. Theodore Sutro was hired to defend the tunnel company against the lawsuit and proceeded to develop a plan. His primary difficulty derived from the opinion generally held by stockholders that the suit was indefensible, and a broad lack of cooperation held him back. Eventually, he was able to convince a small but energetic and affluent group that a combination of reorganization, bond investment, increased tunnel earnings, and vigorous negotiation could generate a successful conclusion with the bank. Theodore was named president of the company at a trustees meeting in May 1888. The group of interested stockholders was increased, and arrangements were made to have the cooperation of the Union Trust Company of New York as holder of the new loan resulting from negotiations with the McCalmonts. Theodore persisted, and the loan was settled within a few months.[193]

One year later, the company was re-organized again and emerged as the Comstock Tunnel Company with the Union Bank holding a mortgage on what remained of the loan. New shares were distributed to stockholders. It didn't take long for some dissatisfied shareholders to become aroused at the manipulations which had taken place. Three original Sutro Tunnel investors, Frank J. Symmes, Joseph Aron and Fairfax H. Wheelan, joined together in a suit against the Union Bank for irregularities in the process of conversion between the two entities. Aron had returned to Paris and issued a voluminous open letter to Comstock Tunnel shareholders containing inflammatory remarks about both Sutro brothers and urging against giving proxies to Theodore for the next stockholders' meeting. The letter was published as a pamphlet and received wide distribution. Included in this document were copies of letters written by Theodore Sutro to the stockholders filled with accusations and denunciations of Aron. Theodore Sutro and Aron exchanged a number of bellicose communications accusing each other of malice and distortions. A genuine dislike grew between the two which continued until the case was concluded in March 1894. More than "…three years were consumed in pleading and submitting evidence; the typewritten testimony and record covered 5,000 pages, and there were 1,000 closely printed pages of briefs." In conclusion, Judge Thomas B. Hawley ordered that "complainants' bill should be dismissed, and judgment entered in favor of respondents for their costs." Newspaper accounts proclaimed this as a "complete victory" for Theodore Sutro and described Aron as having been "scored badly."[194]

Aron never quit. In February 1895, he authored and paid for publication of a newspaper article in the English language supplement of *Les Mines d'Or,* a French journal, in which he denounced Adolph Sutro at length. This was an open letter to the President of the United States and the Congress. Reaching back to early pre-tunnel days, Aron excoriated

Sutro for alleged falsehoods in his addresses to Congress and his speech to the miners, for fraudulent stock manipulation, and other offenses in connection with funding the tunnel. Additionally: "Mr. President and Members of Congress! The great German adventurer, Mayor Sutro of San Francisco, is simply the secret partner of Huntington, Crocker, and the other financial pirates who control the Pacific Railroad." Two more entire pages of newspaper were devoted to reprinting letters from Sutro to Aron ostensibly to show his evil character and disrespect for Congress. A third complete page was a reprint of an interview of Sutro regarding the Central Pacific Railroad Funding Bill being considered by the Congress at that time. Aron implied that Sutro's extreme opposition to the bill was actually intended to create support in the Congress by opposing him.[195]

From 1886 until the end of his life in October 1905, Aron lived in France. He became involved deeply in defiance against anti-Semitism particularly in the case of Captain Alfred Dreyfus. He exchanged letters with leaders of the French government including President Felix Faure; Zadok Kahn, the chief Rabbi of France; Emile Zola and others. In 1892, Adelaide Aron passed away. Four years later, a daughter was born out of wedlock to Amelie Rose Mace to whom Aron was married in 1897. The pair produced a son in 1900 and another three years later when Joseph Aron was 67 years old.[196]

Twelve

SUTRO HEIGHTS

On New Year's Day 1885, *The Daily Alta California* printed Sutro's plans to build a "large, handsome, costly and architecturally interesting building" on the top of the bluff overlooking the ocean near the Cliff House to be used as a family residence. Sculptures of both humans and animals, acquired in Europe, would adorn the grounds which would be open to the public about twice a week. Also, Sutro's library of 30,000 books and his collection of works of art would be located in the new building temporarily until a new library building was erected to house the books. Mr. Sutro was planning to accumulate a "large and valuable" library comparable to the great seats of learning in the old world. Eventually, his plans included having this library given to the city of San Francisco. Sutro's tastes and intentions were admired by the editors.[197]

Indeed, Sutro was back into high gear managing a variety of complex projects simultaneously. Relative to the library, he had hired George Moss of Sacramento to take the position as his librarian; conducted negotiations with architect John Lyman Faxon about designing a new library building; received from Brooks Warehouse proprietor Robert Warner and stored a large quantity of books in a temporary facility in 107 Battery Street; sued the French steamship *Bordeaux* for damages to books during their shipment to San Francisco from Brooks Wharf in London; and had begun the laborious process of sorting the huge volume of materials he had acquired. Late in March 1885, representatives from all the local newspapers were invited to spend a day examining the collection and several extensive articles were published describing the assorted materials. Every writer expressed admiration for the extent of the collection and for the variety of incredibly valuable items. Many predicted great fame for the new library and wrote with pride that this would be a San Francisco showpiece. But, the library wasn't the only project under way. Construction of a road from the Mission District along 17th Street to the vicinity of Golden Gate Park was expected to start immediately and be completed in sixty days — all on Sutro's land.[198]

The road and the work on a railroad line from the city to the Cliff House were all part of an overall plan to build a major entertainment center at Sutro Heights. In his view, the number one priority was the necessity to make traveling to the Heights easy and inexpensive so that families in town would not hesitate to make the journey which had been so difficult and costly just a short time ago. The new railroad line would traverse the edge of the cliffs above the Pacific some 170 feet above the water "... and when completed will afford one of the grandest views and most charming excursions to be found on the continent." The fare was to be set at five cents from the center of town to the end of the line. Decisions had not been made about the type of engine; steam, electricity, and pneumatic power were all under consideration.[199]

Adolph Sutro's round-the-world trip had opened his eyes to many things. He saw how the finest entrepreneurs on the planet established and maintained the highest quality in goods or services and created a baseline for how he would conduct his ventures in the future. He had seen the best of everything all over the world and knew what it would take to compete – to deliver a world-class product of his own and to say so with confidence. But that wasn't all. Sutro also learned that he didn't have to be there all the time himself, tied down by the day-to-day workings of a project. In fact, it was not only possible but reasonably easy for him to maintain a competent staff in every area of his interest and drive them to accomplish details of programs by communicating from afar. He planned to do that in the future.

Sutro had engaged the services of several real estate agencies and sales of lots in the western lands began to ramp up significantly yielding funds for construction of roads, train track beds, a large aquarium, walkways, a conservatory building, and the purchase of huge numbers of trees, other shrubbery and statuary. In the spring of 1885, nearly two hundred lots were sold as future home sites. On many of those sales, Sutro took back mortgages generating a steady cash flow stream. In that same time period, Sutro made occasional trips to Paraiso Hot Springs, California, to enjoy the mineral baths for repeated episodes of "catarrh" (inflammation of the mucous membranes). The coughing may very well have been the result of smoking "segars" which he had Adamson send him even while treating the illness. These diversions didn't interfere with his oversight of projects. More significant, however, was the fact that Sutro was living a fine life and was spending money at a rate exceeding the income from his lot sales and mortgages. He continued buying books through his agents, building his construction projects, and sending monthly stipends to family members and needy friends. His plans outstripped his incoming cash flow as badly as they had in Europe and he found it would be necessary to sell the Inwood house and to borrow money again. Also, he had to turn down his brother Louis who asked for funds.[200]

On top of his entrepreneurial life, Adolph Sutro had engaged in an almost endless series of charitable acts. He had provided land for a wing of the County Hospital which was named for him. He sent books to the schoolchildren in the town of Sutro, Nevada, and to the Pacific Hebrew Orphan Asylum in San Francisco. Children from that orphanage were then treated to a day at Sutro Heights with lunch and entertainments. A similar day was arranged for the San Francisco Roman Catholic Orphanage. One of Sutro's strongest interests was support for various kindergarten associations which were not part of the conventional school system at that time. He had a close working relationship with Sarah B. Cooper who had founded the Golden Gate Kindergarten Association, a consortium of fifty kindergartens throughout the city. Annually, she appealed to Sutro for funds and he never failed to help. Further, Sutro collaborated with, Joacquin Miller, a prominent poet, in organizing the first of the continuing Arbor Days in San Francisco and he donated 40,000 tree seedlings to schoolchildren for the purpose including all those in the kindergarten associations. Plantings and celebrations took place at three locations that day – at Yerba Buena Island, at Goat Island, and at the Presidio. All the trees had been provided by Adolph Sutro who planted the first one at Yerba Buena and delivered a short speech predicting a celebration to honor the 100th anniversary of that date which, unfortunately, none of them would be able to attend. Sutro supported the San Francisco Art League by paying tuition for two students for a full year. There was virtually no end to his charity.[201]

Beyond that, he had other interests. The sea lions on the rocks below Sutro Heights fascinated him and he was outraged by pranks and cruel acts perpetrated against them. Sutro promulgated publishing a legal document which resulted eventually in a United States Congressional Act deeding the Seal Rocks below the Cliff House to the City and County of San Francisco. Those agencies were required to "hold said Seal Rocks inalienable for all time, in trust for the people of the United States, and shall commit to the commissioners of Golden Gate Park the custody and care of said Seal Rocks, and shall keep said rocks free from encroachment by man, and shall preserve from molestation the seals and other animals now accustomed to resort there...." Further, it enjoined local authorities to "...control and limit or diminish the number of seals resorting to said rocks so as to protect the fisheries and fishing industries."[202]

Despite these interesting sidelights in his life, Sutro never lost sight of his main objectives. He was going to create a center of interesting and crowd-pleasing enterprises all around his corner of the peninsula. He focused on anything and everything that would contribute to that result. Within weeks of each other, Sutro offered land to the state university and surfaced plans for his aquarium. The land would be very close to the Cliff House and Sutro Heights and was intended to house the university's marine biological laboratory. Proximity to the ocean made the concept quite appealing to Adolph Sutro. At the same time, the aquarium would be at the shoreline virtually adjacent to the laboratory. It did not take long for the idea to receive a poor reception among the faculty. Many of them thought the university buildings were already too isolated from each other and that additional travel between venues would be extremely inefficient. Further, the gift included only land and required the university to spend considerable money for the facility to be built there. The gift was discussed at the state Board of Regents meeting and was tabled. Sutro went ahead with his plans for the aquarium. It would consist of a round wall of rock fifty feet in diameter, fifteen feet thick, fourteen feet high without a roof. Solid rock pathways would weave through the interior with small ponds here and there. Tides would fill the entire cavity through a tunnel some three-hundred feet long and eight feet high capped at the seaward end with a gate of wire screen. This would permit the great variety of sea life to enter with high tides and would let water escape through the screen when desired. leaving low water levels in the pools containing sea anemones, devil fish, angel fish, starfish, crustaceans, and many types of small ocean life. A series of heated pipes was provided to keep the water at proper temperature for the briny inhabitants.

The aquarium was a relatively short-term objective with completion expected approximately one year later. However, this was just one part of the scheme which, in the long run, would include the baths. Some two acres of sandy beach had been identified as the likely area for the baths and the ingenious methods of filling, controlling and emptying the huge vessels would be proven by operation of the aquarium. In September 1887, tests demonstrated the feasibility of the filling and emptying processes leaving the work of enlarging flow passages as the principal goal. Reinforcing the wall structure was thought to be difficult but well within the bounds of conventional structural techniques. That didn't turn out to be true. The first wall constructed collapsed and basically sank into the sandy soil below it. Sutro had a second wall built using the first as a foundation. This wall also sank as had the first. Undaunted, a third rock wall was mounted upon the two below and success was achieved.

One night in 1887, a bizarre episode halted progress on the Heights. The schooner *Parallel,* lacking sufficient wind for sailing, was beached just below the Cliff House in the early evening. The stranded ship attracted a large crowd interested in helping the crew and saving the vessel. Unknown to the visitors, the crew had gotten out safely and moved away from the area without warning sightseers that the ship's cargo was forty or more tons of explosives. Three or four hours elapsed and, fortunately, people slowly drifted away from the scene to their homes. About one o'clock in the morning, the ship exploded with a huge, loud fireball heard all the way to the center of the city. Early examination yielded reports that the Cliff House had been destroyed substantially but this proved to be false. However, virtually every window in the building was smashed. Large pieces of the schooner were found at great distances away from the point of percussion. The following day, a crowd estimated to exceed 60,000 people found its way to the beach or to Sutro Heights to witness the destruction first hand. Men and women had traveled from Oakland and other distant locales to see the mess. It turned into a day of revelry for the many wanting souvenirs or merely fun on the shore. Sutro had a powder magazine underground near the Cliff House and its security prevented the contents from also exploding although inspection revealed that boxes and cans had been scattered "in great confusion on the floor of the magazine." Had this been ignited, there would have been little of the Cliff House remaining. As it was, Sutro, seemed hardly bothered saying that "…you can buy a good deal of glass for $200." Miraculously, no one had been killed. That was the "public Sutro." He asked Moore if they could "bring about an investigation of the *Parallel* case, by having the captain arrested on some charge of malfeasance – I think he abandoned the vessel in order to get away from here."[203]

In the midst of this flurry of activities, Rosa Sutro became engaged to Pio Alberto Morbio, a young and talented Italian businessman, and the two were married a few days later in February 1887. The wedding took place at the Hayes and Fillmore mansion attended by just fifteen people including Adolph and Leah, Carla Sutro as maid of honor, best man Stanislaus Antoldi, (Alberto's closest friend), Italian Consul Francesco and Mrs. Lambertenghi, Mr. and Mrs. Cesar Splivalo (proprietor of the largest pasta producer in the west), Dr. and Mrs. Wolrad Winterberg (Adolph's sister Emma and her husband) and their son Walter Winterberg, and Sutro's son Charles, brother of the bride. Interestingly, Adolph and Leah had made a practice of avoiding each other at social events and their presence together was a concession to Rosa. Not even their daughter Emma's wedding had been sufficiently magnetic to attract them both. Services were performed by Judge Elisha W. McKinstry, one of the various legal experts upon whom Adolph depended frequently and with whom he maintained something akin to a friendly relationship.[204]

During July, Sutro's son-in-law Moritz Nussbaum (Kate's husband) visited from Germany and spent several days touring California lakes and streams with Professor Harvey W. Harkness, president of the California Academy of Sciences. Their purpose was to examine vegetable and animal growth in the small bodies of California water and obtain specimens for Professor Nussbaum. Surely, Adolph Sutro had arranged this research in anticipation of potential issues at the aquarium and later at his bath house. He utilized Nussbaum's services with confidence and without significant cost. The same was true of sons-in-law George Merritt and Alberto Morbio.[205]

Adolph Sutro spent the better part of the entire year 1887 at the Heights only occasionally leaving for one purpose or another. During that time, he issued more than eighty notes with instructions for Adamson which were delivered from the Heights to the city by train. Some were in the same vein as his letters from the world tour. Sutro thought Adamson overpaid a group of construction workers. When the check came for his approval, he wrote to Adamson, "As far as the blasters are concerned, that [$1.50 per day] is all they will receive until they go blasting when an allowance of 25' per day will be made. I can get a thousand men in a day at that price and they will be glad to get the work. This applies only to the two or three days they have been at work on 17th St and if there is anyone whom this does not suit he can quit." Sutro never withheld criticism when he felt it was appropriate. The notes to Adamson were remarkable demonstrating Sutro's encyclopedic knowledge of his business matters. He knew almost everything about each block of property – its boundaries, whether or not it was leased, the duration of leases, and the amount of lease payments, relationships between adjacent properties that had impact upon the utility of the building next door, and status of facilities and equipment at every location. Of course, this was supported by the constant stream of reports he received weekly from Moore, Adamson, and the accountant, Mr. Kent. A great many of his personal issues outside of the real estate world were also managed in this way. Nothing escaped his purview and if it ever did, he asked about it until he understood. Some samples:

A tenant was leaving – Sutro had Adamson offer a logical portion of the property to another tenant adjacent to the impending vacancy. Another tenant moving out owned the elevator in their suite; Sutro had Adamson study elevator prices preparing to make an offer for the one installed. Rents and collections came up frequently – one tenant was "inconvenienced somewhat by not having the upper floor over their store, but that cannot be changed and so far as our occupation of a part of the floor is concerned, we can remove our things as well as not if they desire it, but as to reducing the rent that is entirely out of the question for the rents of all the floors have now been settled for good and no further change will be made." Also, "I see Mrs. R ..... is behind in her rents for two months; I must again insist that rent collections do not run behind – delinquents must be dunned <u>daily</u> until paid." Sutro got wind that another tenant was talking about leaving and offered, "Does he really mean to leave or is it only a bid to have his rent lowered again?" Adamson was instructed to check deeds and send Sutro the length and width of the land strip between two large ranch properties. "I am afraid

Hughes has fenced in more land than belongs to him." One tenant sublet the basement of his store illegally; Sutro had Adamson issue a warning that, in case of fire, they would be responsible for any damages and that the iron door had better be closed every night. Sutro co-signed every check going out of their offices. The checks (usually a half-dozen or so) were sent to him weekly; at least one was sent back unsigned for some valid reason. Accounting reports were checked before sending them to him but occasionally there would be a note like this, "Enclosed find daily account of July 18 showing a balance of $23,494.36 – should it not be $25,494.36?" And then, "Please get someone competent to examine our water meter." It was read incorrectly resulting in a billing ten times what it should have been.

During that year, Sutro added three people to his monthly "pension list." The first was Jacob P. Leese, then 78 years old, who had built the first permanent house in San Francisco in 1836. A roving merchant and land owner, he had returned to San Francisco two years earlier after a large project had failed and he was in dire financial condition. Sutro put him on the books for $10 per month. The same amount went to [J.] F. Heston, formerly a carpenter and builder who had done construction for Sutro and was no longer able to work. Adamson was instructed to deliver the first payment himself and to check on Heston's condition and report. Third and last was Colonel James L. L. Warren, then 92 years old, who had lectured on the speaker circuit about the Revolutionary War and who was a member of General Lafayette's guard of honor at the foundation laying for the Bunker Hill Monument in 1825. He was known as the oldest member of the Society of California Pioneers and he also received $10 per month from Adolph Sutro.[206]

Sutro went downtown in late March to voice opposition to a sewer construction which would interfere with a road he was building toward the beach. Shortly thereafter, he returned to host various kindergarten associations at a luncheon party on Sutro Heights and, in June, sat for portrait artist Alexander Archibald Anderson who completed the painting at Sutro Heights. He made several trips around the state to mineral springs where he both bathed in and drank the waters intended to promote health. Among those he visited in central and northern California were Bartlett Springs, Lower Lake, Siegler Springs, Adams [Springs], and Saratoga. At Bartlett Springs he observed, "These waters seem to have a wonderful effect on one's system and we all feel better for drinking them. It seems they are alterative [sic], slightly purgative in their effect, and have a powerful action on the kidneys. They say that 'they' [the waters] are the Paradise for those, who suffer from the effects of too much whisky; but in fact they seem to be good for anyone who requires a general cleaning out of the system."[207]

While Sutro was thriving upon the waters, an army of employees was turning Sutro Heights into a magnificent park. Elaborate gardens were planted, raised and trimmed throughout the area and some two hundred statues were placed artfully around the grounds. The sculptures were copies of works Sutro had seen on his round-the-world tour and which he had arranged to be fabricated by a Belgian company. At one time, Sutro joked about having paid more to transport the statuary from the docks up to the heights than to bring it from Belgium to San Francisco; that was probably an exaggeration. But the end result was impressive with serpentine roads and paths throughout the manicured park. He had announced his intention to make these grounds available to the general public. The preparations were admired by one newsman calling them "a thing of art and beauty." The unfinished aquarium and the future baths would only broaden the interest and enjoyment of the citizens.[208]

Not long after, Sutro arranged for another sculpture to be imported and displayed prominently in the city. The location was a knoll known as Mount Olympus at a street junction which no longer exists. The statue was a copy of one he had seen on his travels named "Triumph of Light" depicting a woman raising a torch with her right hand after having vanquished a figure depicting Despotism at her feet. Many who had not seen the Statue of Liberty in New York harbor, which had come to America shortly before this one, confused the two using "Stat-

ue of Liberty" as the name for both. Sutro had arranged electric lighting inside some of the statue details (the torch and the sword) for the
formal unveiling which was held, after several postponements, on
Thanksgiving Day. The ceremonies were extensive with speeches by
Mayor Edward Pond, Judge Solomon Heydenfeldt, poetess Ella Cum-
mins, and Adolph Sutro. His remarks included handing over the deed
to the property, including the statue, to the mayor as a gift to the city. A
band played, children sang "America," and three more speakers felt motivated to compliment Sutro's generosity. A group of invited guests
then went to Sutro Heights where they were treated to "an elegant re-
past" and more speeches.[209]

Elsewhere in America, serious issues were ongoing which would
draw Adolph Sutro's attention eventually. The Philadelphia and Reading
Railroad, after years of contentious leadership under Franklin Gowen,
had been taken over by a consortium of bankers led by J.P. Morgan. The
company had transformed from the world's most prosperous business
enterprise through two bankruptcies into receivership raising the spec-
ter of scandal in many of its dealings along the way. Railroad managements across the country had begun to arouse suspicion and contempt
as monopolists and financial manipulators and were certainly earning
increased observation by both government and news reporting agencies. A competition to complete the first transcontinental railroad had
been waged between the Union Pacific and the Central Pacific railroad
companies since 1862. Abraham Lincoln had signed the Pacific Railroad Act into law including issuance of government bonds and award of
land grants to the railroad companies. Now, more than twenty years later, the promised benefits to the government for its largesse had become
more difficult to see. In early 1887, President Grover Cleveland established a Pacific Railway Commission charged with investigating the
government's cost/benefit outcome from their relationship with companies that built and operated railroads in the United States. A total
$62,500,000 of thirty-year loans had been issued to six companies; in-
cluding interest, the government was to receive more than $142,000,000

133

in return between 1865 (the first loan) and 1897 (the last payment). The Union Pacific Railroad and the Central Pacific Railroad were the principal beneficiaries of that plan receiving $52,000,000 of the total between them. Neither railroad company had made regular payments and both used their influence with congressmen to have laws proposed extending payment schedules significantly. A battle began to rage in the halls of Congress and in the media over these proposals. The commission consisted of three prominent political individuals: Robert E. Pattison, ex-Governor of Pennsylvania; E[dward] Ellery Anderson, a corporate attorney reputed to have "borne a foremost part in cleansing of public affairs in New York"; and David T. Littler, an Illinois State Assemblyman who gave up his seat to participate on the commission. Knowledgeable outsiders were pleased with the selections and with the choice of Pattison as Chairman.

Throughout the year, the commission moved from city to city where headquarters of the various railroad companies were located and where files of financial transactions could be accessed for inspection by the commission's staff. Key owners and administrators were subpoenaed, and extensive inquiries were conducted by the three commissioners, all of whom had significant legal training and experience. The media followed these proceedings closely and daily reports went from coast to coast. The first meetings were in New York and included a brief questioning of Collis P. Huntington, but the bulk of the early sessions were devoted to the Union Pacific which was the prime target of investigation. Their management was accused of a variety of illegal practices including rebates, pool settlements, and overcharges. Accounting practices had been used to obfuscate some of these; the company had used accounts at allied rail lines to cover up transactions. Chairman Pattison compared these to the use of Crédit Mobilier, a phantom company, in earlier Union Pacific scandals during construction of the eastern railroads. When the Central Pacific came on the agenda, Leland Stanford made an aggressive stand to represent the company and to insist Central Pacific (CPRR) had performed incredibly well, had saved the government and the citizens a lot of money, and had been dealt with unfairly by having competitors aided by the government causing CPRR to lose business it had been promised. Stanford was alone on the witness chair for some two and one-half days offering one excuse after another for what appeared to be major lapses in financial integrity. Stanford expressed his personal opinion that the government should forget about the Central Pacific's debts because the nation had obtained huge benefits from its efforts. A small army of upper-level railroad employees shuttled back and forth between the hearing room and company offices to produce documents the commissioners requested. Many documents were "lost" or still being hunted. The hearings were still on the West Coast and Pattison looked forward to weeks later when they would get back to New York where Huntington and Crocker could be questioned on the same issues.[210]

Huntington's performance on the witness stand was a textbook lesson in evasiveness and "forgetfulness." He simply could not tell much about what went on in California because he lived in New York and only visited occasionally. His testimony was useless. When interrogations ended, the three commissioners were not in agreement about what to recommend. Anderson and Littler conceded that the railroad companies had acted outside the bounds of the law in many of their dealings and, further, that they had done everything they could to hide their illegal and shady activities. However, the two commissioners felt the best course of action was to grant a less objectionable payment extension than that requested by the railroads so that some reasonable portion of the government's investment would be recovered albeit much later than contracted. Pattison was unalterably opposed to that plan. Anderson and Littler produced their own report which came to be known as the "majority report" whereas Pattison's "minority report" was his alone. Pattison's fifteen pages included this: "The original purpose of Congress was to promote the public interest, and the companies were made trustees for that purpose, but the public interest has been subordinated by these companies to the stockholding interest. Nearly every obligation

135

these companies assumed has been violated. Their management has been a national disgrace." He went on: "In their relations to the Government they resorted to every device their ingenuity could invent in their efforts to evade the plain requirements of the law." An editorial summarized it thus: "the four men who controlled the Central Pacific, Messrs. Stanford, Huntington, Hopkins and Crocker, had diverted the earnings of that company through contracts made by themselves with themselves for construction, leases and repairs and divided over $142,000,000 in cash and securities ... and took leases of their own lines from themselves for the Central Pacific at the rate of 13 per cent per annum." Pattison recommended that Central Pacific and Union Pacific have their charters forfeited. He pointed out that "every officer of these roads who testified before the Commission overwhelmingly proved by the evidence submitted that the payment of debts at maturity in 1895 and 1897 can under no circumstances be expected." Consequently, waiting was futile. He recommended that lawsuits be commenced.[211]

Adolph Sutro followed these proceedings closely and very quickly agreed with the chairman's viewpoint. Stanford, Crocker, Hopkins, and Huntington called themselves "The Associates" but were known as "The Big Four" to outsiders. Sutro knew all of them from earlier business and social connections. Stanford, Crocker, and Hopkins all lived in San Francisco and were prominent in the community. Sutro traveled in the same circles as that trio. Huntington lived in New York, but they had encountered each other during Sutro's Washington, D.C. days when both were soliciting funds from the government for major projects. Sutro did not care for Huntington or Stanford particularly and held negative views about the monopolistic character of the railroad companies. He was outraged by their attempts to extend the loan repayment period interminably; their attorney, Alfred A. Cohen, had suggested perhaps 150 years would be reasonable. Sutro fumed at that. Of course, at this point, only commission testimony and recommendations were on the table. He knew Stanford and Huntington would not go down easily; he determined to keep an eye on the four "Associates" permanently.

136

Early in 1888, Edward Adams visited Sutro Heights with his wife and a group of friends who accompanied them on their western journey. Sutro had been available to play host and arranged for George Moss and an assistant to show them the library and the incredible treasures it held. Adams later expressed his "anxiety for the safety of the volumes in the far from fire-proof building" where they were stored. Adams recommended that Sutro look into special stones that were used to construct the Sweetwater Reservoir in San Diego County. He had contacted the general manager of the quarry company and could arrange for a discounted price when Sutro was ready. Sutro was not ready then but he did engage Adams and the Winslow, Lanier Co. to help dispose of the Inwood house which they accomplished over a five-month span.[212]

That was just the beginning of a busy period with library issues. Adolph had contacted his cousin Albert Sutro, one of Gustav's brothers in the financial company, about one interesting volume in the collection. The text had been written in 1692 and was entirely in Hebrew. All the family in that Sutro branch were pious Jews and conversant with Hebrew language. Albert had been the New York City representative for the banking house but had returned recently to San Francisco where he was semi-retired. Albert read the volume and was excited by its contents which appeared to contradict by some 90 years the birthdate of Jesus of Nazareth. He reported this to Adolph and suggested contacting the principal documentation experts at the Vatican to initiate discussion of the issues presented in the book. Albert wrote to Cardinal Jean-Baptiste Pitra, Librarian of the Holy Roman Church, explaining some of the details he thought would interest the church fathers. The response came from an intermediary who agreed there may be some interesting points in the text and his eminence would like to have someone look at the book – they would most certainly not be interested in buying the book without having their man inspect it. Albert wasn't sure that Adolph was actually interested in selling it, but he was so caught up in what he saw as revolutionary information that he kept pushing Adolph to pursue the issue. He thought Adolph would become involved in the correspondence and warned him not to appear too eager to sell – let them make the suggestion first. Adolph didn't write and neither did the Vatican.[213]

Besides Adams, the Sutro Library attracted a variety of interesting visitors not the least of whom was Hubert Howe Bancroft. The now-famous historian was gathering information for his two huge documents, *Chronicles of the Builders of the Commonwealth* and *History of the Pacific Coast States.* He had been a serious competitor for books that Sutro wanted and he was very interested to see what Sutro's collection contained. When he came to Sutro Heights, he brought with him two of his associates who wrote portions of Bancroft's edited texts. David R. Sessions had been the first president of the University of Nevada, which had its origins in Sessions' academy in Elko before the state legislature endowed a university. George H. Morrison was one of Bancroft's "assistants" who wrote factual notes for inclusion in the compiled works that Bancroft produced. Bancroft asked for information about how the collection was assembled and Moss sent a fairly detailed summary to Sessions that concluded with this:

"Under the superintendancy of Mr. [Karl] Mayer large consignments of modern books in the various branches of science have reached the library which now approximates 120,000 volumes at a cost of about $250,000. The granite building for which Messrs. [John] Wright & [George Hippisley] Saunders have supplied plans will, with the interior fixtures, cost $300,000. The site at Sutro Heights, with the endowment which Mr. Sutro promises shall be ample to cover working expenses and keep up the supply of the most advanced books and periodicals relating to science, will not fall much short of $1,000,000. However, Mr. Sutro has much book buying yet to do, terming his present collection but a nucleus, and is resolved to spend several years in the East and Europe devoting the time to filling up vacancies that may exist that the ancient, medieval and modern scientists may be readily traced with unbroken and continuous line."

None of the information about the library ever saw its way into Bancroft's works.[214]

The separation agreement between Adolph and Leah Sutro, which had been had been signed and agreed in July 1880, was filed at the office of the city Recorder in May 1888. Newspapers from coast to coast carried the story generally emphasizing the amicable nature of the contract. The timing seemed a bit strange; almost eight years had passed, and the separation had been quite obvious to those who knew the family. Why had it become necessary to establish a registered record and make the issue public? Carla, the youngest child, would come in for her own monthly allotments five months later so recording was not influenced by that anticipated change. The only new provisions were payment of unspecified debts ($20,000) which Leah may have accumulated and an allowance of $2,000 for Leah to travel to Europe where she announced plans to stay for three years. Perhaps Leah had finally been able to acquire her "settlement" which was small considering the deep pockets that her husband possessed. But, it was better than nothing which is what she had before. Leah did not depart for Europe until early April 1889 but she left with greater independence than she had ever known in the prior thirty years. On the other hand, Adolph Sutro had ulterior motives for settling and having the separation recorded. Leah's plans for an extended trip provided an opportunity to sell the house at Hayes and Fillmore, which was far too large for two people. In addition, Sutro needed the cash. The house was put up for sale. There was more as we will learn later.[215]

Adolph Sutro didn't wait for Leah's departure. He and his secretary, Archibald C. Unsworth, left in February for an extended trip which took Sutro almost half way around the world before it was completed. Traveling by railroad during the first part of the trip, they stopped for varying stays in town after town, often pre-arranging a meeting with some individual acquaintance who served as a tour guide for them. Fresno was the first stop and Sutro visited with his son Charley, who was staying there for a time, and with retired Judge John Wesley North who had been President Lincoln's appointee to Nevada's highest court in 1863. Sutro invited Charley to join them for the long journey but he "flatly refused."

Sutro told Emma that Charley had "no inclination to go into the country." They went through Los Angeles and on to Arizona and continued to El Paso from where they embarked into Mexico. Sutro had arranged for a private Pullman car and they slept through the night arriving in Chihuahua in the morning. The stay in that town included a night at the Hotel Robinson where the beds were "not over comfortable" and the dinner was "well cooked in fat or lard which makes the food ….quite indigestible." They proceeded to Jimenez and Lerdo where they did some more sightseeing and then to Zacatecas where they had planned to stay for a few days. This was the middle of an old silver mining community and Sutro was interested in seeing it. The mines were serviced by *malacates*. which were horse-driven winches for lifting ore and water from the mines. Sutro's record of the visit included his detailed analysis of the costs of operating these winches (feeding the horses, daily payments for the miners, silver yields and replacement of major parts). He was impressed that they operated round the clock. He noted all the similarities and differences between the Zacatecas mining experience and what he knew about Nevada.[216]

During a short stay at Agua Caliente, Sutro was amazed to find ice produced on maguey plants at temperatures above the freezing point. Local vendors produced "ice cream" (probably sorbet) using this material. Both travelers were also surprised to see large numbers of residents, young and old alike, both male and female, bathing unclothed, communally, in a spring-fed channel running through the center of town. Sutro and Unsworth opted for the local bath house.

Heading for Mexico City there were additional stops in Leon, Silao, and Guanajuato, all offering opportunities for Sutro to observe mining operations unlike what he had seen in Nevada. However, vast amounts of silver had been taken from this mining region over the years and he was constantly impressed with the competence of their management. Further, the similarities in terrain evoked memories of Mt. Davidson and the Comstock although the poverty and filth of the general population distressed him. Finally, they reached Mexico City where Sutro planned to stay for a week or ten days.

Adolph Sutro complained at every opportunity about Mexican food and what he described as its "indigestible" character. He told his daughter Emma there were more choices in the big city but that represented only a "slight improvement"; he had frequent indigestion, was unable to sleep very well; and had lost weight. He enjoyed one dinner at a noted restaurant where he met and joined Porfirio Diaz (President of Mexico) at his table for a meal and some interesting talk. A number of prominent Americans were in town – Huntington, the Vanderbilt family, and the Garretts of Baltimore all of whom were staying at his hotel, The Iturbide. But, of greatest importance, during his first few days, he scoured the book stores in town looking for rarities and he was rewarded beyond his most extreme expectations. One of the most distinguished bookstores in all of Mexico was located on the ground floor of Sutro's hotel – Abadiano's Ancient Book Store. Sutro bought the entire contents of the store including "thousands of titles published in Mexico from the sixteenth to the mid-nineteenth century, [including] exemplars of the earliest printing presses in America, religious tracts and Church documents, colonial manuscripts, and early chronicles of the Spanish conquest and colonization;...rare periodicals and approximately 35,000 pamphlets and broadsides...As a documentary and bibliographic source for nineteenth-century Mexican history, the material acquired by Sutro was unrivaled." Unsworth was put to work immediately creating a rough catalog of the acquisitions. This collection appeared to depart widely from Sutro's stated desire to emphasize technology in his library. In a comprehensive essay about Sutro's book life, Dr. Russ Davidson suggested that having seen so much mining activity on his trip, Sutro hoped to find material about the history of Mexican mining operations in the Abadiano lode and referred to "...the strengths of the collection in the history of mining and civil-ecclesiastical conflict" as areas Sutro had consistently emphasized.[217]

While away from home, Sutro received reports from all his key assistants – Elliott Moore, George Moss, his new "agent" Alexander Watson, Lagenicht the gardener, and his new real property overseer, son-in-law George Merritt. Most of Merritt's news was good. Sutro had motivated several real estate agencies in San Francisco to resume selling his properties and they were doing so in large quantities. Almost daily, the real estate columns in local newspapers recorded sales of his lots and houses and listed mortgages which had been concluded with the buyers. Easton, Eldridge sold 100 lots in one day. Merritt had suspended his medical practice to help Sutro. He chauffeured Emma to and from her work at Children's Hospital and went to work throughout the day collecting rents, answering tenant complaints, arranging for repairs and fences, and responding to directions from his father-in-law. Sutro wanted the family home at Hayes and Fillmore sold or leased. It is not clear if Leah was aware of this. Merritt had to report a lack of interest in the property; he advised Sutro that all the people who could afford to leave town at that time had done so. He told Sutro that, during the period after Adolph had left on his trip but before Leah and Carla departed for Europe, the "whole family" (no list included) met at Leah's house for dinners from time to time. Merritt often referred to Leah as "Mother" in these notes which probably irritated Sutro. Merritt addressed some of his letters to "Father."[218]

The plan for a short stay in Mexico City was upset by Adolph Sutro coming down with a sick stomach requiring the services of a doctor. He was advised to leave the high-altitude region and to alter his diet, which should have been understandable in the light of his frequent complaints. Merritt, a physician, referred to treatments that Sutro had received with approval: "…leeches, application of acetate of lead, a sticking plaster bandage, etc.; what more could have been done? The treatment given to you is the recommended treatment." In retrospect, it appears Sutro was lucky to have come out alive. Between his illness and processing the books he had purchased, it was not until three weeks after arrival that the pair finally made their way out of the capital heading for Vera Cruz.

Without stopping to look around, they boarded a steamship which embarked immediately for Havana. Sutro finally got a good night's sleep but, upon awakening, learned he could not go to Havana lacking a new passport. A visit to the military commander there took care of that.[219]

Havana provided Sutro with reminiscences of his early days in the tobacco business. He visited some cigar factories whose names had been familiar to him and he bought cigars a half-dozen at a time. However, only two days were spent there and they left for Key West and upper Florida. Sutro found very little to like in Florida; the terrain was flat and boring and the humidity uncomfortable. The potential for contracting malaria bothered him as did the huge and dangerous snakes and alligators. He did have to admit that, though the orange trees looked unhealthy compared to those in California, the oranges were sweeter and "more palatable." He thought that was strange. He also admired the three hotels that Henry Flagler had built in St. Augustine – the Ponce de Leon, the Alcazar and the Cordova – which Sutro said were "probably the largest cement structures anywhere and present a fine and striking appearance." Other than that, he scoffed at claims by Floridians about their superior climate and living conditions compared with those in California.

Sutro decided to go to Europe. He was pleased with the arrangements he had made to keep his businesses moving forward in his absence and he was enjoying the luxury of new experiences every day. A visit to the family in Baltimore and the prospect of seeing Kate in Germany were very appealing. While in Baltimore, he explored local libraries, including the recently opened Peabody and Pratt facilities, gathering information about how they were built, their security and fire protection systems, storage techniques and the like. Then, it was on to New York where he picked up another new passport and sailed off for Europe. Before his departure, Merritt informed him that Moss volunteered to stay and care for the Heights but did not want Watson to know he had applied for that. Jealousy had surfaced within the staff. However, Emma told her husband that Rosa would like to live there. Rosa and Pio had a small house and a one-year-old son and Rosa was pregnant. Soon after, Rosa moved into the Heights mansion. And, despite, numerous lectures from all the family members including several letters from Papa himself, Charley was not applying himself. This was hardly what Adolph Sutro wanted to hear as he left for perhaps a year abroad.[220]

Sutro did not spend a year in Europe. He did go to London in June 1889 and attended an elaborate banquet tendered by James Whitehead, Lord Mayor of London, honoring various ministers to Queen Victoria. He visited his brother Hugo who was miserably sick and poor in Dresden. Next, he traveled to see his daughter Kate and son-in-law Moritz Nussbaum with four grandchildren in Bonn. Finally, he went to Bavaria to partake of the medicinal baths which he found so enjoyable everywhere. But, all good things must come to an end and, after a brief stay in Paris, Sutro returned home with many books, trees, seeds, and ideas for his projects.[221]

Thirteen

THEODOR SUTRO

Adolph Sutro was not the only one of his immediate family to achieve success and fame although, very likely, he is the best remembered. Two of his brothers enjoyed fruitful, though radically different, careers that placed them among the elite in their communities.

The bulk of the clan that Rosa Warendorff Sutro had brought to America landed in Baltimore and made their lives in that city. Otto Sutro, the fourth son in line, found his mark in the world of music in Baltimore. As were the rest of his brothers and sisters, Otto was born in Aachen, Prussia, on the border of Belgium and he studied organ with the renowned Jacques-Nicolas Lemmens in Brussels. After arriving in America, he followed his older brothers to California and spent several years there as organist in various churches. In 1858, he returned to Baltimore and resumed his organ performance studies at the Peabody Institute (now part of Johns Hopkins University). Later, he joined in founding the Oratorio Society of Baltimore in 1880, and became its principal conductor. Otto was a prime figure in the concert and recital world in Baltimore and it was a rare performance which did not include his sponsorship or participation. In addition to composing songs, he was best known for his piano store, Otto Sutro & Company, where he enjoyed dealerships with Steinway, Knabe and Briggs pianos among others. Years later, his brother Adolph purchased a Steinway grand from Otto for the Sutro Library. Otto was very proud of performances by his daughters, Rose and Ottilie, who toured extensively and established a worldwide reputation for their two-piano renditions. On the 75th anniversary of their parents' wedding in 1944, the daughters donated an impressive memorial sculpture to Otto and his wife, Arianna, which was erected in the Franklin Street Presbyterian Church (Baltimore) depicting him playing the church organ.[222]

Otto's career was long and successful, but hardly a match for the baby of the family, Theodor Sutro. Born in March 1845, Theodor was the youngest of the eleven surviving children born to Emanuel and Rosa Sutro. He adopted the Americanized spelling of his name, Theodore, throughout his business life. When mother brought eight of her children with her to Baltimore, Theodore was five years old. He attended public schools in the Baltimore City system until he entered Philips Academy in Exeter, New Hampshire from which he graduated in 1864. From there, he went to Harvard University earning an A.B. degree in 1871. Two years later, he began study of the law at Columbia University and received his LL.B. in 1874. Theodore passed the New York State bar examinations and was admitted to practice before the United States Supreme Court in 1878. Unquestionably, he entered the world of business and commerce with far more preparation than any of his brothers or sisters. He established a practice in New York City including a variety of legal branches and began a close working relationship with the distinguished firm of Shellabarger & Wilson of Washington, D.C.[223]

When Theodore opened his law offices, Adolph Sutro was involved deeply in construction of the Sutro Tunnel. Most of all, he was constantly working at raising funds for the project. New York City was the seat of financial power in America and Theodore was on the spot there. Further, the United States government had provided seed money for the project and Theodore's association with Shellabarger & Wilson was an important Washington connection. Adolph used these connections to maximum advantage keeping Theodore busy responding to requests for a variety of favors and tasks. With a growing practice and the promise of a lucrative future for the tunnel, Theodore was a willing and often uncompensated aide to his brother. In doing this, Theodore became very close with the Sutro Tunnel hierarchy who were equally eager to take advantage of his skills and availability. When Joseph Aron ended his term as President of the Sutro Tunnel Company in 1878, he moved back to New York to resume his position with Weil & Co. But, he maintained a close involvement with management of the tunnel and particularly of its stock. He stayed in touch with the trustees and with Adolph and devoted hours every day to preserving and enhancing the value of the company's shares. Theodore Sutro became Aron's local confidant in these efforts. A strong business bond grew among the threesome of Aron, Adolph, and Theodore until late 1879 when, contrary to all agreements, Adolph was discovered to be selling some of his tunnel shares. Aron was furious, citing his now futile efforts to stabilize the stock price in the face of considerable selling in the markets. Theodore was equally enraged when he found that another broker had been used to sell Adolph's shares rather than himself. The loyal, cohesive threesome burst apart much faster than it had coalesced just two years earlier.

The relationship between the two brothers deteriorated rapidly. Theodore had been left the task of managing conversion of a purchased home near the northwestern tip of Manhattan so that it could be used as a residence for their mother. Of course, Adolph paid the bills for purchase and overhaul of the structure and for furnishings. Still single at age thirty-four, Theodore was going to share the home with their mother. Once construction and furnishing were completed, contact between the brothers ended for some fifteen years except for notes following their mother's passing in 1883, just three years after moving into the elegant, beautifully appointed Inwood neighborhood mansion.[224]

Theodore's knowledge and experience with the tunnel proved to be of great value. After Adolph withdrew from the company, its fortunes plummeted. The major silver mining operations ceased as no new highly profitable veins were discovered. The promised abundance of tailings and improved extraction methods turned out to be more trouble than wealthy owners were willing to endure for steady but smaller returns. The McCalmonts loan loomed large against the minuscule income the tunnel produced. A lawsuit was instituted against the tunnel company by the McCalmonts and the outlook was bleak. The original loan, signed in January 1877, had been for $124,321.10, which had appeared easy enough to repay in the four years allotted. But, as income dwindled in the first years after Adolph's withdrawal, failure to make payments against the loan triggered increases in the principal, and invoked interest requirements way beyond what the tunnel could support. By March 1878, the debt had increased to more than $400,000 and a supplemental agreement was reached extending the time for payments to January 1891. Theodore was hired to reorganize the company and to defend the suit. He completed the reorganization re-naming it "The Comstock Tunnel Company" and was chosen president of the company. Most of the stockholders held the opinion that the impending lawsuit had no defense and that the claims were going to exceed $1,000,000 by the time the suit reached the courts. In the prelude to the court action, Theodore and Aron became passionately antagonistic with each other. Theodore's annual report included, "It is sincerely hoped that the coming year will see an end of the irrepressible Mr. Joseph Aron and his campaign of mis-representation, vilification and abuse." Aron's lawyer, R.E. Houghton, responded with, "I am satisfied, the Court will never accord Mr. Sutro... ...it will put the stamp of disapproval on his actions, and in terms more emphatic than any found in our briefs." Fortune smiled upon Theodore as receipts of the company suddenly increased significantly. Theodore decided to fight for the company and built a small cadre of stockholders willing to raise money and pay back the loan. Unlike many of the mining organizations at the Comstock, the tunnel had never had any assessments. A bond issue was arranged and, combined with increased tunnel-company earnings, a beneficial settlement was forged with the McCalmonts. Theodore was a hero.[225]

He held that position for some seven years, turning the tunnel into a profitable enterprise once more, and then withdrew from the company in 1894. His handling of the foreclosure against a battery of the finest legal minds in the East resulted in a national reputation for Theodore

Sutro. That fame was the key which opened many doors of business opportunity for him. He represented the widow of artist Edward Moran in a suit against the executor of Moran's estate to recover thirteen famous paintings. After winning the case, the paintings were shown at the Metropolitan Museum of Art in New York and later at the Smithsonian. Sutro's participation was advertised broadly and his reputation grew again. In all that time, there had been no contact between Adolph and Theodore.[226]

Legal and financial activities weren't the only things on Theodore's mind all those years. In 1884, he had married Miss Florence Edith Clinton, descendant of George Clinton, colonial governor of New York. Florence Sutro was judged to be "beautiful, gifted and accomplished" and earned her place among the ladies of high society in New York City. Among her closest associates in charity work were the wives of Andrew Carnegie (Louise); William Steinway (Elizabeth[227]); Jacob Schiff (Therese); Carl Schurz (Margarethe), and of Theodore's cousin, Louis Windmuller (Hannah). Florence was a concert-level pianist and often performed publically but did not attempt to make a career of it. Between 1887 and 1894, Theodore and Florence traveled extensively, reportedly to almost every state of the Union and to Alaska as well.

Theodore joined forces with Edward Salomon, former governor of Wisconsin, and Rudolf Dulon to act as counsel for the Consul Generals of Germany, Austria, and Switzerland. Additionally, they represented German-American corporations in their international dealings. In 1895, while widely known as a Democrat, Theodore was appointed Commissioner of Taxes and Assessments for New York City by the Republican Mayor William L. Strong. That year, Theodore broke down and contacted Adolph asking for a substantial loan. Some fifteen years earlier, Adolph had offered "a favor" which his brother was now collecting. Thodore had acquired various parcels of real estate with habitable structures. Several of these were occupied by in-law relatives who were unable to pay toward their upkeep. Another housed Adolph's son Edgar Jordan and Theodore's sister Juliana, who took handouts from his mother. The mortgages on these properties were burdensome for Theodore and the salary from his municipal position was insufficient to get him out of debt. With all his new contacts he expected to be able to pay off the loan in six years from earnings outside the commissionership. No response to this request was found in files, but it is likely that, despite the fact he disagreed in principle, Adolph did not refuse to make a secured loan to a brother who had never collected payment for numerous professional tasks in years gone by.[228]

Theodore and Florence lived in Manhattan when Adolph passed away in 1898. Though they were seasoned travelers, neither attended the funeral.

After a seven-year term, Theodore returned to legal practice with considerable success. The 1911 election of United States Senator in New York was conducted in the historical practice of selection by state assemblymen and senators. Slates were offered by the various political parties and ballots were voted until one candidate received a majority. Candidates were added and removed from consideration repeatedly throughout the process. That year, sixty-three ballots were required before James A. O'Gorman was selected over Chauncey Depew with a 112 to 80 margin of votes. On the 60th ballot, Theodore Sutro was entered as a Democratic candidate receiving three votes. Interestingly, that was three more votes than Adolph had received in four Nevada senatorial elections many years earlier.[229]

Throughout his career, Theodore had pursued connections with Americans of German origin vigorously. He held memberships in the German-American Reform Union (of which he was president in 1894), the German Publication Society, the German-American Alliance of the State of New York, the German-American National Alliance (GMNA), and a half-dozen other organizations with German connections. He was president of the New York State chapter of the GMNA and an honorary president of the national group. In 1918, during World War I, a bill was introduced into the United States Senate to cancel the charter of the GMNA. A Senate sub-committee was selected, chaired by Sen. William

H. King of Utah, which conducted hearings to consider the merits of the bill. Top-level leaders of the organization arranged for Theodore Sutro to address the sub-committee in opposition to the bill. In a split session, Sutro spoke with senators for nearly half a day setting out his views on the purposes of the organization and why it should not be destroyed. His fundamental feelings were based upon the cultural benefits enjoyed within the group and the widely-held anti-German views of Americans. Though unsuccessful, Sutro's performance was generally applauded by the congressmen.[230]

In addition to his connection with German-American organizations, Theodore held memberships in more than forty clubs and societies engaged in artistic, legal, charitable, or educational pursuits. William Randolph Hearst asked him to assume the editorship of the *Deutsches Journal* which had lost favor with its readership. In a three-year effort, Theodore brought renewed respectability to the newspaper which led him into a period of writing and publication. He authored text material for a book about the Edward Moran paintings, *Thirteen Chapters of American History*, which had been the subject of an earlier litigation. He was president of the German Publication Society which produced a twenty-volume set of the best work of nineteenth and twentieth century German authors in English translations.

In 1906, shortly before her forty-first birthday, his adored wife died prematurely. Theodore, shaken by this turn of events, traveled to Europe including some time in Germany. Later, in 1913, he made an extensive trip to Germany delivering lectures on a variety of subjects to promote business interests involving German and American cooperation. Much as his brother Adolph had done, Theodore had become a man of the world.[231]

Fourteen

GOOD TIMES; BAD TIMES

Sutro was not quite sixty years old, had accumulated a fortune, and had turned that into huge swaths of land which were becoming more valuable daily. He had learned to judge the quality of individuals and had assembled a team of competent employees and associates permitting him to assign tasks, monitor performance, and manage necessary changes and improvements without his presence. He understood the difference between money and cash and used his cash as a tool to control everyone he knew. Sometimes, he wasn't careful as he spent his cash a lot more quickly than he acquired it and had to borrow to continue his life style. But, that was easy. Having foiled attempts at divorce and having refused to provide a one-time settlement, he controlled his separated wife through trust payments which provided comfort without opulence. He paid key employees well justifying the tongue lashings he delivered for perceived shortcomings. He tipped serving people excessively which purchased intense loyalty and quick reaction. He donated money and property of all kinds to an endless list of agencies and people of all faiths and persuasions and his name was in the local newspapers on the order of one hundred days per year. He sent monthly cash allocations to his children and to a variable list of relatives and others he considered needy or deserving. He was particularly generous to his siblings. At each year end, a longer list of children in the spreading Sutro family received gifts from him. Though he socialized with a very small group of

152

local dignitaries in San Francisco, it would be difficult to say he had one genuine friend. But, he did have a comely mistress.

Clara Kluge had begun working as a part-time seamstress at Sutro Heights in 1885. She was twenty-two years old at the time and pretty enough to have caught the eye of the famous owner. She lived in rented rooms and worked some days at the main house. Sutro maintained the ultimate discretion throughout the duration of their liaisons – at least in written documents. He appears to have told no one in writing about the affair. At this time, he was less well-known than he would become a few years later and was not as likely to be recognized visiting at her lodgings. Despite his best efforts, he was recognized visiting her lodgings.

In February 1890, he confided in his brother Louis that, once the weather improved, he planned to live at the Heights and work in town about an hour a day. He had found an excellent cook, so his early morning, breakfast and lunch routine could be enjoyed. He did not mention how that would also facilitate extended proximity to his lady friend. He complained about his land-rich, cash-poor situation confessing his bank account was overdrawn some $8,000. That circumstance never intruded upon how he lived. "Everybody thinks that our real estate market will be booming during the coming spring and summer, but I am a little afraid that when everybody expects a thing, it is sure not to happen. These movements rather come unexpectedly." A great deal of money was needed to complete the new library building he wanted. He admitted, "I have been warned, over and over again, by almost every intelligent man who has visited the library that I should not wait a single hour to remove it to a safer place. But, to remove it temporarily and then again, by and by, I would never consent to." He had no idea what a bad decision that was but construction activities for the baths were already under way and his hopes for a real estate boom needed fulfillment to pay for all the construction projects he had in mind.[232]

Sutro engaged Easton, Eldridge & Co. to auction 100 lots in the Park Lane tract near Mount Olympus. Shortly thereafter, McAfee, Baldwin and Hammond were called upon to auction 170 lots on Clarendon Heights. Topping these, Carnall-Fitzhugh-Hopkins completed arrangements with Sutro to place some 1500 lots on the market in what was called the Lakeview section (now Ingleside). Adolph Sutro could not have been disappointed with the real property market that flourished during the spring and summer of 1890.[233]

Sutro enjoyed one exceptional social week that spring. Celebrating his sixtieth birthday, he tendered a party for all the family members in town plus his library director George Moss. The list included the families of his daughter Rosa (Morbio); daughter Emma (Merritt), sister Elsie (Schücking), sister Emma (the Winterbergs), son Charles and children of the others. Though also invited, Adolph's brother Theodore and his wife were unable to attend after Florence was thrown from her horse while riding in Golden Gate Park. Of course, Leah was still in Europe with daughter Carla. The party featured a string band which entertained during and after dinner as the guests all walked from the main house to the Cliff House railroad depot. Just three days later, Florence was recovered sufficiently, and Theodore held a dinner party at the Occidental Hotel honoring her birthday. The cousins from the financial branch of the family at Sutro & Co. were guests in addition to the same roster of family members.[234]

Fortunately, sales of real property were literally booming in the Lakeview area and throughout sections of the community that Sutro owned. By year end, several hundred home lots had been sold and mortgages had been taken for a substantial percentage of these to produce a steady cash stream for Sutro over and above the immediate cash infusion from the sales. Everything was going just the way he wanted and there would be enough money for the library and the baths. His personal life was comfortable and pleasing almost beyond description. However, there were distractions. Near the end of the prior year, three disgruntled stockholders of the former Sutro Tunnel Company had filed suit against both the Union Trust Company and Theodore Sutro who had become president of the successor Comstock Tunnel Company. Not surprisingly, one of the three was Joseph Aron. From Paris in May 1890, Aron leveled a blast at Theodore and the people supporting him, including Adolph, whom he accused of participating in a conspiracy against the corporation's stockholders. This took the form of a lengthy, detailed open letter to Comstock Tunnel Company shareholders including an exchange of messages between Theodore and Aron filled with contentious accusations in both directions. While Adolph Sutro no longer had any connection with the tunnel, he wanted to avoid getting drawn into the conflict brewing around the issue. Further, Aron had been a bulwark of support in Adolph's disputes over securities with Coulter. Now, Coulter was seriously ill, and Aron took Coulter's side against Adolph. In the midst of this hostility, Coulter died having left letters defaming Adolph Sutro which Aron circulated widely. One said, "Mr. Sutro has accumulated a large fortune, a very large portion of which came out of me… It can, indeed, be proven… that all he has is traceable to me and my efforts for him in the past. I was his faithful assistant for years. My only compensation has been fraud, falsehood, and despicable ingratitude, sandwiched with a treachery as base as it has been cruel and cold. He erected an altar to his lust and ambition, his vanity and greed; I have been the sacrifice." Irrespective of how little truth this statement contained, it must have been difficult to live with that deathbed condemnation.[235]

Two weeks after Coulter's demise, Leah and Carla returned from Europe. Their plan to stay for three years had been abandoned; Leah wasn't feeling all that well and wanted to return home. Fortunately, the family house had not been sold or leased and she was able to move in. While Leah was away, George Merritt had arranged for maids and other maintenance services to keep the property presentable for prospective buyers, so it was readily available. With Leah back and not well, Sutro had to defer thoughts of selling the property.[236]

Sutro received reminders of his Jewish origins one after another. His close associate and legal advisor, Solomon Heydenfeldt, passed away and Sutro was tapped as a pall bearer. Responding to a solicitation, he purchased lifetime membership in the Jewish Publication Society of America. Then, renowned Jewish scholar Cyrus Adler sent a request that Sutro donate one of his duplicate copies of a rare Midrash text to another famous scholar, Solomon Schechter, at Cambridge University. Sutro contributed toward the annual banquet of the Eureka Benevolent Society and offered land to the Hebrew Home for the Aged and Disabled for a new facility. The offer was rejected; a new home was built and Sutro donated money instead.[237]

There were other distractions taking Sutro away from his comfort zone. Two separate road construction projects had turned into repeatedly confrontational sessions at the Board of Supervisors Street Committee meetings. The first was a dispute between Sutro and the Spring Valley Water Company over how Seventh Avenue should be extended southbound in the vicinity of Lake Honda. Sutro's interest was to maintain his properties in the surrounding area as level as possible to maximize residential lot usage and facilitate laying railroad tracks with minimum slopes from town to the Cliff House. The water company needed elevation of a waste pond for hydraulic flow purposes. Sutro's former employee and respected working associate, Hermann Schüssler, was the chief engineer of the water company and it was unfortunate they had become the spear carriers for opposing sides in this conflict. Schüssler had designed and supervised construction of the aqueduct system that brought water to Virginia City over a great distance and rough country. He had been a hero when previously employed by Sutro having computed precise locations of connections between the Sutro Tunnel and its intersecting vertical shafts. Conventional wisdom dictated that the intersections could be somewhere between two and five feet away from ideal; Schüssler had achieved intersection within less than an inch variation in both directions. But, that was years ago; this was now. The negotiations and meetings surrounding this proposal appeared endless. Sutro, George Merritt, and, sometimes, Elliott Moore attended session after session ending in postponements and new proposals without resolution. It went on for months. A second dispute arose between two groups of property owners over the proposed closure of a street to create a cul-de-sac. Sutro was leading one group and a real estate colleague of his, Behrend Joost, led the opposing owners. This case continued week after week as did the other and was a source of great frustration to Sutro, to his opponents, and the Board of Supervisors as well. At the final session, before the committee approved Joost's proposal, Sutro was thrown out of the hearing room. All these seemingly unrelated issues were part of the mosaic surrounding creation of Sutro's elaborate entertainment center. The baths, the museum within the bathhouse, the aquarium, the amusement park, the Cliff House, and the low-cost railroad line from the city to the shore were each less than complete without all the others. Together, they were Sutro's dream. To fund these projects, Sutro was depending upon Carnall-Fitzhugh-Hopkins to sell more than 133 acres of graded lots upon which hundreds of trees had been planted to line the streets and decorate individual lots. Nearly 1,200 of the 1,500 lots were sold in the first two weeks.[238]

Sutro was delighted with the results and other exciting things were ongoing. Benjamin Harrison, President of the United States, was planning a visit to San Francisco and Adolph Sutro was a member of the Executive Committee developing arrangements for the occasion. In addition to the requisite parades and sightseeing tours, Sutro was able to schedule a gathering at Sutro Heights and serve a spectacular luncheon for a party of forty-two guests including the President and his wife and family, cabinet officers, city and state officials, and some of his own children. Seven different wines were served to accompany the various courses plus champagne, cognac, kirsch and chartreuse. Postmaster General John Wanamaker drank only water. Sutro always enjoyed the company of politically powerful men and never passed up an opportunity to provide them with meals and gifts and compliments. His years in Washington taught him a great deal about how favors to politicians were received and remembered. To a lesser extent, his many gifts to charities, to the city and state governments, and various organizations of teachers, civic employees, "visiting firemen," and even antagonists constituted bread upon the waters which would earn him positive feedback at some future time.[239]

Between March and August 1891, Sutro concluded a series of purchases, transfers and sales of small properties in the vicinity of Sutro Heights. This was in preparation for the birth of Clara Kluge's son whom she named Adolph Newton Sutro. In addition, a dressmaker's shop was acquired which would facilitate Clara Kluge's launch into her own business once the baby and she were settled in their new house near Sutro Heights.[240]

All this coincided with the first newspaper reports including some details of the Sutro Baths project. The immensity of the structure would not surprise anyone who had seen the beginnings of its foundation being constructed. It was intended to be the largest establishment of its kind in the world. There were to be six salt-water tanks and one fresh water plunge; the largest tank, L-shaped, would be 300 feet on the long leg, 150 feet on the short leg, each leg approximately 75 feet wide. The five smaller salt-water pools would be 75 feet long and vary between 28 and 50 feet wide. The fresh-water pool would also be small and extremely cold. The six salt pools were planned to be heated individually creating noticeable temperature differences from one to the next. Bathers could enter the water in various ways – toboggan slides, swinging rings, spring boards, and trapezes. There was to be an amphitheater seating 3,700 patrons and an equal number of promenade seats for viewing the pools. More than 500 dressing rooms would be available for patrons to change into bathhouse-provided bathing suits. The entire facility would be enclosed within a single structure with a glass roof.[241]

Several years earlier, shortly after Sutro purchased the Sutro Heights properties, he was reported to have invited Huntington, Crocker, and Stanford to visit the site. After lunch, he conducted a walking tour with them pointing out the spectacular views and his plans for turning the area into a park and, eventually, giving it all to the city. He was disappointed with the cold response from the railroad barons and suspected they harbored plans to somehow secure the property for themselves. The Southern Pacific Railroad owned the most dominant monopoly over transportation in America (if not the world) including cross-country rail passage, local commuter lines, and possession of docks and waterways at the western coast of the country. Anyone who wanted to see the beauties of the Golden Gate had to pay the Octopus for the privilege. Sutro opposed the concept of extracting maximum payments from working-class citizens – at least he expressed those feelings in frequent interviews printed in local newspapers. Now, years after that meeting with the barons, the Market Street Railroad, which brought San Franciscans from the inner city to the proximity of Sutro Heights, was a property of the Octopus and their cars were filled with passengers on many weekends heading for the shore, Sutro Heights Park, or Golden Gate Park. The fare was ten cents each way and more for passengers from the Mission District from which there were no free transfers. Sutro felt this was much more than working families could afford and began talking about a five-cent ride. His detractors were quick to accuse him of feathering his own nest looking for low fares to his entertainment center under construction. Sutro countered these arguments by publicly offering to deed the Sutro Heights property to the city in exchange for reducing the fares to a nickel. The railroads wouldn't budge. Adolph Sutro decided he would fight them; later that struggle would continue for several years. As the Sutro Baths progressed towards completion, the contentiousness resumed.

Leah Sutro's illness continued to plague her. Adolph transferred a property of his to daughter Rosa and Alberto Morbio down the street from the family home at Hayes and Fillmore. Having the more mature Rosa nearby, in addition to Carla, seemed sensible. A Steinway piano was bought from Otto Sutro & Co. in Baltimore and shipped to the house, although there is no indication anyone in the family knew how to play it.[242]

As construction of the baths continued, Sutro Heights had visiting dignitaries or guest organizations almost every day. The L.S. Infants

Shelter, National Library Association, Pioneer Kindergarten Society, Cogswell Polytechnic College Zoology Department, National Press Club, Polyclinic Medical Charity, Boys & Girls Aid Society, State Medical Society Ladies Auxiliary, and City of Boston Aldermen all enjoyed picnic days at Sutro Heights during a six-month period. Andrew Carnegie had lunch with Sutro and Emma and visited the Montgomery Block library. In September 1892, Clara Kluge left for Berlin with her young son expecting to stay for nine months. Two months later, she gave birth to Adolphine Charlotte Sutro.

Sutro's philanthropy took a new turn in January 1893. The local Salvation Army group inaugurated its "Life Boat" service wherein one dime would purchase either two meals or a meal and a bed at the agency's shelter. Meal tickets were sold and used for the purpose. Sutro liked the idea and purchased 1,000 tickets. He had been in the habit of giving coins to some of the ragged and hungry horde that inhabited the downtown area; he had known some of them from his earliest days in the silver mines. He was a soft touch never refusing some small amount for anyone in need. The word got around that he would distribute meal tickets at three o'clock in the afternoon at his office. On the first day, a dozen showed up in the hallway outside his offices. Next day there were twenty, then thirty-five and soon there were crowds. The building managers insisted the line move outside. Sutro bought a second, third and fourth $100 batch of tickets. The police were afraid of street blockage and a new system was arranged. Meal tickets would be distributed at the Salvation Army food and shelter depot at 3:00 pm daily. Only 100 tickets were given out each day by the Life Boat managers but there were mobs every day for a long time.[243]

Leah's condition appeared to worsen and, in early April, Adolph purchased a family plot at the Home of Peace cemetery in Colma just outside the city line. Congregation Emanu-El operated the cemetery and their temple had been Leah's choice of a place for worship since the move from Nevada. Local newspapers carried articles every day throughout late April indicating the end was near for her and that the family had gathered to be there in that eventuality. Emma had been providing routine medical services, but had called in several specialists. Unexpectedly, Leah took a turn for the better and public reporting of her condition slipped into the background. By mid-June, Adolph was back working on major details of his library. He had visited libraries around the world investigating organization of their contents and how that related to structural features in the interior of the buildings. He announced a new unspecified location "very near the geographical center of the city of San Francisco." Preliminary layouts of two floors were shown as part of the planned seven stories for the entire building. In addition, he had arranged for electrification of the buildings and walkways at Sutro Heights. General Electric would supply a generator and some five hundred lamps and sockets.[244]

All his renewed energy may have come at the wrong time as the economy stalled which took some of the wind out of his sails. He escaped to Arcadia for peace and quiet. But, he was troubled. He told his brother Louis that Leah was better but "exceedingly weak" and she does not "seem to pick up fast at all." Emma had not permitted Leah to accompany him to Napa. Further, he complained bitterly about business conditions which he blamed upon the worldwide abandonment of bimetallism and asked Louis to sell his share of his brother's business – he described himself as "hard up for money." However, nothing stopped him from spending. In April, just days after buying the family plot, Woodward's Garden Museum closed its business and put everything in its collection of displays and amusement park machinery up for sale. Sutro had put in a bid for the entire collection which was rejected. When the auction was completed, Sutro had acquired almost everything he wanted. News reports claimed that some $10,000 had been realized from the auction. Most of that came from Adolph Sutro. Another letter to Louis six months later echoed the tone of his April messages – business was hardly better; he had not been able to obtain a loan despite having real property worth more than a million dollars; Leah was "somewhat better and lies in a chair during the day which is an improvement over being in bed. Her sickness however has so far progressed that a complete recovery is impossible." Louis was encouraged to prepare an exhibit for the Midwinter Fair in San Francisco. Adolph offered to travel to Chicago, meet Louis, and bring the family out to California for the winter – the mild weather would do them all some good. One month later, the offer was repeated. However, "Leah still continues in a very sad condition. Her life hangs on a thread, and it is a marvel she has held out so long."[245]

Leah Harris Sutro passed away on December 9, 1893. Her funeral was conducted in the family home at Hayes and Fillmore by Rabbi Jacob Voorsanger who "dwelt touchingly" upon the great number of her anonymous charitable acts apparently unknown even to her family. A train, including several filled cars, took mourners to and from the Home of Peace cemetery where a short graveside service was conducted. Work on the Sutro Baths was suspended and Sutro Heights was closed Sunday and Monday prior to the funeral. Adolph spoke of the long years of struggle they had endured before his success in the tunnel. He disclosed that, "During all this time, I was constantly aided and encouraged by my wife, and but for her confidence in me I think there were times when I would almost have despaired." Of course, there had been more than a dozen years of separation. Last April, when it was thought that Mrs. Sutro would soon expire, "the husband repaired to her chamber and a reconciliation was effected." Leah had made a will in March of that year when her illness had become so serious she was expected to perish momentarily. She had allocated "souvenirs," items of jewelry, furniture, and artworks, to each of her children and specified that her remaining possessions be sold and the proceeds distributed strangely. Five hundred dollars was to go to son Edgar's wife, Etta; one-half of the balance would then go to daughter Kate; the remainder was to be divided equally among all her children. There was no explanation for the questions arising out of this distribution. Alberto Morbio and Emma Merritt were designated co-executors. The total value of Leah's estate was estimated to be $15,000. Adolph Sutro had given the Salvation Army $12,000 that year; obviously, he did not subscribe to the oft-repeated line about char-ity beginning at home. He also had a new family with a beautiful young wife and two bouncing babies.[246]

The past two years had been stressful for Adolph Sutro with numer-ous highs and lows often falling one upon the other. His two major proj-ects continued to proceed toward completion but at entirely different rates. The baths were getting their final structural elements and furnish-ings would commence soon. There were sufficient major pieces for the Merrie Way amusement park that would accompany the baths. More could be added later when customer acceptance was verified. Less prog-ress could be noted for the library. The site was uncertain, no architec-tural plans had been rendered, and more books had been purchased in-creasing the scope of the project. A half-dozen knowledgeable scholars had issued warnings about the nature of storage conditions for the col-lection and Sutro worried about this a great deal. He had also dipped his toes into the political waters. His old friend August Helbing from the Eureka Benevolent Society had run for a Supervisor's position in the last election. Sutro attended the nominating meeting of the so-called Non-Partisans and spoke up for Helbing to be the independent nomi-nee in the Twelfth Ward. Helbing was nominated but lost the election; most people who attended remembered that Sutro sat in the front row on stage and was prominent in the convention. The Non-Partisan move-ment gained momentum and Sutro became a regular at their public gatherings. He was named to leadership positions in one organization after another; political groups were no different. On top of these, Leah's illness had led to an earnest attempt at rapprochement. They met to-gether privately and mostly quietly both acknowledging the bond that had at one time been so strong. Those sessions must have been difficult for him. Leah's passing, followed so closely behind the birth of Clara Kluge's daughter, had to arouse emotional stirrings in Sutro that were difficult to reconcile. As 1894 dawned, what Adolph Sutro needed more than anything was a long rest; he was not going to get one.

LEAH HARRIS SUTRO

Adolph Sutro's life has been documented in capsule versions a number of times ranging from a couple of pages up to the length of a full chapter. In each of these, his marriage to Leah Harris is mentioned as an afterthought and snippets of information about the lady are included. Unfortunately, all these little segments have the same failing – they include supposedly accurate statements about her origins and personality that cannot be verified or traced to authentic documentation. Some examples:

(1) "In 1856 Adolph was married by Rabbi Julius Eckman to Leah Harris, of English Orthodox extraction. It was not a good match. Leah was a simple, good-hearted, traditional Jewish woman, whose idea of happiness was a life devoted to husband, children, the synagogue, and Jewish charities."[247]

(2) "In either 1855 or 1856 Sutro married Leah Harris in a Hebrew ceremony, probably at Leah's request for she was far more religious than her liberal-minded husband. Leah was of English ancestry with simple tastes and a good heart. She had no dreams of grandeur, and would have been most happy to see her life revolve around home, husband, children, synagogue, and the charities of the congregation. Whenever she could, these were the things she did, but as her husband's life expanded she assumed the roles he forced upon her with dignity and charm. Had she found it a little

more possible to be his companion rather than his hostess she might have saved them both considerable heartache."[248]

(3) "He [Adolph Sutro] married the devout Leah Harris in a traditional Jewish ceremony."[249]

(4) "In either 1855 or 1856 he married Leah Harris. It was a Hebrew ceremony, probably at Leah's request, because Adolph and his family had liberal ideas on religion and none of Adolph's brothers was married in their ancestral faith."[250]

(5) "…Sutro found the girl he wanted to marry. She was a pleasant-looking English Jewess, Leah Harris, who had 'simple tastes and a good heart.' Leah did not have lofty ambitions. A husband, a home, children, the synagogue, and doing good deeds for the poor were enough for her. Sooner or later these limited horizons would come in conflict with her husband's appetite for living dangerously. But for now Adolph was in love. He married Leah in 1856 and had to be coaxed to participate in a religious wedding ceremony."[251]

The paucity of information about someone so important in Sutro's life is both surprising and frustrating. Moreover, the lack of traceable citations to authentic documents challenges the credibility of the reports. Each author's notes and references for these statements have been followed to their ultimate conclusion without success.

The repetitive nature of the five statements, several using the same wording and phrases, provides further cause for questions. What were the evidences that Leah Harris was a "simple, good-hearted, traditional Jewish woman"? Where does it say, "Her idea of happiness was a life dedicated to husband, children, the synagogue, and Jewish charities"? There is no record of how, when or where they met, what kind of engagement or betrothal may have been arranged. For that matter, a written record of the actual marriage ceremony cannot be found. The question of whether the marriage took place in 1855 or 1856 is troubling. Their first child's birth in mid-December 1856 narrows the possibilities to about fifteen months. With so many of these reports sounding like carbon copies of each other, it is difficult to attach any confidence to the stories. Furthermore, there is no authentic record of Leah's birth, parentage, immigration, or travels which brought her to the West Coast. The only solid evidences of her life experiences reside in letters she wrote and a few newspaper accounts.

Leah Harris Sutro wrote many letters to her two oldest daughters while the girls were away at school. They reveal a remarkable personality basically imprisoned in a relationship in which she had no control and very little say. In the best of financial times for the family, she received an allowance; in the worst of times, she carried more than her own weight in providing support for her husband as well as the children. When the marriage broke up, she fought to obtain a "settlement," her own financial storehouse, so she could plan and spend as she saw fit. It never happened. Adolph Sutro's favoritism toward daughter Emma didn't escape Leah's observation and, very subtly, she attempted to use Emma as a wedge to get her way in contentious issues with "dear Papa." Unfortunately, most of these efforts were unsuccessful. A selection of passages from some of those letters follows which may help to reveal portions of the inner person in Leah Sutro.

April 11, 1871, a letter to Emma and Rosa both attending Visitation Academy, a preparatory Catholic (high) school in Georgetown (Washington, D.C.):

"I received your kind letter of April 2nd today and although I do not feel much like writing today on account of not receiving a letter from dear Papa as I had anticipated informing me about his return so that I would know how to act and relieve my mind of the constant anxiety I feel about his future prospects. I cant (sic) express how happy I shall feel when we are all to be together once more … … I know my darling children must feel greatly disapointed (sic) at receiving such solemn letters instead of the more cheerful I try to write. I accomplish nothing but gloomy correspondence."[252]

August 22, 1871, to Emma and Rosa who were staying with Sutro's mother and other relatives in Baltimore for the summer:

"My darling Emma, I received your letter this morning and the contents made me feel very happy. I am glad to [learn] that my dear Emma's character is such as not to be carried away by trifling frivolous girls that their sole aim and object in life seems to be to try to captivate young gentlemen... ...I am pleased dear Emma that you have no secrets from your parents as no pure right minded girl should have for you may rest assured dear child that there is no person has your real happiness and future welfare more at heart than we do and I feel proud that you write so unrestrainedly to us. I hope and trust that I shall always be able to counsel you in doing right although your own good judgment will suggest what is for the best..."[253]

September 10, 1871 to Emma:

"I was agreeably surprised at receiving a letter this morning I am much pleased to learn that you are going to Vaser [Vassar] College. I have a poor opinion of the girls of the rising generation. They think more of dress and finery than they do to the improvement of their minds and moral character. I should judge by the sentiments expressed in my dear child's letters that she will not grow up to be one of those vain foolish girls that will be attracted or deluded by frivolous trifles and vain holow (sic) display of persons that are artificial. I feel that with the advantages that my dear Emma will receive by being placed in an institution that stands unrivaled in the United States she will make rapid progress towards becoming an intelligent woman." She went on about her lack of respect for women who "try to fascinate men" and cautions that "...as long as girls are weak and foolish men will treat them as a child does a toy and when they are tired of them, cast them of[f] for some new attraction – but both men and women never tire of an intelligent mind; it is like a magnet [and] is bound to attract." Leah concluded the letter with a small lecture about Emma's reported bodily changes and accompanying "sickness."[254]

Shortly thereafter, Leah wrote separately to both girls telling them about the Rosh Hashanah and Yom Kippur holidays and how she had celebrated with visiting relatives and friends. She urged both to remember that, although they had never been exposed to religious training or synagogue attendance, they were Jewish.[255]

October 18, 1871 to Emma:

"…from all that I can learn he [Adolph Sutro] has been quite successful in England. I received a dispatch stating that Papa would leave New York today for California. I am like you dear Emma. I can scarcely realize success for I have met with so many disappointments, but I shall be relieved of all suspense in about another week from now for if nothing happens Papa will be with us about that time."[256]

November 30, 1871 to Rosa:

"… All last week I was out house hunting and could not find one to suit me. I got so tired out going from one place to another, and I was telling Papa how I felt. So the next day Papa sent a cariage (sic) and driver to take me wherever I wanted to go. So I took Annie [Doherty, the maid/au pair] and Carla and we rode round town for nearly four hours but could not get a house to suit. Papa is so very particular that it is difficult to please him, but I am determined to make a change as soon as I can."[257]

December 2, 1871 to Emma:

"…Katie is making great preparations to send you some presents for your birthday which will be on the 15th of this month. I send you dear Emma my heartfelt congratulations and hope that you will enjoy yourself on that day and that many more happy birthdays are in store for you. And that I shall have the pleasure and satisfaction of being nearer my dear girl than I am at present under the like happy auspices….

…I will tell you again my dear child to be carefull (sic) of your health and take all the reasonable pleasure you can, for youth is the season for pleasure and improvement….

... I hope you will conquer Latin. I know it must be real dificult (sic) at first but after you get acquainted with the first rudiments the difficulty will gradually disapear (sic) and you will see your way more clear. Latin reminds me of a person having to climb a very steep hill. At first it seems almost impossible to ascend but step by step we reach the top but not without much patience and perseverance we then look down the hill and find that we have surmounted all those difficulties and all looks bright and beautifull (sic) and so it is dear child we must always be looking upward and onward."[258]

Leah Sutro's letters during the entire year 1872 are not found in any of the major collections. A search for them continues. During that summer, Emma and Rosa spent their vacation in the town of Sutro and managed to get into serious personal trouble with both parents. Only vague hints of the issues or the episodes have been found. However, in early 1873, the animosities persisted. Leah wrote to Emma on New Year's Day with a potpourri of messages:

"Your kind letter reached me and I was quite surprised to find by the heading that you were in Baltimore. I understood Rosy to say that Papa would not allow you to leave Poughkeepsie...

... Katie and I went into Dayton to see the Christmas tree. After all the presents were distributed we went to the Ball in company with Mr. [Thomas James Tiddy] and Mrs. Tiddy. Katie's dancing was greatly admired; we had a splendid time and did not get home until past six o'clock in the morning...

... Last Sunday night our house was beautifully illuminated with gas. We had forty-six lights burning and about 20 gentlemen gave me a surprise party singing speeches and recitations were made...

... I hope dear Emma that you have seen Papa at Baltimore and that a better state of feelings will exist in the future..."[259]

About that time, Adolph Sutro offered a job to Herman Hoepfer, husband of Adolph's sister Emma who was living with Grandma Rosa Sutro in Baltimore. On January 10, 1873, Leah wrote to Emma:

After repeating her surprise at daughter Emma having gone to Baltimore for the holidays, she continued, "...You did not tell me what Papa said to you. Was he angry? I cannot understand all you write. I have to guess part. I wish you would endeavor to write as plain as possible the news you tell me about Papa giving Uncle Herman a situation here I have no doubt pleases them greatly. I am afraid it will not make things quite pleasant for me. In the first place, they would have to live with me as there is no dwelling houses (sic) to rent and I know they have not money to build. Now of all things I dislike is to live with another family because they would remark everything and should things not suit them or me it would make it quite uncomfortable. Papa has not told me anything about it at present."²⁶⁰

February 21, 1873 to Emma:

"...I am real sorry to find that Papa objects to have you go and stay with Miss [Jane] Palmore particularly at a time when she feels so lonesome in consequence of her father's death. If the matter was left to me I would give my consent with much pleasure, but Father has an idea that there never was any people so near perfection as the Sutro family and consequently he may object on that account for I know that the only place that he cared for any one to go to is Baltimore and I never could find much attraction there; everything seems so much on the surface nothing is genuine and real about them. I don't believe one of the Sutros cares two straws about us, only that they think that your father can be of some benefit to them..."

Leah went on to other painful subjects in this letter. Her spat with daughter Rosa had not been patched up, and she wrote at length about how distressed she remained about it and how it would preclude her creating geographical separations between the other children and herself which now she blamed for Rosa's rebellion. She would try convincing Papa to let Emma visit her friend Jane Palmore in New York at the next holiday.²⁶¹

March 2, 1873 to Emma: Papa has to go back to Europe and things did not appear to work out with Uncle Hermann Hoepfner so he will very likely not show up.

"...I am much pleased to learn that Uncle Herman will not arrive here at present, and as Papa has to go to Europe perhaps he may change his mind in the meantime and not come here. I am so happy and contented at present that I dread the thought of having strangers break in my solitude and destroy all the castles I have been building of the future happiness in store for me perhaps all my castles will evaporate into air but if they only dwell in my imagination it is a happy feeling as long as it lasts and we don't like to have it crushed or trampled on...

...If any person had told me that I would ever settle myself with any degree of comfort in this land of sage brush I should have imagined that they were certainly not in a sane state of mind...

...I think that I am becoming somewhat of a philosopher and view things in their true light and when I reflect how much we have to be thankful for it does away with my little discontentment[. O]ne may at times feel our house looks real cheerful and I am never at a loss for company[. W]e have a great many little social parties and I am treated with the greatest respect and kindness by the people that live here[. W]ith regards to the country there is a great sameness about it which makes it not so agreeable as it otherwise might be but we can't expect all the comforts with[out] some little inconveniences..."

Leah went on about her successes in raising animals for food and growing an abundance of food crops and her abilities in canning and smoking foods, in producing an abundance of ice and wonderful ice cream and, "...so you see dear Emma that we are very comfortably fixed." It was very clear that Leah was lonesome and wanting her husband to come home and stay there with her.[262]

After the episode at the Virginia City International Hotel, Leah listened to too many stories and rumors about her husband which were easy to believe after seeing him with the lady in the hotel room. He persisted in denying any serious involvement with the woman, but Leah was too angry to believe him. Adolph was really the only one who knew his intentions that day and he protested accusations the rest of his life. In the intervening years, Leah prepared a divorce proceeding, actually filed for divorce, and then withdrew the suit. So many questions remain about that day and Adolph's other relationships with women which have gone unanswered. What did he hope to learn from a private investigator? What, if anything did he learn? Documents which might have answered these questions have not surfaced. Who was Mrs. C. Howard who insisted he come to her room at the Palace Hotel to give her investment advice? Who was Emma Allen, the woman who demanded "her notes back"? "Just tell me you have destroyed my notes or, if not, hand them to me and I will never ask to see you again." Her letter tells of hours spent waiting for his return to his "summer house" causing her to come down with the croup. Of course, the name "Allen" seems to be too coincidental – was there some connection to the Diamond Lady? Sutro certainly attracted women even in his later years. As for Leah, why did she file for divorce and then withdraw? Did she really want a reconciliation? Her letters only speak of wanting a final settlement with Adolph; a permanent cleavage. However, there is evidence that their relationship mellowed later, and that Leah would visit at Sutro Heights where they sat together and spoke quietly watching the waves and the seals and the fog.[263]

The thirteen-year separation between the events at the International Hotel and onset of a serious illness had certainly permitted Leah considerable freedom of activity. She had entered the social world of San Francisco sufficiently to keep Carla, her youngest daughter, in the midst of the most desirable potential matches in town. Together they attended many parties and dances and other celebrations and traveled to Europe together. However, Carla remained single until after both parents had passed away. Leah also had the opportunity to participate to her heart's content in religious activities. None of the five Jewish congregations surviving today in San Francisco from those years has records to confirm her attendance or membership – most of those documents were destroyed in 1906 during the combination of earthquake and fire. However, we are left with some clues.

Early in 1893, matzohs were purchased for the upcoming Passover at the family house. Very shortly thereafter, Adolph Sutro purchased a grave lot at the Jewish Home of Peace Cemetery in Colma. The lady who had managed rooming houses and created farms to support the family during Adolph's early business career was failing physically. Adolph Sutro found a new mission – keeping her alive and comfortable. At least a half-dozen of the most prominent doctors in the community were called upon to offer medical advice and services. In August, writing from his country place in the Napa Valley, Adolph told his brother Louis that, "Leah is much better, and almost well again, but exceedingly weak. She does not seem to pick up fast at all." Emma, the doctor in charge of Leah's treatment, had not permitted her to go along with him. However, two months later, Adolph told Louis, "Leah is somewhat better and lies in a chair during the day, which is in preferment to being in bed. Her sickness however, has so far progressed that a complete recovery is impossible. She has suffered a good deal and very patiently, but has all the comforts and attention it is possible to render." But in November, all he could muster was, "Leah still continues in a very sad condition. Her life hangs on a thread, and it is a marvel that she has held out so long." Leah's struggles ended on December 9th.[264]

FANTASY

Sixteen

REACHING THE SUMMIT

On New Year's Day, 1894, Collis P. Huntington sent a verbose letter to the Central Pacific's London Agent, C.E. Bretherton, enclosing his rationale for the proposed loan repayment schedule he had offered the United States government. In it, Huntington confessed "The Company owes the United States Government a large amount which it cannot pay at maturity (see reasons in printed letter), but I believe a settlement can, and will, be made that will not only be entirely satisfactory to both parties but be upon lines that will preserve all the equities of both ...." He continued, "Of course, the Company must have a long time in which to pay this debt to the Government, say 125 years, but that will make no difference to the Government, so long as it gets its money sometime whilst it will make all the difference to the Shareholders who need a current income to meet current expenses." The enclosure set forth a litany of difficulties and handicaps Huntington alleged the railroad had been forced to endure and pointed out how much money the railroad saved the government by assuming responsibility for security in the western states. Further, he claimed the costs of mail delivery between the coasts had been reduced by half. He went on, "I think that the government will admit without question that it has made or saved more through the existence of this road than the Shareholders who built and operated it have." In closing, Huntington agonized, "... I am quite sure the statistics of the oldest and ablest roads in the country will show that the mortgages today are much larger than they were on the day of their completion.

I think the case of the Central Pacific will prove no exception. Bonds must be issued to pay bonds, and the most we can hope to obtain is a reduction in the interest. Many companies are now issuing bonds to run 100 years and … one has been issued to run 476 years." Summarizing his offer to the government, he explained, "… for the sake of a final settlement of these much discussed questions, the company will accept a [Congressional] Bill giving an extension equal to something less than forty-four years." This document had been sent to the *Washington Post* and received wide circulation including general distribution among the members of Congress.[265]

Biographical treatments of Huntington have been frank portraying his business participation as "cold, crafty, hard, and frequently dishonest." Oscar Lewis described him: "He had none of the qualities of the militantly good citizen. Social and civic consciousness were meaningless phrases; a man's responsibility was to himself." Arthur McEwen, editor of the *San Francisco Examiner*, called him "a hard and cheery old man with no more soul than a shark." David Lavender's biography of Huntington, appropriately entitled *The Great Persuader*, showed how he was able to convince large numbers of high-level individuals in the government of his viewpoint on issues time after time. However, it includes this: "As a vigilante he [Huntington] presumably approved this rough insistence on goals, not means, as the ultimate consideration. Seen against that background his statement, made years later to Hubert H. Bancroft's scribes, to the effect that the bribery of Congressmen was justifiable if it persuaded them to do "right" – such thinking then emerges with a blunt and consistent logic." In Huntington's own words, "…circumstances arise sometimes when power gets into the hands of corrupt men, who withhold justice and are perfectly willing to ruin others to sustain themselves… and when the only possible way of obtaining justice is by the use of influence in whatever form is essential and inevitable; in such cases bribery may be the last and only means left to honest men… All theory is opposed to this, I know…" Huntington's history of bribery was well-known following the investigations by the Pacific Railway Commission. Hundreds of C.P. Huntington's letters to his business partner, David Colton, between 1874 and 1878, had become public knowledge and revealed the incredible number of subversive payments he had sponsored to officials at every level of government and to individuals in privately owned railroad services. Sutro knew Huntington and knew this was an accurate characterization of the man and was determined to oppose his distorted view of the world.[266]

Sutro had hoped to open the Sutro Baths as early as May 1st, 1894, but one thing after another intruded to push back the opening month by month. Real estate sales tapered off significantly due to a combination of seasonal influence and a slowdown in the economy. He had arranged to put a large number of home lots up for sale in September but there was little enthusiasm in the market. The banks were making fewer loans at higher rates and Sutro's cash flow problems began to intrude upon decisions. The street in front of the family home at Hayes and Fillmore needed paving for which he was responsible. He applied to the City Public Works Department for a delay because he did not have the cash to pay for the work. In addition, Leah's passing had taken more out of him emotionally than he expected and condolences from relatives and acquaintances continued to arrive providing reminders he would have preferred to do without.

On New Year's Day, crowds poured onto the grounds at Sutro Heights and there was heightened interest in the huge structure enclosing the baths. Sutro hinted to a reporter that the opening was expected in February. He told his brother Louis the bath buildings cost him "over a quarter-million [dollars]." The Market Street line, owned and operated by the Southern Pacific of Kentucky, ran the steam rail from the edge of the main city residential areas to the ocean. The line carried thousands of passengers daily and ten times that on summer weekends. Every passenger paid twenty cents for the round trip and some who did not have transfer privileges paid an additional ten cents. Sutro wanted transportation from the central city to Sutro Heights to be both abundant and affordable so that those crowds could be accommodated economically on a regular basis. He received little cooperation from the railroad company which threatened to shut down the steam line to Golden Gate Park when the Midwinter Fair ended in February. Their spokesman, John J. Haley, told members of the Richmond Improvement Club that it would be two years before a cable line provided service to the ocean. In early March, Huntington and Crocker visited Adolph at Sutro Heights and the railroad plans were discussed. Sutro, still hopeful that Huntington and Crocker would deal as honest competitors, proposed two possible rail routes from town terminating at the new bath house. Crocker was reported as saying, "…there was no possibility of Mr. Sutro's suggestions being complied with." All day long the pair of them engaged in hushed whispers as they looked about the splendid vistas of Sutro Heights. Sutro suspected that they lusted after the property. That was Saturday; first thing Monday morning, Adolph Sutro went to the Hibernia Bank and borrowed $100,000 mortgaging twelve blocks of his outside land property in the process.[267]

Sutro was ready to go on the warpath against Huntington and the railroad. A fence was erected at Sutro Heights, its structural beams cemented in place, creating a barrier to entry into the baths or the Cliff House from the end of the extended rail line. His plan was to charge nothing for entry into the baths, the beach, or the Cliff House from those arriving by any means other than the railroad. Those coming on the train would be charged 25 cents to enter. He was quoted as agreeable to removing the charge if the railroad reduced its fare to five cents from the ten cents it was charging. This policy was justified because he had spent some $20,000 each year on Sutro Heights for the benefit of the public for which he asked no admission fee. At the same time, the railroad collected fares from thousands of patrons who visited the Heights all year long. Sutro also spoke of building his own rail line to the area.[268]

Sutro prepared a document agreeing to deed Sutro Heights to a Board of Trustees representing the city of San Francisco "…provided there is only one single five (5) cent fare charged from the Ferries to the Cliff House." There were more details, but the essence of the offer was clear – Sutro would give the Heights to the city if the railroad company created and operated a cable line, charging only five cents each way, from the Ferry slips at the bay to the western beaches. This offer was publicized widely in San Francisco and aroused negative responses from the monopoly which accused him of trying to increase the value of his land holdings. In parallel with this activity, Sutro hired three knowledgeable agents, Charles A. Sumner, J.M. Bassett, and Frederick B. Perkins, to re-locate to Washington, D.C. and perform the functions of Congress watchers and lobbyists against the proposed Pacific Railroad Funding Bill. All three had credentials for the position. Sumner had served a term in the United States Congress in the 1880's where he was remembered for opposing the Pacific railroads and he was later editor of the *San Francisco Herald*; Bassett had been employed by the Southern Pacific and was fired by Huntington after which he wrote nasty letters to his former boss which were published in newspapers throughout California; Perkins worked as a cataloguer under George Moss in the Sutro Library and had previously been fired as head of the San Francisco Public Library. Sutro began to author and publish letters and essays about the dangers and injustices of the proposed bill which he sent to his agents for distribution. They were instructed to give copies to the President, the Cabinet, every Congressman and Senator, the Supreme Court and numerous others with political influence. As many as 1,500 copies of some messages were distributed by face-to-face contact.[269]

The suggestion that Sutro wanted to increase the value of his properties by offering the Heights to the city may indeed have had a kernel of truth, but it is fair to say that was far down the list of his priorities in the early spring of 1894. Further, the Richmond section of town had become increasingly popular and homeowner groups were pushing for more and better services in an area that had received less attention from the city administration. Sutro's battle for reduced fares brought out hordes of supporters almost immediately after his offer appeared in newspapers. A meeting was called for Farrell's Hall (actually a roadhouse convenient to the area) where more people showed up than could be accommodated inside. The meeting was moved outdoors where overcoats and mufflers were seen in wide use, but the crowd stayed. Sutro spoke amid cheers and enthusiasm and promised a series of such mass-meetings and offered to find an appropriate venue for the following week. Newspaper reports about the five-cent fare issue began to appear every day. Less than a week after the first mass meeting, Sutro petitioned the Board of Supervisors for a franchise to build a new railroad, conforming to city codes, which would connect from the terminations of existing lines to the beach. The Street Committee took it under advisement. Concurrently, Mayor Levi R. Ellert tried convincing Southern Pacific to lower their fares. Ellert asked Charles F. Crocker (son of the original partner Charles Crocker and president of the Market Street Railroad) to help the city acquire Sutro Heights by reducing the fare to five cents. Ellert thought he had succeeded; he forwarded a response from Crocker indicating the Market Street line would comply with the request. When Sutro read Crocker's response, he was enraged; a number of "strange" requirements were there that Ellert hadn't either noticed or mentioned.[270]

From Washington, where he was lobbying for the Funding Bill, Huntington also sent word that in return for Sutro's beneficent gift of Sutro Heights, the Cliff House, and the baths, Southern Pacific would reduce the fare and lay a cable. Sutro had been insisting that he wanted the rail line to the beach to be a cable car line. Of course, no offer had been made which included the Cliff House and baths. Huntington knew that. At one of the hearings where the Street Committee was considering his franchise application, Sutro made public his response to Mayor Ellert which ended: "This matter has been talked over a dozen times or more between myself, Mr. Crocker, Mr. Huntington, Mr. [William] Hood, their chief engineer, and others, and they know full well that the great object I had in view was to get a cable road and a depot immediately at the baths [meaning close by], so that visitors would not have to face the cold winds of the ocean after leaving the baths…They talk in a patronizing manner about what they propose to do in the interest of the people. They talk as if it was through a sacrifice on their part that the public would secure the use of Sutro Heights. They ignore me altogether, and forget that Sutro Heights has been open to the public, free as air, for the last ten years, while they were busily engaged in gathering in all the 5-cent pieces they could." All of this was published the next day and another mass meeting was held that night with crowds demanding a five-cent fare and adding their voices in opposition to the Reilly Railroad Funding Bill before Congress.[271]

Less than a week later, the Street Committee agreed to put Sutro's railroad proposal up for public auction. This meeting had been spiced with a contentious confrontation between Sutro and John J. Haley, spokesman for Southern Pacific and the Market Street line. But for physical intervention by other attendees, the two may have come to blows. That there were serious, irreconcilable differences between the two sides was abundantly clear to everyone present. However, Sutro came away with the victory he had sought, and the community was exultant over the result. Of course, this was only one small part of what Sutro was after.

On June 8th, Adolph Sutro opened the Sutro Baths for its first public showing. He conducted a personal tour of the facilities for a select group of women delegates attending the American Medical Association convention. His daughter Emma was active in women's medical organizations and this was very likely a nod in her direction. The first really public activity at the baths was a concert by Fritz Scheel's orchestra plus swimming races involving members of the Olympic Club witnessed by more than 15,000 people in October. Attendees enjoyed the performances but were highly critical of the Market Street rail line which had provided distinctly inferior transportation.[272]

Sutro turned his attention to the action in Washington. He sent 1,250 letters to government officials from the president on down to chairmen of the state central committees of every state and other individuals he knew. Both Sumner and Col. William Little had reported disruptions to distribution of Associated Press telegraph reports and railroad agents were suspected. Sutro thought Huntington was behind that. The government was asked to look into the issue. Leland Stanford had passed away a year earlier; at the urging of Sutro's agents, United States Attorney General Richard Olney notified Stanford's Estate that the government claimed $13 million as their portion of the bond indebtedness due. If so, the new college was in trouble. A mass meeting was called for the evening of June 19th at Metropolitan Temple. Col. Little had been busy soliciting agreement from a number of key individuals to take leadership and speaking roles at the meeting and most complied. The meeting was large and boisterous and Sutro was cheered wildly. He spoke at length detailing the issues confronting West Coast communities due to the railroad company which he referred to continually as the "Octopus." "The United States Government generously aided in the construction of the Central Pacific Railroad. The managers evaded the payment of interest at regular intervals, but the company should have set aside enough from year to year to meet the interest and a sinking fund to meet the principal at the time of maturity. What did they do? They took the interest money and that intended for a sinking fund and put it in their own pockets, and now, when the principal and interest fall due, they tell the Government that they owe nothing and that the road is bankrupt." Simply stated, the speech convinced anyone who was in doubt and the crowd loved it.[273]

Two nights later, Sutro was too tired to attend another mass meeting convened at The Tabernacle in Oakland where, in his absence, more than 3,000 cheered his message delivered by Col. Little. This meeting was sponsored by the Populist Party which was suddenly gaining in popularity throughout the state. The political machines of both Republican and Democrat parties dominated elections and it was rare to see much enthusiasm from other partisan agencies. Sutro's personal popularity among the attendees did not escape the notice of the People's Party leadership.

Sutro followed up approval of his franchise request by visiting the Supervisors' clerk's desk in person to submit his bid. Only two bids were submitted. The first one opened contained a one-dollar bill causing the bid to be rejected. Sutro's bid of $6,010.00 was accepted upon the spot for consideration by the Supervisors. A week later, Sutro asked the Supervisors to return his fee citing the fact that over the years many franchises had been awarded without fees. While no approval had yet been granted, a bargain was struck requiring Sutro to post a $6,000 bond against completion of the railroad under the terms described in regulations. The Supervisors had also authorized charging entrance fees at Sutro Heights so long as the net profits were given to charities. The Catholic, Protestant and Hebrew Orphanages received equal payments of $242.20 for the first five weeks of operation. There were newspaper reports of the Tabernacle meeting, the franchise auction, the bond agreement, and the donations from Sutro Heights gate fees. Another newspaper report from the sleepy town of Mariposa, California, many miles from San Francisco announced that, "Adolph Sutro will probably be nominated by the People's Party for Mayor of San Francisco. His popularity should insure his election."[274]

In the early tunnel days, while he was trying to raise money at any source, Sutro had spent major portions of several years in Washington buttonholing congressmen and senators at every opportunity and getting a thorough education in American politics. He held a general disrespect for most elected government officials, particularly those who made careers of politics and were constantly running for office. He was sickened by the ease with which elections could be bought. Sutro had run for political office in Nevada several times and had witnessed how votes and voters were swayed by money. He arranged that an article entitled "How Members of Congress are Bribed" would be published in a popular weekly newspaper. He told his brother Louis: "The corruption in Political affairs is something appalling, and it is not easy to bring about a reform, for the men who run for political offices do so as a general rule, for gain, and it is difficult for instance, to find a dozen Supervisors who are honest and remain honest during their term of office. The temptation is too great." In an afterthought to his daughter Kate and Moritz, he said, "They also talk about running me for an Office, possibly Mayor of the City, but I do not think I will run into a Political fight, which causes no end of anxiety and labor."[275]

On a Sunday in late July, a delegation from the executive committee of the People's Party visited Sutro at his home where they tried to convince him to accept their nomination for Mayor. The best they could get out of him was a promise to talk with their entire committee on Tuesday. The full committee left the ensuing meeting with Sutro prepared to enter his name as their candidate at the nominating convention on August 14th. He hadn't accepted; he hadn't refused but, it seemed clear, he would be willing to accept in the face of such enthusiastic backing. He did say he would "give it the consideration it deserves."[276]

Finally, the Supervisors convened to consider Sutro's franchise application. The twelve Supervisors voted eleven to one against. Sutro controlled his anger but was quick to say the Southern Pacific had arranged his defeat. "The octopus has a petition in now asking for franchises for nine different branch roads…the real scheme is to obtain possession of these few blocks and thereby block others from getting franchises on the thoroughfares." He added, "…when the Southern Pacific petition comes up on Wednesday, there will be eight votes in favor and four against it." He named who would vote each way. Notwithstanding the actions of the Supervisors, Sutro proceeded as if he had approval. That day, the Sutro Street Railway Company was formed with five directors including Sutro, O.T. Baldwin, O.F. von Rhein, Joseph H. Moore, and Monroe Greenwood. Sutro's trusted jack-of-all-trades, Col. William Little, was named Secretary. At the last minute, Sutro had changed the name on the Articles of Incorporation from "Nickel Railroad" to "Sutro Railroad;" perhaps some time in the future, a nickel wouldn't be sufficient. Subscriptions for shares were being solicited at the real estate offices of von Rhein who had become Sutro's principal real property agent. Sutro predicted the new line would be in full operation by New Year's Day and would feature a five-cent fare from the ferries to the Cliff House including admission to the restaurant and Sutro Heights Park.[277]

Pressure from the Peoples Party continued unabated until mid-August when Sutro capitulated. In a letter to P.O. Chilstrom, Chairman of the Municipal Convention, he offered, "I have no desire to hold any office, and would never consent to take one except on the ground that I might contribute to the general welfare ... I do not claim to belong to any political party, am entirely independent, and recognize but one issue before the people, and that is <u>the destruction of the evil powers of that incubus upon our welfare the Southern Pacific of Kentucky.</u> That is the <u>only</u> plank upon which I stand ... If you choose to nominate me with <u>this understanding</u>, I will accept the honor of your nomination." That same night, Sutro was nominated.[278]

Negative reactions came quickly. One out-of-town newspaper editorial said of Sutro, "The way in which this venerable man has hornswoggled English pounds, shillings and pence is altogether out of the common. He has absorbed on the scale of royal largesse. And yet this aged ex-appropriator does not hesitate to pose as a reformer." Another opinion from yet another city: "... [of all the queer things associated with this election] the advent of Adolph Sutro as a People's candidate for Mayor of San Francisco is certainly the most peculiar of them all... there is today not a more selfish, conceited and arrogant man living in the State of California than Adolph Sutro... [his] philanthropy is only a cloak to cover up his selfish schemes ... Sutro always was and is this present day a shrewd, ignorant, scheming, pushing, overbearing, unscrupulous, arrogant, vulgar fellow, who will not shrink from doubtful measures, as long as they are serving his own selfish purposes." Editorial commentary from both of these organs had been critical of Sutro for years reflecting the views of their owners who were closely allied with machine political organizations.[279]

Sutro did his best to ignore these commentaries. He concentrated upon keeping his word about campaigning on only one issue – the

Southern Pacific of Kentucky. As the keynote speaker in a People's Party rally, he launched into an extended attack upon the railroad and Huntington and was cheered enthusiastically. Despite his narrow focus, a wide variety of groups pledged their support including the Young Woman's Suffrage Club, the Veteran Soldiers & Sailors Republican Club (!), the German-American Independent Party, and the Afro-American League. At one after another of the large rallies, Sutro's name or entrance or introduction brought roars of approval from the large crowds.[280]

At the end of October, the Market Street Railway Company announced it would reduce its fare from the ferries to the beach to just five cents. Huntington and Crocker both stated that the reduced fare would not meet the necessary level of income because the bulk of travel on that line was on the weekends. Further, they anticipated the possibility of converting to electric power from steam power on their lines and had wanted to make no changes in operation until that decision was made. They contemplated the necessity of operating at a loss in order to comply. There was a general feeling that Sutro's threat to build a competing service had motivated the decision. The fare reduction was supposed to take place on November 6th which was Election Day.[281]

Election Day arrived and Adolph Sutro was swept into office on a wave of ardor. When the votes were counted, he had received more than all his opponents combined. Expressing his satisfaction, he said, "It's a triumph. The people have turned out *en masse* for me and carried everything before them like an avalanche." He was particularly pleased by the position in which the railroad forces were left; they now knew they could not beat him locally and they could not buy him and were perplexed about how to proceed. However, Sutro had not been able to extend his popularity to the supervisor races.[282]

Sutro spent a few days at his Napa Valley retreat working on continuing attacks upon the funding bill and setting plans for the launch of his term in office. Congratulatory messages rolled into his office from friends and relatives and innumerable supporters. There were also many requests for positions in the city. His personal business issues continued unabated – contracts for use of the new bath building, street gradings for the new railroad, payrolls for employees at the bath construction, and more. Col. Little filtered all of that, prepared everything for Sutro's signature and passed on daily letters with details. Elliott Moore's brother and partner, John, who had shared legal responsibilities for the tunnel, and who was a director of the new railroad company, passed away. George Moss represented Sutro at the funeral as the new mayor-elect took a short vacation at his Napa Valley retreat. During Sutro's absence, two full weeks including two weekends with beautiful weather had gone by since the Market Street railroad had promised to reduce fares; the ten-cent fare was still in force and newspaper headlines were asking "Was it a bluff?" Huntington continued making promises that would become effective after some "necessary arrangements"; Col. Little showed details of the Sutro Railroad Company construction efforts including massive purchases of rails, ties and spikes and an employee count exceeding one hundred eighty.[283]

The clerk of the Supervisor's Office reminded Sutro that he was required to submit an itemized statement detailing funds he received toward his election and identifying individuals who had made contributions. Further, he and two selected sureties were to post a $25,000 bond and duplicate Oath of Office Forms for filing at separate locations. Otherwise, he could not receive a Certificate of Election. This was exactly the kind of administrative absurdity that Sutro despised and which biased him against running for office in the first place. However, now he was elected and would have to comply whether he liked it or not.[284]

Sutro held a luncheon for the newly-elected supervisors at Sutro Heights. He used the event to propose peaceful cooperation between the ward leaders and himself. In a short speech, he toasted the group and expressed his hope that there would be "...harmony so that much good may result in our city." Charles L. Taylor, speaking for the collected officials, hoped that "...this pleasant meeting was only the beginning of two years of cooperation and friendly feelings," and proposed a toast to the host in return. While no business was conducted at the gathering, Sutro let it be known he had sorted the Supervisors into what he considered logical groups for assignment to the various committees that oversaw city activities – finance, judiciary, streets, fire services, public buildings, water supply, health, police, licenses, hospitals, printing, salaries, street lights and outside lands. He was astonished to hear in return that the Supervisors themselves traditionally made those appointments. The Supervisor's clerk, Mr. Russell, confirmed what the Supervisors had been telling Sutro. He could hardly believe it; it made no sense to him. He ended the conversation not wanting to spoil the mood of the meeting, but he knew there was a fight on this subject in his future. [285]

With the election behind them, citizens of San Francisco appeared to feel secure in the knowledge that Sutro was going to continue the fight in their behalf. Adolph Sutro knew he needed help – particularly financial support – to pursue opposition to the Funding Bill. He wrote a lengthy open letter to the "People of San Francisco" appealing for their participation. In it, he told them the community was sleeping and the media was half-asleep while, three thousand miles away, Collis Huntington was busily engaging his various allies, "... shrewd lawyers, unscrupulous politicians, bribers, thieves and associated villains" in lobbying the new Congressmen. Only the innocents would be shocked at the thought that Congressmen can be bribed. Hundreds of Congressmen were defeated for re-election recently due to financial enticements. Only 150 votes are needed to pass the Reilly Funding Bill. If that number of Congressmen can be bought for $20,000 each, that would cost Huntington only $3,000,000. What is at risk in the bill is $77,000,000 and Huntington stands to profit some $74,000,000. He may not be a highly educated man but "... he has studied arithmetic sufficiently." We all need to defeat this bill and you must help me with your voices and with financial assistance.[286]

On Christmas night, the Cliff House burned to the ground. Firefighting equipment and personnel were four miles away and virtually no defense was established against the conflagration. For a time, it appeared the Sutro Baths were threatened but, fortunately, they were spared. Two days later, Sutro was quizzed about his plans for the site and calmly explained that an architect had already been consulted and the restaurant would be rebuilt very likely on the same spot. The last thing Sutro needed at this time was a new problem involving significant expense and the kind of attention he was accustomed to paying to construction projects. His nuanced reaction required a considerable amount of self-control. The Cliff House had been a very special place for him. He had transformed it from a dump to the finest eating establishment in the community, an assessment it had earned originally when first built and was attracting the likes of Governor Stanford, William Randolph Hearst, and Charles Crocker. Over time, it lost that panache. Nothing less than the best place in town would satisfy Adolph Sutro now that the baths and the amusement park were close to opening. So, he had a new challenge.[287]

January 7th, 1895 was a busy day for Adolph Sutro. Final preparations were under way for his inauguration the next day including polishing the inaugural address. That same morning, he was asked to put his name in nomination for president of the California Academy of Sciences. This was no small honor; even in the late 1800s, scientific investigation and pursuit of modern technology were important elements of California life. Unfortunately, Sutro had been too busy with other issues and wasn't aware of being thrust into a highly charged political battle in the Academy. The fact he was identified as the Reform candidate should have given him a clue. Later that same day, Sutro learned that Police Commissioner Dan Burns had resigned and had already been replaced by outgoing Governor Henry Markham who was serving his last day in that capacity. Sutro was furious; he contended the Mayor and not the Governor should have made that appointment. He confessed high regard for Mose Gunst, who had been selected to replace Burns, but considered he had none of the required attributes or experience for the job. Further, it appeared that this had been arranged to give Gunst the position and that Burns had agreed to step down to facilitate the change. Sutro was quoted, "Mose Gunst is

not the man I would have appointed. The fact is the whole government has been perverted, and is not being carried on squarely for the
people at all."[288]

The following day, Adolph Sutro delivered his inaugural address
which laid out plans for the community in every area of civic interest.
His words touched upon honesty in office; elimination of boss rule; encouragement of the Grand Jury; separating local elections from national
and state contests (therefore localizing the issues); increasing funding
for public schools, emphasizing gymnastics, technical training and kindergartens; radical reformation of the city charter; eliminating the
Spring Valley Water Company's monopoly by taking over water supply
as a city service; similar treatment of both gas and electric supply; improvement of Fire Department manpower and equipment; standardiza-
tion of street construction methods and materials including the sewer
system; control of the sale of spirits; increased availability of drinking
fountains; growth of the public library system; work programs for the
unemployed; and various improvements in processes of government
relative to how it dealt with suppliers and other state and federal institu-
tions. It was a bravura performance which demonstrated how thoroughly Sutro had studied and analyzed the problems of the city and set out a
huge list of things which would produce a better community. If Sutro
had control, matching how his own projects were run, it could have
been a merry time in San Francisco.[289]

While Sutro was being inducted into his new position, members
of the Academy of Sciences were visiting Academy offices throughout
the day to vote for their officers. One of the "Reform" leaders was interviewed late in the day and pointed out how strange it was that there
were a large number of members committed to the Reform movement
who did not show up to vote. Reform leaders expected to win the election but, in the end, were defeated soundly. Sutro lost to Professor
Harvey Willson Harkness for president by a vote of 67 to 44. Harkness
actually had one more vote than he had garnered the prior year. Harkness was disliked for his overbearing leadership methods but his long-

time friendship with Leland Stanford brought him considerable support from the octopus group to which his continuing victories were attributed.[290]

Sutro didn't have time or energy to take on another dispute. Still committed to defeat of the Reilly Funding Bill, he succeeded in having State Senator William J. Biggy propose a resolution urging California members of the United States House and Senate to vote against "... any bill to extend the time for the payment to the Government of the Pacific Railroad debts and vote for a measure to foreclose at maturity the lien of the Government on these roads..." Both the state Senate and Assembly approved the resolution which was sent from newly-elected Governor James Budd to United States Congressman James G. Maguire who had actively collaborated with Sutro. Maguire led the forces opposing the bill. In the House of Representatives, a debate raged over the bill for several days in late January ending on February 2nd. The Reilly Bill was defeated by a seventy-one vote majority. Huntington's lobbyist, John Boyd, assigned blame for the loss to Sutro. In interviews, Maguire defended Sutro who was attacked for the stridency of his letters and telegrams and his relentless charges of bribery against Huntington. The Congressman said, "Collis P. Huntington is greatly interested in a measure before the House, and he has never hesitated to resort to bribery for the accomplishment of any purpose of this kind in which he has been interested." He referred to Huntington's letters to his partner David Colton and how they justified Sutro's statements which may have been "over-zealous" but merely represented the sentiments of his constituents in California.[291]

Sutro thanked his brother Louis for a congratulatory message. He added, "...there never has been such a combination of money powers than was assembled at the Capitol to carry through the Reilly Bill. I started and organized the whole fight and, if anyone knows who beat them, it is Collis P. Huntington, though the newspapers do not give me full credit for what I have done." He went on to predict the bill was not dead; that "...they will try and hang something to an appropriation bill which will partly carry it through." He was right; they never stopped trying. Dan Patten, Sutro's caretaker at the Arcadia site, observed, "You hit Ellert &&& heavy, but they deserved it. I say hit them right & left, high & low. This time Huntington will meet the Mayor of San Francisco instead of the dutch crank with a bath house on the beach."[292]

Huntington was indeed persistent. A new charter had been proposed for the city of San Francisco including a section on transportation. One of its features was a requirement to reserve certain streets as "boulevards" precluding the use of these thoroughfares for tracked vehicles. In addition, the existing network of tracked lines would be reserved for the current users for extended periods of time. One Freeholder connected with Huntington, Irving M. Scott, was a principal in Prescott, Scott & Co. manufacturers of metal products principally in the boating business. Sutro and Scott engaged in several debates at Board of Freeholders meetings which included name-calling and elevated emotions. Sutro maintained that "…railroad influences were working to shut off avenues by which competing lines might be built…every person in San Francisco, even to the children, knows a certain malignant influence – an octopus – spreads its arms over San Francisco and that its iron heel is on the government of the municipality."[293]

Shortly after these discussions, the Market Street Railroad had several hundred men suddenly working to tear up Church Street in preparation for laying tracks. Mayor Sutro visited the Street Committee to complain that the railroad's charter for Church Street had been abandoned by lack of use; a written notice of abandonment had been submitted and accepted by the Board of Supervisors. Sutro ordered the cessation of work sending word to the police and the Superintendent of Streets. The railroad gang refused to stop and completed a large portion of the work they had begun. The superintendent of the railroad crew was arrested and summarily bailed out upon a promise to stop work at 6:00 pm that day. In violation of that agreement, work continued throughout the night. Thomas Ashworth, Superintendent of Streets, was slow to respond but finally did see the Deputy Chief of Police who agreed to have a large-enough force of officers assembled to stop the work.[294]

By mid-February, just six weeks after his term began, Sutro expressed great frustration over his disappointing relationship with the supervisors. A hard core eight of the twelve members opposed everything he advocated and persisted in proposing and passing measures he considered insignificant. All eight were machine politicians from the Democratic or Republican parties and he was certain they had been given gifts originating from railroad sources. He felt they not only opposed him but "… appear to delight in showing their hostility." They desired to erect a pest house (quarantine facility) in close proximity to the local almshouse; he considered this absurd. They wished to build a new hospital despite the general opinion among the city's physicians that the current facility was "admirable." The old city hall building could be repaired and spruced up economically rather than replaced with an expensive new building the eight supervisors proposed. Sutro wished he were 1,000 miles away. This mood continued for several days which was long enough for him to be interviewed by a newspaper reporter. He remarked about his annoyance over politicians and office seekers. The printed article aroused the supervisors who thought he was referring to them. At the next Board of Supervisors meeting, Sutro gave a short speech explaining he had been misunderstood and that his remarks had no connection with "your honorable board." He used this non-apology as introduction to a discussion of the city's water delivery issues for which he recommended the city acquire all the water resources and serve itself. The suggestion was greeted with silence from the Board. A resolution was adopted to meet and discuss water rates for the coming year.[295]

Sutro was determined to win his point against the Spring Valley Water Company. Aside from the concept of city-owned utilities, which he was promoting vigorously, the safety and quality of the water delivered to households needed to be beyond criticism. He was convinced this was not uniformly true. Sutro had engaged Thomas Price & Sons, a quality control agency in the chemical and mining communities, to evaluate the water in Lake Merced and to render judgment about its purity. Price found one of the three samples taken to be "foul and dangerous" and unfit for drinking purposes or domestic use. This was presented to the Board of Health which resolved to perform its own microscopic and chemical evaluation. One board member, Dr. Martin Regensburger, made a point of disagreeing with everything Sutro said or proposed. It appeared certain Sutro had acquired another critic who may have had some connection with the railroad.[296]

For several weeks, the supervisors, the Board of Health, Adolph Sutro, and Hermann Schüssler wrestled with the quality, the quantity, and the cost of water to be delivered by the Spring Valley Water Company under the new contract. Much of the discussion was bitter. Shutting down any supply from Lake Merced was considered. Most of the participants visited the site and saw the proximity of large numbers of roaming animals, large and small, and the likelihood of runoff from ranches and pig farms during rainy periods emptying into the lake. Opposing chemical and biological analyses were obtained by both sides of the dispute and, of course, conflicting reports were issued. When the Board of Health's chemist found no problems in the waters of Lake Merced, Sutro threatened to summon a Grand Jury investigation.[297]

While Sutro was distracted in the water-supply battles, the Market Street railroad, representing the Southern Pacific of Kentucky, conspired to pass a bill in the California Assembly which would have allowed the commuter line to double its fares. The just-lowered 5-cent fares could be charged for each three miles of travel on the line under this new law. Sutro learned it was coming to a vote from one of his hired Assembly watchers who reported that the voting was held up intentionally while lobbyists "worked on" members of the Assembly to change their votes. The managed timing had been successful, and the bill passed. Sutro was certain Governor Budd would veto the bill and he delivered a petition to the Governor asking that he do so. He gave copies to the newspapers including an appeal for all citizens to request the same of the Governor. It didn't take long for Budd to put an end to it. However, for Sutro, the message was clear – the octopus would never quit trying and had numerous methods.[298]

The eight supervisors who continuously opposed Sutro had, by then, been assigned the name of "The Solid Eight" by news media. They caucused together and established scenarios for a variety of actions particularly giving employment to unqualified candidates of their choosing (including many relatives) while replacing competent civil servants. The eight proposed and passed an absolutely outrageous ordinance that was blatantly political, and which was specifically designed to injure Sutro. The new ordinance went into another realm of dreadful government by establishing a monopoly in procurement of bituminous rock for street construction and a corollary monopoly in the delivery transportation of this material. The delivery agent was to be the Southern Pacific of Kentucky through its local service – the Market Street Railroad. The proposal went back and forth in Board sessions over a period of several months with Sutro issuing vetoes when he could. The eight knew every trick to craft the ordinance so that only one supplier could meet terms of the specification. Further, nine votes (out of twelve) were needed to overturn a Mayor's veto so the Solid Eight turned the ordinance into a resolution which was not subject to veto. Sutro promised he would not sign any bills contracted under a resolution. The delivery issue was aimed at Sutro more directly by providing profits to the octopus. Prior to this time, bituminous rock had been delivered primarily by boat. The rationale for changing to rail shipment was based upon the costs of bagging and removing the rock at delivery. Of course, this process was needed no matter how it was transported but that was ignored in the volume of discussions about other factors. By the time the proposal was brought before the Supervisors for discussion and approval, a franchise had already been prepared for the Market Street Railroad and a purchase order was ready for signature. The *San Francisco Call* pointed out that the franchise "contained limitations and conditions which were not authorized by law." That did not prevent the inevitable approval by the Solid Eight.[299]

There was no more uncertainty about the situation in which Sutro found himself. The railroad barons, particularly Huntington and Crocker, had constructed a conspiracy to blunt Sutro in all his endeavors. Very likely, they had bribed the eight supervisors and offered assistance in identifying issues for contention. A battery of legal experts was able to study civic laws and expose loopholes that would benefit the Market Street Railroad and place impediments in the way of the Sutro Railroad. Decisions of the Board of Health were subject to consent and approval from the Supervisors and were never going to favor Sutro. Supervisor and Health Board sessions constantly led to arguments and anger which thwarted the Mayor beyond anything he had ever faced before. Coming from a world in which he made all the rules and all the decisions without dispute to a place where he was outnumbered and outshouted was intensely frustrating. That he was able to maintain a modicum of composure throughout this period took incredible self-control.

Meanwhile, Adolph Sutro was busy with his personal life as well. He finally closed the house at Hayes and Fillmore Streets and moved the family (Charles, Edgar, and Carla) to Sutro Heights. He also completed property transfers giving Clara Kluge ownership of the house and property at Point Lobos Avenue between 38th and 39th Streets just a short ride from Sutro Heights so that he could visit his second family very conveniently. The Sutro Railroad car barn was under construction and would provide storage space and services for sixty rail cars. Offices, machine shops, and maintenance areas were included. Plans called for completion in time for rail service to begin in September. The *San Francisco Call* pronounced the new structure "one of the handsomest and best equipped carhouses in San Francisco." Slightly more than a mile away, construction of the new, elaborate Cliff House continued. Looking like a French chateau, the building had five stories with spires and a four-story tower above. Each floor was designed for different types of services. The ground-level floor was to house a large dining hall, parlor, bar and private dining rooms. One floor up contained twenty private luncheon dining rooms plus an art gallery featuring many items from

Sutro's personal collection. The third floor would house a photograph gallery, reception rooms, and parlors. One floor down from street level, there would be a popular-priced eating establishment with a view of the seal rocks – ideal for tourists at lunch. Beneath that, was the boiler room, laundry, and other major service areas. There would be kitchen facilities where needed on the upper floors. Also, the amusement park specialties at Merrie Way, adjacent to the baths, were being installed and spruced up with paint and other decorations. This all represented an incredibly ambitious program for a man with a full-time job elsewhere. That was Adolph Sutro.[300]

Some half-dozen years had gone by since Sutro first offered property to the Affiliated Colleges for a scientific research facility of some kind. During that time, numerous conversations had been held about issues related to the gift. University committees were organized several times to review land offers which changed from time to time. There were simply too many viewpoints and opinions, and nothing had been accomplished. Sutro made one last effort to propose a gift of land. Six years earlier, he had set his mind on a site exceeding 26 acres in an area near Golden Gate Park as the place for his library. He prepared an elaborate offer letter to the Regents of the University expressing his willingness to share that site so that it would include 13 acres for the use of the colleges and an equal space for his library which would be available to students and researchers as if it were part of the university complex. The document included an extensive sales pitch about the library which then contained "…counting all titles… approximately 300,000 [volumes and documents]." A complimentary letter about the content of the library from the former president of Cornell University, Andrew J. White, was quoted at length as was a laudatory statement from Professor George Lincoln Burr, assistant to the president and librarian at Cornell. The letter was given wide distribution in printed form. Although it was not written in his promissory note, Sutro told the world he would be giving the Library to the city eventually. This was a theme he repeated over many years and the same promise was made for Sutro Heights park. This time, the Regents accepted his offer for the colleges and the transfer was recorded in early October.[301]

That same week, *The Sacramento Daily Record-Union* published a lengthy editorial lauding the works of "The Railroad Builder of the Pacific Coast" which ended: "If ever a community of civilized people had reason to hold any single individual in grateful remembrance for his contribution to their material prosperity and the commercial and industrial development of the part of the world they occupy, the people of California have reason to hold in grateful remembrance the life services of C.P. Huntington." The news organ which had been the home for Mark Twain, Bret Harte and Dan Dequille was now safely "in the pocket" of the octopus.[302]

Test runs of Sutro's new railroad line were conducted through the Richmond neighborhoods on their way to Sutro Heights. As a result, Sutro was going to secure the fare reductions he had sought and would have adequate transportation to his venues at the coast on schedule.

That railroad issue was settled. But, the Central Pacific Funding Bill began to surface once again. Huntington came to San Francisco and was interviewed by the media. He had been given ten questions which he chose to answer with a lengthy written response. Nothing he said was new – the CPRR owes the government $50 million which it does not have and cannot pay upon the required date; a new version of the Reilly Funding Bill will be proposed and passed at the next session of Congress to relieve the railroad of this onerous obligation somehow; services provided by the railroad worth $1.8 million should be credited to the railroad; the government made more money from the construction and operation of the railroad than the company did; and the railroad should be credited for providing "policing services" through the territories where the trains run. He went on to talk about the "... labor and privation which the builders of the Central Pacific undertook and suffered." Huntington's ability to distort was unlimited. The following day, Sutro was interviewed similarly on the subject pointing out various large discrepancies in detail and forecasting the use of bribery in CPRR's dealings with members of Congress. The war was starting all over again.[303]

Construction of the new Cliff House was nearly completed and Sutro made final payments to Campbell & Pattus. As scaffolding was removed, the building "stands out in all its majestic grandeur...a landmark that masters of incoming vessels can distinguish twenty-five miles out." The Pfister Knitting Company delivered the bulk of 1,000 new bathing suits for the Sutro Baths. Rabbi Joseph Krauskopf appealed to Sutro for an additional $10,000 to complete purchase of land for his Jewish Farm School. Sutro paid the Home of Peace Cemetery for annual care of the family plot after which he borrowed $200,000 from the Hibernia Bank.[304]

Then he got back to work. He organized another mass-meeting to arouse the public about new threats from the railroad. A standing-room-only crowd filled Metropolitan Temple and heard Sutro and others speak eloquently in opposition to yet another attempt to alter funding payments of the Central Pacific Railroad. The speakers were cheered lustily and Sutro was given great encouragement from the masses. He directed election of a Committee of Fifty [citizens] to lead the effort in San Francisco. The group included many prominent men including Mayor John L. Davie of Oakland; Levi R. Ellert, ex-Mayor of San Francisco; lawyers Henry E. Highton, Judge Elisha W. McKinstry and Stewart Menzies; George K. Fitch, owner of the *San Francisco Call* and the *San Francisco Bulletin;* Charles M. Shortridge, Editor of the *San Francisco Call;* and Levi Strauss, the famous clothing manufacturer. Sutro also made clear he had been the sole financial support for the opposition in the past and was looking for local citizens to participate in financing to fight the octopus. He claimed to have spent about $10,000 per year during the last two battles against the Reilly Bill (just a bit less than $300,000 in today's currency). He could no longer go it alone.[305]

Seventeen

ADOLPH SUTRO, THE BIGOT

It is unlikely that Adolph Sutro ever sat through a Passover *seder* at which the story of the Israelites escape from Egyptian bondage is told every year in the homes of the pious. However, there is no doubt Sutro knew all about Moses and the forty-year trek through the desert and, particularly, details of how the Jews had been treated in the years of their enslavement. In his later years he was quoted in an interview saying, "Even today, after the Negro has been emancipated and is no longer a slave, there is that deep-seated prejudice against the colored race that prevents the white man and white woman from sitting at the same table with them. That is not desirable – we want only one class of men – all on the same basis – before the law and before society. The distinction of classes is not desirable in a democratic country." There is much to admire in that pronouncement. He would have attributed that idealistic viewpoint to guidance from his mother whose whole aim in life was "…to bring up her large family of children and give them a good education and correct ideas of morality."[306]

However, the very next line of that same interview continues: "I think most decidedly there is fear of the Chinese over-running the country if there is no law to prevent it." How could a man so worldly, intelligent and altruistic come to believe that?

Jews in America had developed unusual patterns of behavior toward minorities. In colonial days, some Jews owned slaves. There appeared to be no tribal memory of those ugly Egyptian times when the Jews themselves were the slaves and it is easy to imagine the confusion of continental children going through their *haggadah* on Passover knowing there were slaves out in the back house. In the post-Civil War period, new and strange views surfaced locally. As the bulk of United States Jews accepted Negro emancipation and settled down to worrying about how Jews would be treated, some western American Jews, particularly in California, who had benefitted greatly from an environment with very little religious bias, developed strong negative feelings for their Chinese neighbors.

Anti-Chinese feelings had begun at the conclusion of the California Gold Rush when competition for jobs began to increase. Mining unions and other informal organizations lobbied their managements to exclude Chinese from the workers lists. In addition to job security, the willingness of Chinese laborers to accept lower wages threatened the pay level of Caucasians. Throughout the western states, and principally in California, anti-Chinese sentiment grew steadily through the 1860s and into the next decade. Denis Kearney, leader of the Workingman's Party, and Governor John Bigler politicized the practice including enactment of a policy to prevent Chinese from moving into California. Special taxes were imposed upon Chinese and new ones were added throughout Bigler's four-year term. All through the 1870s the bias against Chinese accelerated in the West and the slogan "the Chinese must go" was heard throughout California. In the Comstock region of Nevada, anti-Chinese meetings had culminated by organizing an Anti-Chinese Club. Every member pledged himself to "not patronize anyone who employed Chinamen, nor to vote for any political aspirant who employed them or sympathized with them."[307]

Historian Rudolf Glanz tells us, "The experience of the California Jews with the Chinese made them more immune to the cry, 'the Chinese must go', that was so popular among other sectors of the population…there were no Jewish names on the rosters of the anti-coolie clubs. Nevertheless, there can be no doubt that in the end they, too, fell for the anti-Chinese psychosis to a considerable extent, thereby earning bitter reproach from their brethren in all other regions of the country." The majority of California Jews believed that the Chinese were merely cheap labor and minimal consumers making little contribution to the economy. Glanz goes on: "Unfavorable descriptions of San Francisco's Chinatown, with lurid tales of the opium dens became part of the account of the situation of the Chinese in California." A group of San Francisco clergymen sent a telegram to President Rutherford B. Hayes asking him to approve a bill restricting Chinese immigration. The list of those who signed the message included three rabbis – Elkan Cohen of Congregation Emanu-El, Henry Vidaver of Congregation Sherith Israel and Aaron S. Bettelheim of Congregation Ohabai Shalome. Eastern Jews were shocked.[308]

In 1882, the United States Congress passed the Chinese Exclusion Act creating severe restrictions upon free immigration of Chinese into the United States. Coincidentally, that same year marked the largest immigration of Jews into the United States reflecting the need to escape pogroms in Eastern Europe. Originally intended to last ten years, the Exclusion Act was renewed in 1892 and made permanent in 1902. In 1943, fifty-one years later, it was repealed.

Not all California Jews supported the anti-Chinese viewpoint. Adolph Sutro's friend and frequent legal advisor, Solomon Heydenfeldt, said, "California owes its prosperity very much indeed to the industry of the Chinese... I think we would not have had as many white people if the Chinese had not come... they give white people homes and employment... without them the Southern Pacific would not have been built." And as for their moral qualities, "I think they are the best laboring class among us..."[309] Unfortunately, that was a minority opinion. When asked, Adolph Sutro rendered his judgment of the situation.

"I do not believe in having this country overwhelmed with Chinese. I do believe that the mechanics and laboring men of this country have a right to join together and cast their votes for such men as will protect them against the influx and competition of the Asiatic labor. An

American laboring man who has got a wife and children whom he wished to support and dress decently, bringing them up in a respectful way and give the children a common school education must not shrink from the degrading competition of the Asiatic who lives on a few cents worth of rice and who dresses himself in a bit of cotton fabric and who has no family to take care of and no children to educate. I think that no man of any sense of dignity would readily submit to be placed on the same footing and in competition with such men as those, and besides that, it is not desirable to introduce a population into the United States which will never assimilate with the Caucasian element, and which will in time produce as great evils as that of slavery in the South by introducing different castes."

He went on: "I think most decidedly there is fear of the Chinese overrunning this country if there is no law to prevent it. China, with her 400,000,000 [population] could quietly send over one million. The [American] people think that they have the right to use cheap labor as well as labor-saving machinery. The Chinese are a people of a different race, different religion, different intelligence, with their prejudices and superstitions handed down to them for thousands of years, who would not, in centuries, rid themselves of their peculiarities, and for that reason alone they should never be permitted to come here. I can say one thing, that among all the thousands that I have employed during my life in California, I have never employed a Chinaman, and I am one of the few in this state that have not. I will bet that you can't name another man that has employed as many men as I have (some thirteen or fourteen thousand at a time) that has not employed a Chinaman. I am opposed to the Chinese, on the political grounds of the future. I think it is introducing an element that will never assimilate, and it is not desirable that in a republic there should be two kinds of people...the very worst emigrants from Europe are a hundred times more desirable than these Asiatics. We do not want them here. Chinese labor is not exactly slave labor, but it will always be looked upon as a lower grade of labor."[310]

204

Very likely, Adolph Sutro would have had a difficult time believing that, just 120 years later, Asians would outnumber Caucasians by large percentages at seven of the nine campuses of the University of California including the two largest at Berkeley and Los Angeles.

In mid-March 1896, the Sutro Baths opened formally for public access and quickly became a top-notch entertainment venue for the entire community. Crowds came during the week and in greater numbers on weekends enjoying the reduced transportation costs and protection from wind and weather that the enclosure provided. Adolph Sutro had completed his term in office as mayor effective December 31, 1896 and he was officially retired. On July 4, 1897, John Harris went to Sutro Baths with a group of friends and purchased a 25-cent ticket which entitled him to general admission, a bathing suit and access to the changing room lockers. Harris took his ticket to the counter issuing bathing suits and was refused. The agent had observed that Mr. Harris was a man of "African descent, known as a negro and colored man" and the refusal was "on account of his race and color and for no other reason whatsoever…" On July 11th, Mr. Harris returned to Sutro Baths and made a second attempt to obtain the rights and privileges attendant to having paid the admission price and was refused again. Harris filed suit against Adolph Sutro seeking $5,000 for each incident during which he had been accompanied by a group of Caucasian friends and where he was held up as "inferior and degraded" in their presence.[311]

The story was reported in local newspapers and Mr. A.O. Harrison, superintendent of the Sutro Baths responded: "Negroes, so long as they are sober and well-behaved are allowed to enter the baths as spectators, but are not permitted to go in the water. It is not a matter of personal feeling with us but of business necessity. It would ruin our baths here because the white people would refuse to use them if the negroes were allowed equal privileges in that way. No one could in equity expect us to make such a sacrifice. I do not think such a case could ever be won against us. Public sentiment would be too strongly in opposition for any law to force such a commingling of the white and colored races. I do not believe the case will ever come to trial."

Sutro's son, Edgar, held a supervisory position at the Baths and agreed "... it would be ruinous to allow negroes in the baths, because the white people would be unwilling to mingle with them. There were not colored people enough to justify separate baths for them on a large scale, and he could see no remedy." Harrison was wrong and young Sutro was short-sighted. Harris brought suit which lingered in the courts for more than half a year. In February 1898, Harris was awarded $100 damages by a jury just one week after Adolph Sutro was judged to be mentally incompetent. There is no evidence that he had discussed this issue with his son or with Harrison but, very likely, a mentally competent Sutro would have agreed with his staff that business risk trumped social justice and refusal was the sensible thing to have done.[312]

$\mathcal{E}ighteen$

FINAL YEARS

As he began the second year of his term as mayor, Sutro was fully aware of his disadvantage in the struggle with the railroad. Huntington had spread substantial amounts of money around the California communities including newspapers in the large cities and, most significantly, throughout the San Francisco city administration. In Sutro's mind, Huntington could afford to spend two or three million dollars to protect the seventy million the railroad barons had obtained. Further, living in New York, Huntington was not a local target for publicity and had no other issues to interfere with his railroad activities. If he chose, he could go anywhere and concentrate upon the re-funding plan stealthily. On the other hand, Sutro was bogged down with what seemed like infinite meetings and documents and interviews which intruded upon his ability to focus on the Central Pacific and its monopolistic leadership. Every day, Sutro was attacked editorially in Sacramento and Los Angeles as well as locally regarding elements of his mayoralty. Worst of all, it seemed he could not get problems to resolve in some permanent way; every issue dragged on interminably. He had wanted to have the Cliff House open and the new electric rail line running concurrently as the year began. An opening celebration actually took place for the new restaurant on January 4, 1896. Additional delays made it necessary to forecast opening to the public at the end of the month. However, an unusually severe storm blew out many windows on several floors of the building causing damage to the new dining areas and another one-month delay was predicted. The railroad line was held in abeyance until both could open together.[313]

At City Hall, it was no better. The dispute over water quality between Sutro and the Spring Valley Water Company had been going on for months and showed no signs of being settled soon. Water samples from several reservoirs had been sent to three separate agencies for evaluation. Samples were unmarked as to source location so that collusion and preconceived notions would be precluded. A Board of Health meeting was held in March 1896 to feature opening the analysts' reports. In spite of differences among the three analyses, the Board of Health voted to accept the Spring Valley water purity. Only Mayor Sutro voted against approval because of the inconsistencies.[314]

Sutro's veto had necessitated a series of meetings to discuss bituminous rock specifications for street paving. As with the water purity issue, weeks turned into months before the Street Committee of the Board of Supervisors was content to send the issue back to the full board for another vote. After all that discussion and the many appeals from potential suppliers who would be shut out of competition, the specifications were going back to the Board unchanged from the last vote.

According to local regulations, the mayor was the designated chairman of a three-man Board of City Hall Commissioners consisting of the City and County Attorney, the City and County Auditor, and the Mayor. The attorney, Harry T. Creswell, and the auditor, William Broderick, appeared to be in league against Sutro and were able to outvote him on every issue. Further, they were disrespectful and abusive in conversation with him. Sutro alternated between ignoring their attitudes and responding in rage. The results were not productive for the committee or for Sutro's health. One of the subjects this committee oversaw was the construction project on the new City Hall building. Creswell kept his eye on the contractual issues and Broderick on the money. Sutro watched everything. The three met weekly and consistently ended in shouting matches and bitter words. The source of many disagreements was a building directory which would be placed in the hallway specifying office locations for the occupants. The city's Merchants Association had volunteered to produce the directory and both Creswell and Broderick were vehemently against the idea considering themselves competent to do the job and not thankful for what they labeled "outside interference" from the merchants. Sutro persisted in questioning the "real reason" they objected causing Creswell to suggest "… it is about time to call in the Lunacy Commission to pronounce judgment on you. Your mental faculties are evidently on the wane." Sutro ignored the remarks and intimated the influence of the railroad was likely. At the next meeting, one week later, the same subject ended in another shouting match with Creswell heaping insults upon Sutro. The two commissioners voted for a resolution inviting directories from outsiders at-large which they planned to ignore and use the one they themselves created.[315]

Sutro's aggravation over City Hall issues was relieved somewhat as the Sutro Railroad had its formal opening. Within days, weekend ridership exceeded 10,000 passengers each way despite winter weather and the fact that swimming was not yet available at the Baths. The crowds of visitors were content to stroll around the huge interior and about the grounds. His son Edgar was working at the Baths as an inspector and reported growing daily receipts until a particularly rainy stretch and a cave-in within the railroad tunnel which temporarily cut down attendance. Everything was on schedule for the anticipated March 14 opening of the swim venue. Temperature studies were near completion assuring the planned differences between each of the seven swimming pools. Amusement rides and games on Merrie Way were likewise ready to go. All of this was ongoing while Sutro took a brief vacation at Arcadia, his Napa Valley retreat, accompanied by the Adamsons. Edgar's sudden burst of motivation was matched by his older brother's real estate activities under von Rhein, the real estate broker who also was a Sutro Street Railway Company trustee. In his absence, business was picking up in all of Adolph Sutro's ventures.[316]

While Sutro rested, the United States Senate committee investigating the proposed funding bill had begun their interrogation of Collis Huntington. U.S. Senator William Frye of Maine, President pro tempore of the Senate, questioned Huntington briefly allowing him to defer a general statement until the next meeting. In closing, Frye asked, almost humorously, if large sums had been paid to Sutro to stop his attacks in the press. Huntington took the opportunity to offer a story about discussions between Sutro and himself regarding the railroad from the ferries to the Heights, which had ended badly with both vowing to fight the other over the issue. The testimony was reported to Sutro who responded calmly in a letter to the *San Francisco Call* disputing many of the claims Huntington had offered and telling his version of the conversations in great detail. He explained the earlier confrontations in which the railroad barons had been unable to conceal their desire to possess Sutro Heights which led to Sutro calling them "the Octopus." Not content with that, Sutro went back in time to his days in Nevada telling of disputes he had with Stanford and Crocker over excessive freight charges for tunnel building materials which had made him wary of dealing with them over many years. He ended with a condemnation of the federal government as having become an oligarchy by submitting to the will and demands of the large corporations. His choice for the best example of this was the Southern Pacific of Kentucky and its "head manipulator, Collis P. Huntington; and especially now that this question of refunding is pending before Congress and the passage of which would not only defraud the government of its just right, but would enslave the people of our coast for half a century."[317]

Upon his return to the city, another Board of City Hall Commissioners meeting was held where Broderick and Creswell persisted in disagreeing with every statement Sutro made. Nasty inferences were exchanged and Sutro repeated accusations he had made in the recent past concerning Huntington's influence on elections. The auditor and the attorney took exception vigorously denying either of them had benefitted in their election from efforts of Huntington. They appeared to be looking for ways to oppose the mayor. He seemed to have resigned himself to their perpetual contradiction. As the meeting closed, he told them he planned to attend no more of these meetings; he would send a substitute. Broderick replied that the substitute would not be recognized. They adjourned.[318]

In Washington, D.C., Congress continued evaluating the funding bill. Huntington was back on the stand and testified he had never read either the majority or minority report concerning the Pacific Railroad Commission's earlier investigation. Senator John T. Morgan did not believe that statement and insisted that a week's delay would be observed providing time for Huntington to acquire and read both documents. During that same period, discussions went forward in the Congress. One member of the House advised that there were no extra copies of Pattison's minority report to be had and that the Railroad Committee was holding discussions though "not a member of the Committee has a copy of the report." A proposition to reprint a supply of copies was rejected as railroad supporters in the Congress outnumbered their opponents.[319] Sutro's "watchdog," Frederick Perkins, reported frequently on discussions he held with Congressman James Maguire and Senator John T. Morgan of Alabama who led the opponents of the funding bill. They were waiting to "fry Huntington" over issues in the Pattison report and Perkins was looking forward eagerly to hearing it. Morgan had been enraged when Huntington called the opposition from California a "lot of chicken thieves;" the Senator wanted an opportunity to force Huntington back to California for questioning.

Adolph Sutro arranged a superb ceremonial opening for the Sutro Baths making certain that each speaker addressed some virtue of the mayor, including how he had overcome difficulties, the contrast between Huntington, who was at that moment "traducing this State in the East," and Sutro who was "earning and receiving the praise of his fellow citizens," and how the community was benefitted by having these "Pleasure Grounds." The band played "He's a Jolly Good Fellow" which stimulated a five-minute cheering outburst from the assembled crowd. Sutro spoke briefly listing the many entertainments available at the site and patting himself on the back for persevering when things went wrong. Then, to no one's surprise, he declared the Baths open. The weather was miserable; a cold wind was reported blowing from the ocean and there was little sun breaking through the heavy mist. In spite of that, the crowd was estimated to be about 7,000 people and the interior was warm enough for summertime fun. For first-time visitors, the Baths were an incredible sight. Nearly three acres under its glass roof, the immensity alone was overwhelming; the contents were beyond imagining for most people. Seven pools, six of ocean water and one a fresh water plunge, stretched nearly 500 feet from one end of the building to the other. Each pool was regulated to a different temperature; the largest contained unheated sea water while each of the other salt water pools was heated a few degrees apart from those adjacent, giving swimmers a wide choice of personal comfort. The fresh water pool was ice cold to most and created a challenge for teen-aged boys. As with Sutro's aquarium, the salt water pools were filled by tidal flows directly from the ocean; it required just one hour to fill the tanks with more than 1.8 million gallons. The heating system had been tested and tweaked until each of the pools could be regulated to a desired temperature. Pools could be accessed by seven toboggan slides, thirty swinging rings, diving boards, and rope ladders. Swimmers were required to wear bathing suits provided by the Baths. An impressive laundry facility supported management of the swimwear. The architects had designed the facility to handle up to 10,000 bathers and an amphitheater surrounded the pools containing 3,700 seats for non-participants.[320]

Sutro's introduction had promised other delights including a museum with "collections of natural history, of coins and intaglios, curios from Egypt, Mexico, Palestine, Assyria, India, Japan, all parts of Europe, Alaska and other countries...to help instill in the minds of youthful visitors a desire for learning." True to his word, there were mummies, stuffed birds and animals of all kinds, totem poles, plants, insects, and much more. Outside the Baths, on adjacent property, was Merrie

Way amusement park. Sutro had acquired all the exhibits and rides from Woodward's Gardens when it closed in 1893 and a great deal from the Midwinter Fair in Golden Gate Park in 1894. These were assembled around a midway featuring a large Ferris Wheel variant known as a Firth Wheel, a Mystic Maze, and a "Haunted Swing" ride. Later, a Scenic Railway was added. In the nine and one-half months following the opening until the end of the year, Sutro's pleasure grounds (excluding the Cliff House) produced more than $80,000 of revenue in nickels and dimes. That week, von Rhein's auction of Sutro home lots yielded fifty-seven sales throughout the Richmond area surrounding Sutro Heights and the Baths.

The same day that Sutro took office as Mayor of San Francisco, James Herbert Budd was sworn in as Governor of California. Though they belonged to different political parties, Budd and Sutro began a pleasant and cooperative relationship which promised much for the citizens of California. Ten years earlier, Budd had served in the United States House of Representatives as congressman from the Second District of California which included a large portion of the state north of San Francisco. He was respected widely for self-effacement and great interest in getting the right things done for his constituents. In his lengthy inaugural address as governor, Budd managed to include some recommendations to the newly elected legislators, "...I also suggest that you instruct and advise against all Pacific Railroad refunding bills. The Government might with profit to the Pacific States foreclose on the property and operate the mortgaged roads, under proper regulation, at a rate of charges to be measured by the cost of service." Sutro must have been delighted when he learned that Budd was against the funding bills. At the end of March, Sutro telegraphed to Budd, "Please permit me to congratulate you upon the great service you have rendered the citizens of San Francisco by preventing the streetcar fare bill to become a law. I know the pressure which was brought to bear upon you. You stood as firm as a rock – and today we look upon you as the "noblest Roman of them all." But, that had been a year earlier.[321]

213

Sutro's gift of land to the state university was intended to house the medical school. Several earlier site selections had been discussed and rejected for a variety of reasons. The area chosen had not been very popular with university leaders as it would require students and faculty to travel from one location to another during the day causing disruption in schedules. Additionally, it was not very close to public transportation and imposed a hardship on those without their own vehicle. Sutro succeeded in closing the deal by a promise to build his library on adjacent property and locating his 300,000 scholarly treasures right next door to the school. When the regents and Sutro agreed on details, the contract included two unusual features. In one, the colleges were committed to commence building their facilities within six months from the date of the agreement. Additionally, Sutro offered to select a board of trustees who would guide establishment and management of the new library. Six months later, in early April, a joint meeting of the Board of Regents and Sutro, including an assortment of attorneys for both sides, ended badly with both claiming the other had failed to meet its obligations. Sutro said he was willing to grant any reasonable time for the regents to begin their part. University representatives suggested that he merely deed the land to them, forget about the six-month commitment, and things would take place on a schedule which pleased him. Neither side accepted the proposals from the other and the meeting concluded with no decisions. After the meeting, Sutro expressed his opinion that, somehow, Huntington and the railroads had their hands in the sudden opposition he was facing; he was beginning to see conspiracies everywhere.[322]

A few days later, another meeting was held attended by the same participants plus Governor Budd and more lawyers on both sides. Sutro wasted little time getting to accuse the "Octopus" of being involved. He referred to Huntington as "thief, scoundrel, satellite, flunky and nincompoop." Governor Budd was not pleased at Sutro's outbursts; after trying unsuccessfully to get Sutro back on the subject, he attempted to proceed with the business at hand. Lawyers had been meeting on the side as recently as the previous day to get the issues settled and a university attorney presented their position. Sutro had been given a copy of the agreement drawn by the attorneys and his signature was needed. Sutro had informed them that he had lost or mislaid the agreement and was given a second copy the day before. Sutro's response began quietly as he traced the history of the discussions going over much area that everyone knew about. He pointed out that he had "opened and graded streets" throughout the composite area in question. He suddenly shifted gears and complained that he had been given just twenty-four hours to review and approve the agreement and with all the other demands upon his time, "being jumped on in this manner" was more than he could stand.

Budd and Sutro had contentious words with each other and the longer the discussion lasted the worse it became. The meeting degenerated into a shouting match after which the whole issue was returned to the hands of the combined law committee which had been working together. Sutro harangued about the octopus several more times and Budd showed his anger saying, "Mayor Sutro, take your seat; you have been heard enough." As he was leaving, Sutro volunteered to sign an extension of time for the university to begin work. Budd left for San Jose and then back to Sacramento. Once home he gave an extended interview reviewing the situation with Sutro and the gift to the college. He ended with "In my opinion the declarations of Sutro are simply a pretext under which he will endeavor to avoid keeping his promise to the regents, and I now predict that when the time comes he will find some technicality or excuse for not carrying out his agreement. I defy any man to show me a single instance in which he has kept his promises to the public except in those schemes for the avowed benefit of the populace which are marked by the jingle of nickels and dimes as they pour into the Sutro pocket."[323]

Budd was surely no longer the "noblest Roman" in Sutro's eyes. The tragic part of this breach between them was the apparent loss of Sutro's cool-headed rationality. He seemed obsessed with the octopus finding Huntington and the railroad operations at the root of all evil in the world. There was no reason for the disagreement over the college land gift to have gone out of control but now it had become an uphill struggle to get it back on course. Sutro claimed he had never agreed to give a deed "unless the site be freed from taxation." The lawyers were back together attempting to settle that issue but "they seemed to see no way of meeting the difficulty." Sutro continued to maintain the position that he wanted to settle amicably. He wanted to go to Washington and hoped to "fix it up" before departing. Of course, he was planning for a battle with Huntington but regretted his inability to handle all the issues he confronted. He told his brother Louis, "... I am overworked. I made a foolish step when I went into politics; in fact, I knew it when I went in but I could not very well escape."[324]

Sutro suffered physically from the combination of problems and disagreements he had encountered through the early part of the year. He asked for and arranged a two-month leave of absence to put himself back in better health. Staying at Arcadia, he pulled the strings as best he could with letters and telegraphs to his various agents. Most important were the messages to and from Frederick Perkins who was watching the Congressional debates and back-room discussions closely. So long as the funding bill did not come up for a vote, Sutro was content to stay out of the fray. However, his mayoral responsibilities were something else. He had been absent from his position for two months leaving a great deal of administrative detail on his desk including many documents which required his signature. Supervisor Charles L. Taylor had assumed a quasi-leadership role during Sutro's absence, but he had no official standing as Acting Mayor. Even some of Sutro's strongest supporters were beginning to wonder "who is mayor of this town?"[325]

Sutro returned in time for the July 4th celebration. A great deal of documentation needing his signature had crossed paths on its way upstate and had to be returned. But, Sutro was "cheered enthusiastically" as his carriage rolled along Market Street in the annual parade. Later that weekend, he prepared his monthly "Allowances List" including some daughters, his daughter-in-law, various nieces and nephews, sisters and sisters-in-law, two Kindergartens, Children's Hospital, the Boys and

Girls Aid Society, and Mrs. Sarah B. Cooper, the head of an immense Kindergarten program in the city. More than $500 each month was distributed in this way to the oft-changed chosen few.[326]

Sutro wanted to concentrate what energy he had on the battle against the funding bill and its follow-up strategies. He told people that "the time when an enemy seems to sleep is the time to be most alarmed" and he warned the Committee of Fifty to begin preparing for a new struggle during the short upcoming session of Congress. He promised to bombard Congressmen with anti-funding literature. But his responsibilities in the city persisted and became wearisome. Creswell and Broderick attacked him two or three times each week and, try as he might, he could not control his anger at their behavior. A civic organization called the Western Addition Improvement Club distributed circulars demanding a 2 ½ cent fare on his railroad which they claimed he offered at one time. No such offer had been made but Sutro was invited to "set an example for all the other roads." He refused flatly.[327]

The Civic Federation, a self-appointed citizen organization, arranged a large meeting at Metropolitan Temple to chastise the "Solid Seven" supervisors (and the not- so-bad eighth) for their fiscal irresponsibility in lowering tax assessments of corporations serving the city and taking the maximum from lower- and middle-class residents. The Spring Valley Water Company, one of Sutro's targets, was shown to be worth $21,650,000 and its assessment was based upon $3,820,000. There were others. The supervisors did not explain the rationale for these disparities. Sutro had declined an invitation to chair the meeting as it would be an "impropriety" for him to discuss criminal charges against a committee over which he was elected to preside. The leaders of the organization hoped that the Grand Jury would find a criminal basis for further action against the Seven. One hundred members of the Federation were listed as vice-presidents in newspaper reports and three of the major local newspapers, *The Call, The Examiner* and *The Chronicle,* consistently supported the intentions of the group. A resolution commending the Grand Jury for "promptly presenting these Supervisors for removal" was accompanied by resolutions thanking the news media for their participation and another thanking Mayor Sutro and the four minority members of the Supervisors for "championing the rights" of the citizens.[328]

Sutro was away at Arcadia again literally worn out from his political life. He was invited and, owing to ill health, declined nomination as supervisor from the Twelfth Ward in the upcoming election. He was looking forward to the end of his term in office and withdrawal from the mayoralty. The land gift to the Regents of the University was coming together finally; at least Sutro's role in the gift had become clear to everyone and he was free to resume work on establishing his library. But, that would have to wait until the funding bill issue was settled.[329]

Huntington deferred his annual trip to California, so he could pay close attention to the progress of his lobbying activities in Washington. His legal staff maintained constant contact with many of the Congressmen and continued to press the value to be obtained by keeping the railroad in the hands of those who had built and run it for so many years. No one was more persuasive than Huntington himself and he began the process well before the opening of the session. The railroad men had a new "line" – they professed to actually want the government to take over ownership... or so they said. Colonel Charles Crocker was quoted, "We would be perfectly satisfied to have the Government take over the Central Pacific Railroad... none of those railroad demagogues, such as Senator [Stephen] White and Congressman Maguire of this State, are really sincere when they talk of Government ownership of railroads. They simply talk for effect. Why we would willingly turn over the Central Pacific in payment of the debt due the Government if the United States would accept the property at its fair valuation. In fact we would rather have the Government take possession than secure the passage of a refunding measure." This was nearly impossible to believe; surely Sutro did not.[330]

Tuesday, November 3rd, came and went and, to Sutro's relief, James D. Phelan had been elected mayor of San Francisco effective on New Year's Day 1897. Early in December, Sutro invited Phelan and all the newly-elected supervisors to a luncheon at Sutro Heights. The gathering provided opportunity for Sutro to advise the group regarding City matters and he lectured on street paving techniques, sewer systems, and other issues relative to infrastructure which very likely were mysteries to many of those assembled. He began to unburden himself of responsibilities of office but retained enough determination to oppose proposals he disliked. He refused to sign the contract for construction of the new Hall of Justice, he vetoed two railroad measures approved by the old Board of Supervisors, and fought tenaciously to prevent relocation of the Pesthouse onto the same property as the Almshouse. This last outburst came on December 29th, just two days before he was to relinquish his office; he blamed Huntington for the proposal and claimed it was intended to injure him. There was hardly an issue raised anywhere which Sutro could not connect with Huntington and it was often difficult to follow his logic.[331]

On January 7, 1897, debate on the Railroad Funding Bill began in the United States House of Representatives. Congressmen from all over the country voiced their opinions about the proposal over a four-day period. A great deal of it was not pretty. Only one California member favored the bill. Grove L. Johnson of Sacramento delivered a rousing speech insisting that the supposed opposition from the State of California was false. He claimed "If the members of the House from that State should vote their honest sentiments, all but one of them (William Bowers) would vote for the bill. But, they were terrorized by the two men who were responsible for the alleged opposition to the measure – Mayor Sutro and W.R. Hearst of the *Examiner*." He went on to make a "remarkable, vituperative attack" upon Hearst and Sutro described later by Congressman Henry A. Cooper of Wisconsin as "the most disgraceful attack in the legislative annals of the United States." The following day, California Congressman Samuel Hilborn spoke eloquently in opposition to the Funding Bill. Summarizing his analysis of the proposal he said,

"The United States advanced for the construction of these roads, in principal and interest which it has paid or will pay up to maturity,

$178,884,249, and donated over 26,000,000 acres of land worth $65,073,836; in all, $243,935,595. These advances of money were not donations to the companies, or to the individuals controlling them, in consideration of the construction of the roads. On the other hand, the terms of the act require them to repay the Government every dollar of principal and interest." Further, "...the sum advanced by the Government was greatly in excess of the necessities for construction. These men could have dealt honestly with the Government and still have become millionaires; but they chose the opposite course. Nearly half of the great sum placed in their hands by a confiding Government for the performance of a trust was misappropriated and diverted to their own use by the parties charged with the trust, who are now fabulously rich, while the companies in whose names they acted are left at last stripped of all means to pay while the individual directors are all millionaires. In other words, the directors have the money and the companies owe the debts."

Much of Hilborn's information and motivation had come from Sutro, Hearst, and Charles Sumner, a former California Congressman working as a lobbyist for the Committee of Fifty and being paid by Sutro. Sumner had used his familiarity with the members to infiltrate caucuses of the railroad supporters while distributing printed literature opposing the bill which was defeated finally with 102 in favor and 167 opposed.[332]

Sutro was delighted with the result, but cautioned his followers against relaxing too much. This was the fourth time the re-funding concept had been defeated and he was certain more was to come. According to Sutro, "...the war is not over, not by any means. I tell you this man Huntington does not recognize defeat...he will try again." But this day was one for celebration and he arranged a phone call to the Heights to have all the flags flown. Mayor Phelan delivered a stirring address at a mass meeting that night and Governor Budd declared January 16 as a legal holiday.

Less than two weeks later, Congress received a proposal to establish a commission which would review indebtedness of the Central Pacific and offer possible solutions to the problems this posed. Sutro was enraged. He authored and had printed an open letter expressing his opinion that there were no more issues for Congressional consideration – that the only issue remaining was one of law, honestly applied. It closed with these words, "Does Congress intend to compromise fraud? There is nothing else to compromise. Let foreclosure go on. The debt is good. Prove to the people that BEFORE THE LAW Mr. Huntington is no better than any one of the seventy millions of individuals that constitute the United States." He considered the idea more dangerous than the re-funding had been and should be "placed in the courts where it belongs." The letter was distributed nationally.[333]

Sutro tried to get back to his normal life throughout the late winter and early spring of 1897. Real estate sales began to pick up after a sluggish period and his skirmishes with street grading and sewer lines and other real property issues kept him busy. He told his brother, Louis (calling him by his formal name, Ludwig) that "It is a perfect blessing for me to be relieved from the political duties I had to perform for of all the wretched people that I have been thrown in contact with during my administration, the politicians are by far the worst I ever had anything to do with in my life. By doing what was good for the people, honest and right, I have earned the abuse of a lot of criminals, who consider the man who keeps them from stealing is a man who is robbing them of their rights and that is about the standard of the ordinary American politician." He was very proud of his role in defeating the Funding Bill despite the minimal credit he received in histories of the events. He told Ludwig, "... [What I] started myself single handed has become a national question." The year, from August 1896 to August 1897 , saw the passing of Adolph's cousin Gustav Sutro, his old friend August Helbing, and his cousin and former business partner Bernard Frankenheimer. None of that could have brought him joy and he failed to attend any of the funeral services.[334]

By the end of August, Sutro was feeling weak and sick. Emma and George Merritt accompanied him to Baldwin's Tallac House resort on the shore of Lake Tahoe where they spent a month hoping to "recover his impaired health." This was apparently not successful; less than a week after their return newspapers reported that family and friends were alarmed by his enfeebled condition. He was said to be very ill in late October from what appeared to be a "stroke of paralysis" which was denied by the family. Emma told reporters he had been overworked the past two years and was suffering from nervous exhaustion from which he would recover soon. That week, Sutro deeded the Reese property to his children, one day after Carla's 30th birthday which was the last condition possibly preventing the transfer.[335]

A variety of events went by very likely without Sutro being aware of them; his attention was no longer easy to gain. John Harris, the African-American man who was denied use of the Sutro Baths, sued Sutro and the Sutro Baths. Local media had carried stories about the events which were probably shielded from Sutro. Edgar, working as a supervisor of sorts at the Baths, had been quoted along with the superintendent as having made a business decision – Caucasian customers would refuse to use the facility if Negroes were allowed to swim. The $10,000 suit was settled in favor of the plaintiff for $100. Sutro's business manager, Col. Little, (he preferred "agent") wrote a desperate message to the boss pointing out that some $32,100 was owed and he had no cash in the accounts to cover these debts. Other minor lawsuits were concluded with Sutro owing plaintiffs. By late January 1898, it was clear that he had lapsed into dementia back in September and that his business agenda needed full-time professional management. There was no longer anything to be gained by hiding the fact from those outside the family. Consequently, on February 7th, Col. Little, took charge of Emma's petition to the courts for appointment as his guardian. A $100,000 bond was provided to assure faithful performance of the duties attached. Charles, Edgar, and Carla joined as sureties of the bond. The guardianship was approved by Judge Isaac Sawyer Belcher.[336]

The following day, Edward Pond, Reuben Lloyd, and Elisha McKinstry met with Emma Merritt at Sutro Heights to search for the last will and testament of Adolph Sutro and, as we learned previously, the only will they could find had been written in 1882, sixteen years earlier. Edgar Sutro had not waited till the next day; as soon as Emma was named guardian, he applied for the "old position I used to fill, that of general outside manager, purchasing agent, overseer of repairs &c [at Sutro Baths]." Two days later, *The San Francisco Chronicle* published an article widely copied across the country disclosing the claims of Clara Kluge who declared herself the "contract wife" of Adolph Sutro and announcing her intention to "stand up for her interests if any move was made by the family to keep her out of what was due her." The King wasn't even dead, but everyone wanted a piece of the crown.[337]

By the end of March, Sutro had improved somewhat and his imminent demise was no longer expected. Emma turned her full attention to managing her father's business empire. She obtained permission to sell properties raising funds to pay debt obligations. Col. Little's letter back in December had surely been useful for quantifying what was owed and had very likely been written in response to a request some months before it became necessary. With Emma's approval, Charles W. Sutro, Adolph's older son, was put in charge of real estate management for the estate with a combined salary plus commission on sales he promoted himself. Already holding the bulk of the stock, Emma Merritt was elected president of the Sutro Railroad Company. All her siblings and their spouses signed an indenture as sureties for tax debts of the estate. It all seemed very smooth and efficient.[338]

Adolph Sutro was living at the family mansion on Sutro Heights. Both unmarried, Charles and Carla lived there with their father and Emma looked in from time to time with medical guidance. Three prominent doctors made regular visits to the Heights to check physical and mental progress of the patient. Early in May, a strange incident unfolded. Emma arrived at the Heights home accompanied by a horse-drawn ambulance with two burly drivers and announced she had come to take Adolph to her home/office where it would be more convenient to care for his medical needs. Charles and Carla objected strenuously; Sutro Heights was his home where he was comfortable and knew and loved the surroundings. He would not be that comfortable anywhere else. Emma pushed past Carla and instructed the drivers to place Sutro in the ambulance. The ambulance drivers began moving Adolph to the front door ready to place him in the conveyance. Carla ran to the ambulance, grabbed the whip from the seat and struck the horses who took off across the lawn of the mansion. With that, she had hoped to destroy the ambulance preventing removal of her father. Some of the statuary on the grounds was overturned but the horses turned around and headed back to the front of the mansion. By then, the drivers had re-taken control and put Sutro into the ambulance and drove off to Dr. Merritt's house. This episode signaled the beginning of serious disagreements between Emma and her siblings. Several of them feared the possibility that one of the others could influence Papa to sign a document which would disadvantage one or more of them. *The San Francisco Call* printed a lengthy article raising possible issues which might separate the family members from each other and which predicted legal avenues that might be taken. This included, "It is probable that the court will be petitioned to appoint a new guardian and trustee, and if so the allegations that will be made in support of the petition will no doubt enumerate all of the causes that have led to the division of the Sutro family against itself. When the family skeleton, if there be one, is haled (*sic*) into court there will be a rattling of dry bones that may not prove uninteresting to those who are interested in the fortunes of the stricken capitalist."[339]

Emma made some peace overtures to Carla and the others to no avail. Her refusal to return Papa to the Heights constituted a brick wall between them. Carla withdrew from the list of sureties. Rumors floated almost daily about Sutro's health – he was better one day, worse the next. On and on it went. Early in June, Carla announced her engagement to marry William J. English, reportedly a wealthy and prominent attorney in Chicago. No wedding date was set and future plans would depend upon the situation with her father. Real estate sales progressed at a merry pace. Likewise, tales of upheaval in the family were reported almost daily. Actually, in the midst of this apparent normalcy, Adolph Sutro was growing weaker and less responsive every day until August 9th when he breathed his last.[340]

$\mathcal{N}$ineteen

ADOLPH SUTRO, THE JEW

Adolph Sutro readily discussed his ancestry from Jewish roots on both sides of his family.[341] His paternal grandfather appears to have been a pious individual and Judaism was practiced throughout the families of his father's [Emanuel] siblings. The oldest brother, Abraham Sutro, was Chief Rabbi of Westphalia and was reported to have been an early mentor of Isaac Leeser, who became a renowned American rabbi.[342] Adolph's mother, Rosa, came from the Warendorff family and it is not clear whether she observed Jewish religious tenets when young. However, many years later, one of the Warendorffs solicited Adolph for a handout through the good offices of the Community Synagogue in Cologne.[343] As she chose, Sutro's mother was buried in a Christian ceremony after funeral services conducted by Reverend F.P. Henninghausen of St. Stephen's German Lutheran Church in Baltimore.[344]

Adolph Sutro was unquestionably a secular Jew, professing total disinterest in the rituals and dogmas of the faith. On a trip to the Holy Land in his later years, he sneered about those who prayed at the Wailing Wall: "One of the sights here is to see the Jews weep and cling to an old wall suppose (*sic*) to be a remains of the temple of Solomon; they are there for hours, men and women, weeping and praying. Most of them polish (*sic*), dirty beyond description."[345] However, Sutro was disdainful of organized religion ecumenically. He also said, "It is astonishing what a lot of cattle the human species is composed of; they go crazy year after year celebrating the birth of Christ all over the world, when I am sure more mischief has arisen in the name of Christ than from most all other causes combined. Christ was no doubt a very exemplary man and better than those who surrounded him; but it is too absurd to believe that he was the son of God who performed wonders. People in those days were full of superstitions and ... I am sorry to say that a large portion of mankind is still in the same condition."[346] He expressed his personal views on religious observance thusly: "I for one, firmly believe in the moral code, which is very much the same for all religions, and if people would simply follow its principles and throw aside all the humbuggery invented by priest craft, mankind would be much happier."[347]

While his daughter Emma was waiting for admission to Vassar, she attended Baltimore Female College and apparently asked her father about participation in religious activities. He advised that, "There can hardly be any objection of your going to church with the other girls, that is to say if you feel any inclination to do so. The teachings of the Christian Church and that of the Jewish, as far as the moral part is concerned, are precisely alike; the only material difference is that Jews do not believe in Godlike character of Christ. It will probably be inconvenient for you to attend the Synagogue, and when I get over there I shall talk all these matters over with you." There is no record of that discussion.[348]

This disdain for formal religion and any of its practices didn't prevent the world from identifying Adolph Sutro as a Jew. Further, he spent a lifetime seeking and enjoying the company of Jews, of belonging to Jewish organizations and, most significantly, being charitable to Jewish causes.

Sutro reportedly attended a Jewish elementary school in Aachen for a short period of time before transferring to a public school.[349] It was certainly long enough for him to have learned to read some Hebrew. During his time in Memel, he visited Königsberg and wrote to sister Juliana, "Every shop has its adress (*sic*) and firma [company name] in German and Hebräisch. I believed that it would be jews where I saw this Hebräisch schreiben [Hebrew writing], but every christian merchant has also his shield in hebräic, because the poluvan (?) jews can't speak and read german and this man make the whole Geschäft [business] here."[350] Sutro was twenty years old at the time and spoke and read at least four languages.

In general, there are few evidences of Jewish connections within the Sutro household. Sutro expressed it thus: "[My mother] in religion was [a] very liberal woman – extraordinarily so. She was more so than my father... ....I never was a very strong religionist. My parents were not either; nor any of my brothers. If you call religion taught as it is generally taught I say no, but when it comes to religious feelings, I think they are strong in the family, if religion consists of charity and kindness, which we considered always the true religion of the world. When it comes to religious rites and superstitions handed down in all directions, you find very little belief in our family – in other words, the whole family were thoroughly liberal in their ideas. I never made any particular distinction between one religion and another; in fact no one of my brothers was married in the Jewish faith. I did."[351]

When Sutro left his family behind in Baltimore and moved to the West Coast, he arrived dependent upon relatives and family friends for assistance in getting settled and finding a source of income. Almost all those early contacts were with Jews as much by choice as by default. He carried with him the address of August Helbing, a young friend who preceded him and who had established a dry-goods business with a partner. Sutro had his effects taken to Meyer, Helbing & Co. and Helbing invited him to sleep in the store. Sutro "gladly accepted as it is impossible to afford living in a hotel. Most of the business people have young men sleep in the store so as to have help if it should get afire."[352]

Helbing was twenty-seven years old and had been instrumental in creating an organization for Bavarian Jewish settlers in San Francisco. He was the first president and held that position on subsequent occasions. The Eureka Benevolent Society had regular meetings, conducted in the German language, and was dedicated to nursing the sick, assisting the widowed, and burying the dead as well as helping poor and needy Jews. By 1860, the society had upwards of 300 members many of whom became community leaders and world-class philanthropists. Among those were Levi Strauss, who turned rugged clothing into its ubiquitous ultimate; Michael Reese, a real estate tycoon of major dimensions; financiers Louis Sloss, Isaac Glazier, Lewis Gerstle, Simon and Elie Lazard of Lazard Frères; Henry and Jesse Seligman of J&H Seligman; and various members of the Sutro family. At least a half-dozen members of the Eureka organization served later as *parnas* [president] at Temple Emanu-El in San Francisco. Adolph Sutro maintained membership in the Eureka Society throughout most of his adult life including all the years he lived in Nevada and traveled the world.[353] Helbing went on to head the firm of Helbing, Strauss & Co. and sat as a member of The Local Security Board charged with exercising control of the stock brokerage practices in San Francisco. He was defeated as a Republican candidate for Supervisor of San Francisco's 12th Ward in 1892.[354]

While staying with Helbing, Sutro wrote to his first cousin Baruch "Bernard" Frankenheimer who had a dry-goods store in Stockton in partnership with Charles Haas. The inquiry was to find a business opportunity which turned out to be timely – Frankenheimer and Haas were disbanding their partnership; less than two months later, Sutro joined his cousin in business in Stockton. A scant two months from then, most of the town was destroyed by fire. All but six of the stores in the commercial district were burned down. The cousins found a new store and re-opened with many advantages – more space, lower rent and much higher prices owing to the scarcity of goods after inventories had been wiped out. But, Adolph didn't stay long in Stockton, opting to return to San Francisco. Baruch Frankenheimer forged a distinguished career in the grain business and his family remained in Stockton beyond the end of the century. He and his family were active in the local synagogue and his wife served a term as president of the Hebrew Ladies Benevolent Society. All the family members were interred at the burial grounds of the Temple Israel Cemetery in Stockton.[355]

Where and when Adolph Sutro met Leah Harris is not known. Factual documentation of their meeting, romance and engagement has not been found. The date of their wedding is likewise questionable. Emma Merritt, their oldest child, provided information on a library card indicating they were married in 1855, but other sources specify 1856. One fairly current text advises that they were married by Rabbi Julius Eckman in 1856, but no documentary evidence of that can be found. We are told that she was of "English Orthodox extraction" and was a "simple, good-hearted, traditional Jewish woman, whose idea of happiness was a life devoted to husband, children, the synagogue, and Jewish charities."[356] There is very little else about Leah's origins in files extant. A Leah Harris emigrated from Liverpool, England arriving in the port of Philadelphia on November 22, 1856 accompanied by an Esther Harris. The ladies had traveled aboard the *Tonawanda* as Forward Cabin passengers. Leah's age was estimated to be 21 years. However, a document prepared by Leah Sutro's grandson, Carlo Morbio, specified her birth date as having been August 6, 1833. The latter is more likely to be correct. It should be noted that the Sutro's first child, Emma Laura, was born on December 15, 1856 making the arrival date of the aforementioned Leah Harris improbable considering subsequent events.[357]

Some evidences of Leah Sutro's Jewish affiliation remain. In a letter to her eldest daughter Emma who was beginning college at Vassar, she said:

"I am not at all surprised at Uncle Ottos wife treating the family so distantly. She evidently does not like the Jews from all that I can learn and I don't blame her for when the Jews themselves slight those of their own race instead of feeling ashamed of them. It is to be suposed (sic) that people of other circumstances will treat them with the contempt they merit. It is not our religion that we have any cause to be ashamed of, it is our own actions through life. I hope dear Emma that you will never be ashamed or afraid to say you are a Jewish, for the Jews are Gods (sic) chosen people and although they have had many hardships and persecutions to endure they have always come out triumphant in the end. It seems that Miss Reinhardt did not know that Papas relations were Jews. I don't think that Miss Reinhardt will treat her [Emma's sister Rosa] less kindly on that account. Last week was New Years. (sic) We had a nice time. Next Sunday is Yom Kipor (sic) fast day. We will not have quite such a nice time. The children had a week vacation on account of the Jewish Holidays. All of the public schools [in San Francisco] were closed."[358]

On the same day, she wrote to Emma's sister Rosa, then attending a Catholic school in Baltimore, and offered the following:

"Last week we had a very nice time. It was Jewish New Year and I had lots of visitors. Cousin Alex came from the country to celebrate it. Albert [Sutro] called and Mrs. Wertheim and lots of other friends. Next Sunday will be the fast. All the public schools closed for one week so as to give the children a chance to enjoy the Holidays."[359] (Leah's cousin Alex Harris was the owner of a bar in Eureka County, Nevada. By "Mrs. Wertheim" she probably meant to indicate "Esther Wertheimer," one of a small group of Jewish ladies living in Eureka County. Leah wasn't very accurate with grammar or spelling.)

In the period between Emma's completion of high school and beginning classes at Vassar, she and Rosa stayed on the East Coast principally with relatives of Adolph. Leah wrote to the two of them that, "... it seemed very strange to me that you have had no settled home since you have left the Convent. I really think after all that it is the best place for you girls if it was not for the bigotry and superstitious notions that they instill into the minds of young girls."[360]

Leah Sutro did not like Adolph's family and made no secret of it in many letters to the girls at school. In particular, Uncle Hugo's wife, Maria (known as Mary), came in for special mention more than once. In the summer of 1873, Hugo's business had apparently failed, and his partnership was being disbanded. Leah told Emma:

"It is too bad that Uncle Hugo is out of business; he was not satisfied when he was doing well. Mary advised him to dissolve because his partner was a Jew and was dishonest. I wonder what is the cause of the break up. Now I am real glad that he has a trial of cristian (sic) friends so that he can find the difference. Hugo told me that when he was in partnership with Mr. Cohen that he saved 20 thousand dollars. I think that was doing well. Now that he went with a Christian partner he lost money."[361]

Adolph and Leah were both impressed by the discipline and rigor in parochial schools and opted to send several of the children to private Christian schools in preference to public education. Beyond that, none of the children were offered religious training and there is little in the archival remains to indicate that any of them had strong feelings about religious observance. The children knew they had Jewish origins, but it didn't matter to them. Most of them married outside the Jewish faith. Only one, Kate, married a person with Jewish roots – Dr. Moritz Nussbaum. A biologist, Nussbaum was a cousin of Kate's. His grandmother, Sarah Sutro Michel, was a sister of Adolph's father Emanuel Sutro. Like Kate, he was not a religious practitioner and pursued his career realizing he could not make the progress his capabilities had earned. In 1880, Nussbaum advanced the Theory of Germinal Continuity which competed with theoretical works of Charles Darwin and Gregor Mendel as the general model for heredity. Eventually, in 1907, he was appointed a full professor at Bonn University. Five years later, he attended the annual meeting of the American Association of Anatomists and was elected an honorary member by acclamation.[362]

Moritz and Kate Nussbaum lived in Bonn, Germany, and had six children, one of whom died in infancy. The oldest was Adolph born in 1885. At the age of fifteen, Adolph was baptized and confirmed in the Lutheran Church. He had expressed a desire to pursue a medical career and his father took steps to shield him from the anti-Semitic climate prevalent in professions at the turn of the century. Adolph graduated from Bonn University and passed the required medical examinations in 1909 and entered the surgical staff of the Bonn University Hospital Clinic. He became director of the clinic in 1928 and had private patients at local hospitals. Unfortunately, following "Kristallnacht," his Jewish origins caught up with him. He was stripped of his medical licenses, given a new identification card, and shipped to a concentration camp in Müngersdorf where he was assigned to work as the camp doctor. His mother, though Jewish on both sides of her family, was an American citizen which very likely influenced the selection of his assignment. He survived through the war, was restored to his teaching position and clinical duties in Bonn, and passed away seven years later. In 2007, Dr. Adolph Nussbaum's memory was honored by having the new clinical wing at Bonn University Hospital named for him.[363]

A different scenario developed for Adolph's younger sister, Elizabeth Louisa Nussbaum. In 1930, with both of them unmarried and in their forties, Elizabeth (known as Liz or Liss) and Johan Steenbergen met and fell in love. He was Dutch and had spent many years involved with design and manufacture of high-performance, personal camera equipment. Most of that time had been in Dresden, Germany, which was a world center for cameras. Steenbergen had launched and overseen the Ihagee Kamerawerk Steenbergen & Co. proudly producing the world-renowned Exacta camera. More recently, his countrymen from Holland had recognized his status in the community and he was asked to be honorary consul in Dresden. Johan and Liz were married in 1931 and set up light housekeeping in a small house but shortly found an "impressive house at Justinen Strasse." Business began to flourish reaching an employment level of 500 and featuring a personal visit from Prince Hendrik of The Netherlands, consort of Queen Wilhelmina. All was well until May 1940 when Nazi Germany invaded The Netherlands. Instantly, the Dutch consular official and his Jewish wife were enemies and were interned for a short period of time. Steenbergen attempted to split his business into two to get money out of it but was unsuccessful. Clearly, they had to leave Europe and managed to do so, arriving in New York where they were welcomed by the Dutch ambassador. Unfortunately, there was no financial support waiting and Liz had to call upon her aunts (Emma and Rosa) in San Francisco to help which they did. Johan and Liz traveled to San Francisco and spent the remainder of the war years there. He maintained contacts with key design and manufacturing personnel who had worked for him and, when the war ended in 1945, he returned to Germany leaving Liz behind in California so that he could make suitable arrangements. Now he was appointed Dutch military attaché in the French zone of Germany which had been partitioned by the allies. He wore the uniform of a colonel and received a military stipend. The factory he had left behind was virtually destroyed – only the walls remained plus a few machines which could be repaired. He began the process of rebuilding and arranged for Elizabeth's return. Almost too late, he realized she had suffered a brain hemorrhage, a severely broken leg, and was in the early stages of Alzheimer's Disease. Liz passed in September 1948.[364]

Another indicator of Adolph and Leah Sutro's Jewish identity was that their third child, Gussie Emanuel Sutro, who was born in August 1859 and deceased on December 25, 1864, was buried in the cemetery of the Eureka Benevolent Society in Virginia City. Though Sutro was not actively involved in the local organization, he was very likely accommodating Leah's piety with the boy's burial site selection. As mentioned earlier, he did pay dues and make contributions to the organization over a period of years.[365]

Both Adolph Sutro and the Sutro Tunnel were frequent subjects for newspaper articles. In the late 1800s, it was often difficult to separate news from editorial comment as most newspapers were owned and published by individuals with very specific involvement in local affairs. The major news organs in Virginia City were owned and operated by and for the Bank of California – Sutro's principal enemy. Further, anti-Semitism was openly practiced and the word "Jew" was employed in a pejorative way. Alfred Doten, publisher of the *Gold Hill Daily News*, editorialized about proposed changes to the Congressional Mining Act of May 10, 1872. Shortly thereafter, he attended an "anti-Sutro Tunnel meeting at [Virginia City] Opera House – Big one ..." He met with William Sharon, cashier of the Bank of California, and wrote an editorial for the paper entitled "Shylock Sutro." The one and one-half-column article excoriated Sutro as "unprincipled schemer" and gluttonous for demanding the $2 per ton royalty which mines would be required to pay to Sutro once the tunnel was completed and usable. The analogy to Sutro being Jewish was rather pointed. He concluded with "He has gobbled up all the lands within a radius of miles around the mouth of his tunnel, all the unclaimed land between there and the Comstock ledge, and now wants to gobble up the Comstock itself..... Shylock Sutro claims his pound of flesh. He knows that no patent can be issued upon any of the mines of, or contiguous to the Comstock .... without his royalty of two dollars a ton tacked upon it. He grasps after it, and says 'is it not so nominated in the bond?'" Doten met with Sharon the following day and had the interest rate on his loan from Sharon reduced to one percent.[366]

Four months later, Doten attended one of Sutro's lantern lectures in which Sutro projected pictures and diagrams on a wall and talked about the potential of the tunnel. Sutro had a difficult time with the lantern equipment and Doten regaled his readers with derogatory descriptions. He followed this with a seriously anti-Semitic paragraph mocking Sutro's accent:

"... and, says he, 'mine friends, de baper vots brinted in dis town – der GOLT HILL NEWS – is der vorsht and meanest of dem all. It has always lied about me, and I don't know nottin else. It never dells der droot. It lies vive dollars voort, and den goes to Bill Sharon and gets vive dousant dollars more to lie on. Shendlemen I advise you all not to dake der GOLT HILL NEWS." He went on, "Even der San Francisco *Gronigle* was now owned by der Bangk Wing. I'm not avraid of 'em. I've fought 'em from der shtart, and got away with 'em and I'm going for der shcalps..."[367]

Sutro did his best to retaliate by purchasing his own newspaper, *The Sutro Independent,* published in the town of Sutro which he owned. Circulation was reported to be 750 copies many of which had to be going to the neighboring communities of Virginia City, Gold Hill, Carson City, Dayton, and Winnemucca. *The Independent* occasionally carried articles about Jewish holidays, worldwide Jewish events, and activities at San Francisco synagogues. This was surely arranged by Sutro; it is not likely any of his editors would have included that material without direction. The *raison d'etre* for the newspaper was to trumpet progress and successes of the tunnel and to deflect criticism of Sutro.[368]

Adolph Sutro's gravitation towards Jewish business associates was very likely not intentional, but the result of cultural affinity. A level of communication and understanding, supplemented by the comfort of common language, facilitated doing business with the Seligmans, the Lazards, Joseph Aron, Isaias Hellmann, Solomon Heydenfeldt, Ignatz Steinhart, Alexander Weil, David Cahn, Michael Reese, and his banking Sutro cousins. From the earliest tunnel project days, these were the core of Sutro's business colleagues and he was comfortable engaging in financial arrangements with any of them. Except for Hellmann, every single one held Sutro Tunnel Company stock. Further, they were dependable as associates; none would be guilty of financial impropriety with Sutro or he with them. It is likely these relationships existed without Sutro being aware of the Judaic content of his inner circle. Religion simply did not matter to him; culture did and, had he been asked, he would more likely have considered them Prussian rather than Jewish. However, the fact remains that (in September 1878 when the connection to the mines was made), excluding shareholdings less than $200 in value, 41.7% of shares in the Sutro Tunnel Company were owned by Jews, most of whom were either relatives or colleagues of Sutro. Excluding Mc-Calmonts holdings, that was nearly three quarters of company shares.[369]

Sutro did keep up with news in the Jewish world. He purchased repeated subscriptions to *The San Francisco Jewish Progress, The Hebrew* [newspaper], and continued his membership and contacts with the Eureka Benevolent Society. While he was charitable to a wide variety of organizations, he was particularly generous to Jewish groups. Jewish orphan agencies received large gifts and he was solicited for donations from any number of individuals and groups overseas identifying themselves as Jews who needed financial aid. One of his principal beneficiaries was Rabbi Joseph Krauskopf who promoted the concept of moving young, unemployed Jews out of the congested eastern cities onto America's abundant farm land and teaching them to be farmers. He argued that in their countries of origin, the Jews had not been permitted to own land and, consequently, had no heritage of farming or any of the skills and techniques of the process. The rabbi made repeated personal appeals to Sutro and had some of his supporters also write to solicit help. With donations, Krauskopf purchased 118 acres near Doylestown, Pennsylvania, and created The National Farm School in 1896. That facility is now Delaware Valley College. Sutro made some significant contributions to the birth and growth of the school in the final years of his life. He was right in the middle of his intensive battles against the Pacific Railroad Funding Bill and the parallel war over commuter rail fares in San Francisco when he was solicited intensively by Harry Weinstock, a loyal and devoted supporter of Rabbi Krauskopf. Weinstock's appeals to Sutro's "Jewish guilt" succeeded in having him provide funds for publishing and distributing some of the rabbi's lectures. The timing could not have been worse.[370]

In early April 1893, Leah Sutro's death appeared imminent. Adolph and Leah had re-cast their relationship, so they could at least be tolerant of each other. In keeping with that, he acquired a lot at the Jewish Home of Peace Cemetery in Colma. Leah survived until December, but finally passed away. A large and impressive traditional Jewish funeral was arranged and was conducted at the family home (Hayes and Fillmore) by Rabbi Jacob Voorsanger, spiritual leader of Congregation Emanu-El. Following the service, a seven-car train carried mourners to Colma for a graveside service. The Sutro Baths and Sutro Heights amusement centers were closed for several days. Newspaper accounts of her life spoke of the years he was struggling and penniless and how helpful Leah had been. Adolph was quoted, "During all this time I was constantly aided and encouraged by my wife, and but for her confidence in me I think there were times when I would almost have despaired." His concerns and compliments were about a dozen years too late.[371]

According to Jewish tradition, Leah's gravestone was to be unveiled eleven months after interment. Several weeks before that date arrived,

Adolph Sutro contracted for the removal of his departed son Gussie Emanuel's remains from its burial plot in Virginia City and re-interment alongside Leah at Home of Peace. Arrangements had been made by the sexton at Temple Emanu-El. This was truly a remarkable act for a man who disavowed interest in the dogma and rituals of his faith. The man who was reportedly married by a rabbi [Julius Eckman] in 1856 had very likely not seen the inside of a synagogue between that event and his wife's funeral except as a tourist in the Holy Land or as an attendee at the funeral of an acquaintance. This sudden outpouring of religious accommodation was unusual. No record of an unveiling survives, but an impressive gravesite remains to honor Leah.[372]

Equally mystifying was Sutro's funeral. The will from 1882 had left no instructions about his funeral or the disposition of his remains. None of his children had ever been educated about the Jewish way of death. They probably all knew that Leah had attended services and functions when she could. The default action was to find a rabbi to perform the service; certainly no other religious denomination would have been appropriate. Most likely, Emma Merritt made the contact and Rabbi Jacob Nieto, of Congregation Sherith Israel, accommodated her. Other than Adolph's cousins from the Sutro & Company branch of the family, no other Jews attended the funeral. When the brief service concluded, the body was transported to the Odd Fellows' Cemetery where it was cremated. The family surely knew about the existence of the burial plot at Home of Peace. They may have been advised that cremation was definitely not a Jewish practice; it is also possible they were not so advised.

Twenty

THE MESS LEFT BEHIND

Adolph Sutro's passing brought on a blizzard of commentary in news media from coast to coast, but particularly in California. Considerable speculation about the size of his estate filled the pages of San Francisco newspapers day after day. News organs which had never been particularly friendly to Sutro offered glowing tributes to his accomplishments and his perseverance against accumulated opposition, competition, and bigotry. They praised his charity, particularly that which was anticipated to be given to the city of San Francisco and its inhabitants. Plans for his funeral were announced but the absolute privacy requested by the family very likely stifled some of the interest.

The San Francisco Call listed funeral attendees who totaled about thirty. Of his children, only Emma was listed along with her husband, Dr. George Merritt. Rosa's husband, Pio Alberto Morbio was listed but not Rosa; neither were Carla, Edgar nor Charley. Moritz and Kate Sutro Nussbaum lived in Bonn, Germany, and could not possibly have arrived on time. The remaining family members included cousins in the Sutro/Lowenberg financial branch of the family, Mrs. E.E. Schücking[373], and Adolph's sister Emma Winterberg along with her husband and son. Non-family attendees were Judge McKinstry, Reuben Lloyd, W.K. Van Alen, masonry contractor James Scobie, James M. Wilkins (proprietor of the Cliff House) and his wife, Barna McKinne who managed the Park Lane real estate tract for Sutro, Col. William Little (Sutro's business manager), attorney James T. Rogers and a Mr. Hutchins who was otherwise not identified, [374] but very likely was John Powers Hutchins and old time mining engineer who had apparently instructed Sutro in methods for drilling rock when the tunnel was started. He authored a text on the subject.

Two days after the funeral, the family gathered at Sutro Heights for the highly-clichéd reading of the will. The Nussbaums still had not yet arrived from Germany, but all the other children were there. Attorneys Reuben Lloyd and E.W. McKinstry, who had been in the search party which found the will, were present and Lloyd did the reading. Of course, Emma and the lawyers knew that the will being read had been written sixteen years earlier; the others were genuinely surprised to learn that no later will had been found. A great amount of speculation surfaced, both inside and outside of the family, when details of the will became known. Why had such an intelligent and business-like person neglected to update his will after so many changes in his fortunes, possessions and beneficiaries? The media tried to explain – "... like many other rich men, [if he made a new will] he would die shortly thereafter." Was it really possible Adolph Sutro had been superstitious? Not likely. Also, "... with all his wonderful energy, he was a 'mañana' man, always ready to put off action on any matter until tomorrow." Did this describe the Adolph Sutro people knew? Hardly. It was more likely that another will had been crafted and had either been destroyed or filed where no one had found it. [375]

The 1882 will contained 37 uniquely numbered paragraphs or sections. Specific amounts of money were left to a long list of relatives, friends and acquaintances, identifying their city of residence, with the qualification that they outlived Sutro. The list of those who did not outlive him included his mother; his brother Otto; cousin Gustav; his friend and legal expert Elliott J. Moore; Judge Solomon Heydenfeldt[376]; and Hattie Trundle, the so-called "$90,000 diamond widow," who had been the central figure leading to the separation of Adolph and Leah. Representative J. Proctor Knott of Kentucky was the only one of eight United States Congressmen included, with the same survival restriction, who managed to outlive Sutro. Within days, local newspapers reported correctly that "more than half the persons named in the will are dead."[377]

His six children were each to receive $10,000 from the earliest disposition of properties. Later, when all the other distributions had been made, his children were to divide the remainder of the funds, "share and share alike," except for key portions of his real estate in the City and County of San Francisco. One notable exception to the provisions for his children was paragraph XXIII which stated, "Unto my daughter, Emma L. Sutro [Merritt], all the books, papers, scrapbooks, manuscripts and pictures contained in my library; also all my private papers, accounts and account books, and all other written papers, whether contained in my desk, safes or safe deposit vault or elsewhere." This was an astonishing turn of events. For years, Sutro had made it clear he was leaving his book collection to the city of San Francisco and intended to place it in a new library building on property adjacent to the medical school land he had given to the Regents. Paragraph XXIII provided further evidence that the document being read to Sutro's family could not have been his last will.

If there was another will, where was it or what had happened to it? Considering the issues normally associated with identifying suspects, only one person had the means, the opportunity, and the motive to do away with a more current testament – Emma Sutro Merritt. She had been in charge of Adolph Sutro's entire empire as well as his facilities and his very body for months. If there were a later will and she was not pleased with its contents, it would have been the easiest thing in the world for her to do away with it. Her display of concerned curiosity with the trio of dignified and incorruptible gentlemen searching for the will could very well have been an act of pure deception. If, in fact, this was the case, what was her motive? What did the newer will contain that Emma disliked enough to destroy it? There are several possibilities but, interestingly enough, there does not seem to be any documentary evidence that the issue of her potential culpability was raised publicly. If anyone in the family questioned Emma on the subject, it stayed within the family. Of course, Emma had all the power now; who would (or could) challenge her?

The 1882 will had another puzzling, convoluted legacy. Several lengthy paragraphs identified two important sections of real estate generally known as the San Miguel Rancho and the Cliff House Ranch. The document described both areas in excruciating surveyor-type detail and removed them from the distribution pool for his children. Instead, Sutro laid out a broad plan for creation of a board of trustees which would control distribution of gifts to worthy charitable organizations. The listed executors were to manage these properties for the first ten years after Sutro's death. Thereafter, the board of trustees was directed to sell portions or entire properties and make gifts in accordance with rules of the will. The trustees would include the Governor of California, Chief Justice of the Supreme Court of California, Presiding Judge of the City and County of San Francisco, the Circuit Judge for the District of California, the Mayor of San Francisco, the President of the Chamber of Commerce of the City of San Francisco, the President of the Board of Regents of the University of California and six other members to be chosen by the group named above. Many details of how the trustees could function and how the real property was to be managed were included. Executors of the will would be challenged to administer these directions properly. This section of the will became known as the "trust clause."

Five executors had been appointed – Gustav Sutro, Elliott J. Moore, Solomon Heydenfeldt, W.R.H. Adamson, and Adolph's daughter Emma. Unfortunately, Moore, Heydenfeldt and Gustav Sutro had all died before Adolph leaving Emma and Adamson as the only surviving executors.

The will failed to include provisions for Clara Kluge and her two children. Sutro was known to be extremely fond of his "second family" having made daily lunchtime visits to the home he had secured for them. He appeared to have made efforts to bring the two families together; photographs survive showing them together though only Adolph seems to be enjoying himself. The possibility that he would have excluded the second family from his legacy was unthinkable. Five months before his demise, when Sutro was declared mentally incompetent, Clara Kluge had engaged legal representation and made clear she would fight for her rights and those of her children who she had made certain to name in his honor. Surely, the six siblings of his first family were quite aware of their existence and the affection he held for his second family. Had a newer will provided excessively for Clara Kluge and her offspring, that might have precipitated destruction or hiding of the document, but it would not be possible to deny Clara's claims for inheritance. The *San Francisco Call* article about details of the will concluded thus, "It is intimated by persons close to the family, that the children will acknowledge that Mrs. Kluge, the alleged widow, has rights and will settle with her rather than fight the matter in the courts. Mrs. Kluge has two children, Adolph and Adolphine, both of whom are said to bear all the striking characteristics of the Sutro family."

The will provided $50,000 for Miss Hattie Trundle of Washington, D.C., as a "reparation, as far as it may be possible, for the injury done her by a scandalous charge, falsely and maliciously, at Virginia City, State of Nevada, in the month of July, 1879, then and there brought against her." This will, written just three years after the incident at the International Hotel while Sutro maintained considerable guilt and remorse over the events, probably provided more for Hattie Trundle than any will prepared in the mid-1890s.

Reflecting the status of their relationship at that particular time, Article VI of the will stated, "Unto my youngest brother, Theodore, the attorney-at-law, the sum of one dollar ($1)."

As the significance of Emma's status became apparent, major disagreements began to surface among family members. By the end of August, it was clear that Rosa, Kate, Edgar, and Carla were not going to tolerate Emma's disproportionate inheritance without a fight. Her control of the estate and so many of the high-valued assets appeared unfair to the siblings and they succeeded in obtaining a continuance in filing of the will for probate. The four challengers had Rosa's husband, Pio Alberto Morbio, and their brother, Edgar, apply as administrators of the will which was denied in court. At the same time, Mrs. Kluge's attorneys were making her demands impossible to ignore. Barely a month after Adolph Sutro passed away, the entire family was embroiled in an internecine battle.[378]

Months went by without even an informal settlement of the issues between the various parties and the Sutro family became involved in other activities. Edgar and his wife Henrietta (known as Etta to the family) ended up in court with complex cross complaints. Etta accused Edgar of beating her and depriving her of financial support primarily because he abhorred work. He had filed a suit to compel foreclosure of a mortgage on property for which she was the beneficiary. Both sides had filed papers accusing and denying assertions of one another. On Christmas Day 1898, Carla Sutro was married to her Chicago lawyer in Los Angeles. The site was probably chosen to avoid public curiosity which was certain to be aroused in San Francisco.[379]

Shortly after Carla's wedding and her relocation to Chicago, the trust clause of Adolph Sutro's will was declared invalid by a local judge. The incredibly valuable property was anticipated to be back under the management of the executors without charitable gift requirements. Clara Kluge kept up her fight for a share of the estate. She took a $9,000 mortgage loan from the Hibernia Bank using the property in Richmond, which Sutro had given her, as collateral. That was enough to secure legal representation. Now everyone was prepared for a court battle over the estate.[380]

Sutro's will was admitted to probate on January 20, 1899 just five months after his demise. With the likelihood of challenges to the will, a year went by before suits were filed by Emma's siblings and Clara Kluge opposing the will. During that time, Emma and Adamson worked strenuously to dispose of properties in the estate. The Cliff House stimulated vigorous bidding. The Sutro Railroad was sold to the Sutter Street Line in an auction setting for $215,000. Meanwhile, battles had been ongoing over trust clauses in several large estates including Sutro's. Jim Fair's will still was being contested some four years after his death and the will of Amasa P. Willey was likewise under judicial review for an extended period owing to trust clause issues. Settlements in both these cases were expected to establish precedents for the Sutro estate.[381]

In January 1900, the California Supreme Court rendered its decision on gifts to charities. The statement turned out to be less clear than the convoluted trust clause in Sutro's will. General opinion held that the "peculiarities of the trust clause and its ambiguities" had resulted in its being declared invalid. Within a week following, the "sibling family," without Emma's inclusion, had filed a lawsuit contesting the will. Clara Kluge had also filed a suit for herself and for her children. In March, the heirs of Hattie A. Trundle filed suit to obtain the bequest set aside for her in Sutro's will. The Sutro library collection became a thorny issue. Emma persisted in claiming ownership from the wording in the document. Her brothers and sisters continued to challenge that. Adamson filed application to sell the library to which Emma sued to prevent. By March 1902, all other elements of the distribution had been settled. Clara Kluge had received either $100,000 or $150,000 or $200,000 (depending upon which newspaper report was correct), Hattie Trundle's claim had been rejected in court and relatively equal shares of the bulk remainder had been allocated to each of the siblings.[382]

Between the summer of 1902 and early 1906, Clara Kluge-Sutro (as she called herself for the remainder of her life) sold sixteen parcels of real estate for which acquisition documents cannot be found. These were very likely gifts to her from Sutro during the years of their close attachment. In the middle of that period, she employed an architect to design and supervise construction of a new home in Pacific Heights.[383]

Twenty-one

POSTSCRIPT

I met a traveller from an antique land
Who said: 'Two vast and trunkless legs of stone
Stand in the desert. Near them, on the sand
Half sunk, a shattered visage lies, whose frown,
And wrinkled lip, and sneer of cold command,
Tell that its sculptor well those passions read
Which yet survive, stamped on these lifeless things,
The hand that mocked them and the heart that fed.
And on the pedestal these words appear –
'My name is Ozymandias, king of kings:
Look on my works, ye Mighty, and despair!'
Nothing beside remains. Round the decay
Of that colossal wreck, boundless and bare
The lone and level sands stretch far away."

"Ozymandias" by Percy Bysshe Shelley

As with Ozymandias, very little of Adolph Sutro's works remain. The Sutro Tunnel has collapsed internally; little more than 100 feet can be traversed from the mouth of the tunnel despite considerable work to make the entrance look like new. Philipp Deidesheimer's rugged support structures fell victim to time and the huge pressures resting upon them. None of the buildings that supported tunnel operations remain except for one small shack once used by maintenance crews for storage. The town of Sutro, Nevada, designed and built by Adolph Sutro, which at one moment in time was the most populous community in Nevada, no longer exists. The Sutro Baths burned to the ground in 1966, were left as ruins for years, and then cleared so that only the foundation remains as a memorial to the world's largest indoor swimming venue. Likewise, all the constructions on Sutro Heights – the Mansion, the Conservatory, the Gallery, the Dolce Far Niente balcony – yielded to the ravages of time, the work of Franklin Roosevelt's WPA, and change. There is no more Sutro Railroad. The Sutro Forest is gone; more than one million trees burned or felled and replaced with residential development. At one time, Sutro Heights had more than two hundred imported statues on the property. Today, two lions remain at the walk-in entrance. Adolph Sutro's last Cliff House burned down in 1907. A new Cliff House stands in its place. More than half of his 250,000-book and ephemera collection was destroyed in the 1906 earthquake and fire in San Francisco. The remaining portion that was saved resides in the California State Library Branch at San Francisco State University several miles from Sutro Heights. The sea lions have mostly abandoned the seal rocks and "boundless and bare, the lone and level sands stretch far away."

NOTES

FOOTNOTE ABBREVIATIONS
(Separate collections are located and detailed in NOTES section)

AS - Adolph Sutro

BANC Notes -- Adolph Sutro autobiograpical notes, biographical and character sketches, etc., for the use of Hubert Howe Bancroft {1888ca], Bancroft Library, University of California, Berkeley.

BANC Papers -- Adolph Sutro papers, 1853-1915, Bancroft Library, University of California, Berkeley

HUNT Papers -- Huntington Library correspondence of Sutro and related to Sutro.

NHS Collection -- Sutro Tunnel Company Collection, Nevada Historical Society

SFPL Collection-- Sutro Business Collection, San Francisco History Center, San Francisco Public Library

STAN Papers --Cecil H. Green Library, Special Collections, Stanford University

SUTRO Collection/ Sutro Papers -- Adolph Sutro Collection, (1830-1898) Sutro Library Branch, California State Library, San Francisco.

UN-R Records -- Papers of the Sutro Tunnel Company, Special Collections, Mathewson-IGT Knowledge Center, University of Nevada- Reno.

NOTES FOR CHAPTER 1
(ENDNOTES)

1   In birth order, the children of Emmanuel Sutro and Rosa (Warendorff) Sutro, and their spouses are as follows: (1) Emmanuel (changed to Edward, known as Sali), married Mathilda Meyer; (2) Juliana, married Edward Jordan; (3) Adolph, married Leah Harris; (4) Emil, married Kathinka Schucking; (5) Otto, married Arianna Handy; (6)

Laura, married Gustav A. Drost; (7) Hugo, married Marie Trautman; (8) Ludwig (known as Louis), married Lillie Fraatz; Elsie, married Constantin Schucking; Emma, twice married, to Herman Hoepfner firt, then to Wolrad Winterberg; and Theodor (later Theodore), married Florence Clinton.

2   McKinstry misspelled Van Alen's name twice in the notes

3   Papers in the possession of Scott Trimble inherited from the estate of his grandmother, Frances C. Trimble. Copies can be found at http:// www.ststlocations.com/Arichives/Genealogy/Sutro/

NOTES FOR CHAPTER 2

4   Robert E. Stewart and Mary Frances Stewart, *Adolph Sutro, A Biography,* (Berkeley, CA: Howell-North, 1962), 46-102

5   43 U.S. 426, 2 How. 426, 11 L.Ed. 326, Susan Lawrence, plaintiff in error v. Robert McCalmont, Hugh McCalmont, and William Johnson Newell, defendants, January Term, 1844, US Circuit Court, Southern District of New York; George McHenry, *Philadelphia and Reading Railroad Company: Its Financial History,* (Philadelphia: January, 1881), 6; Marvin Wilson Schlegel, *Ruler of the Reading: The Life of Franklin B. Gowen, 1836-1889,* (Harrisburg: Archives Pub. Co. of Pennsylvania, 1947), 230

6   "Gold Mining in California," *London Mining Journal,* XXXIX (Jan 16, 1869), 49

7   W. Turrentine Jackson, "Lewis Richard Price, British Mining Entrepreneur and Traveler in California," 337-8, *Pacific Historical Review,* v. XXIX, No. 4, Nov 1960, 331-348

8   Ibid, 339-43; *The Pacific Historian,* v. IV, No. 3, August 1960, W. Turrentine Jackson, ed., "Journal of Richard Lewis Price: Voyage from London to San Francisco, 1871," 97-111 (This article's title shows the name of Lewis Richard Price incorrectly both in the heading and in the journal's index. Throughout the printed material, his name is shown correctly. Much of the article is reproduced from a diary of Price's which Jackson obtained from its repository in Shrewsbury, England.)

9   *Ibid*, 343-44; Waywiser (Harvard University, Dept. of the History of Science website) biographical notes for William Ashburner (1831-1887), member of the Whitney California Geological Survey (1863), professor of mining and regent at UC Berkeley, trustee of Stanford University

10   *Ibid*, 344-48

11   Power of Attorney, 30 Apr 1873, Folder 23:6, *Adolph Sutro Collection, (1830-1898)* Sutro Library Branch, California State Library, San Francisco, (hereafter SUTRO *Collection*). During the course of research for this text, the collection was re-organized and new folder numbers were created to match the new arrangement of manuscript materials. Most "old" locations were easily converted to their new numbers but some were not. Librarians at the Sutro branch will be able to assist in finding items listed in "old" numbered folder locations; J. Seligman to AS, 22 May 1873, Folder 47, "J&W Seligman," Box 10, Collection BANC mss C-B 465, *Adolph Sutro papers, 1853-1915,* Bancroft Library, University of California, Berkeley, (hereafter BANC *Papers*)

12   Articles of Agreement between Sutro Tunnel Co. and McCalmont Bros. Co., 8 Aug 1873, Folder I/4, Box 1, Collection NC7, *Papers of the Sutro Tunnel Company,* Special Collections, Mathewson-IGT Knowledge Center, University of Nevada – Reno, (hereafter UN-R *Records*); Fourteen letters between March 1773 and mid-1875, Folder 37, "Freshfields & Williams," Box 5, BANC *Papers*

NOTES FOR CHAPTER 3

13   Birth Certificate, City of Aachen, Prussia, Registration Department, dated 21 April 1830; Stewart and Stewart, *Adolph Sutro,* 9

14   A number of well-known texts were used to assemble this summary of the Bank Ring. Readers are advised to see the original versions. These include: George D. Lyman, *Ralston's Ring; California plunders the Comstock lode,* (New York and London: Charles Scribner's Sons, 1937); Dan DeQuille (William Wright), *The big bonanza: an authentic account......*(New York: A.A. Knopf, 1947) (first edition 1876); Eliot Lord, *Comstock Mining and Miners,* (Berkeley: Howell-North, 1959) (first edition 1883); Michael J. Makley, *The Infamous King of the*

Comstock, William Sharon and the Gilded Age in the West (Reno and Las Vegas: University of Nevada Press, 1906); Myron Angel, Ed., *History of Nevada: 1881*, (Oakland: Thompson and West, 1881); Grant Horace Smith, *The History of the Comstock Lode, 1850-1997*, (Reno, NV: Nevada Bureau of Mines and Geology, c1998); Bancroft Library collection BANC MSS 77/88 c, *William Chapman Ralston Correspondence, 1864-1875,* Items 12021 and 12022.

15 Several well-known texts were used to distill this very brief summary of the Bonanza Firm. The reader would be better served by reading the original versions. These include: Dan DeQuille (William Wright), *The big bonanza: an authentic account....(op. cit.);* Eliot Lord, *Comstock Mining and Miners*, (op. cit.); Oscar Lewis, *Silver Kings* (New York: Alfred A. Knopf, 1947); Robert Sobel, *The Money Manias* (New York: Weybright & Talley, 1974); Dennis Drabelle, *Mile-High Fever* (New York: St. Martin's Press, 2009). The quote about the huge ore discovery is from the Lord text, page 311.

16 George Kraus, *High Road to Promontory - Building the Central Pacific (now the Southern Pacific) across the High Sierra*, (Palo Alto: American West Publishing Company, 1969), 294--297; Oscar Lewis *The Big Four: the Story of Huntington, Stanford, Hopkins and Crocker, and of the building of the Central Pacific*, (New York; London: A.A. Knopf, 1938) *passim;* Stephen E. Ambrose, *Nothing like it in the world: the men who built the transcontinental railroad, 1863-1869*, (New York: Simon & Schuster, c2000), 43-44, 47-48, 53, 72-73

17 Adolph Sutro, *Autobiographical Dictation*, c1877 (dated from reference to Rosa Sutro's death), typescript marked "56111," 9, Collection BANC mss C-D 799, Folder C-D 799:4, *Adolph Sutro autobiographical notes, biographical and character sketches, etc. for the use of Hubert Howe Bancroft*, [1888ca], Bancroft Library, University of California , Berkeley, (hereafter BANC *Notes*); copy also found at Sutro Library *Adolph Sutro Papers*, file 30:2

18 William David Cohan, *The Last Tycoons*, (New York: Doubleday, 2007), 18-21

19 Huntington Library, *Louis Janin Papers* contains material about Janin's early training; AS to Louis Janin, 6 May 1867, Folder SUT 1100 and

AS to Janin, 13 Jun 1867, Folder SUT 1101, Box 2, HUNT *Papers*;
Louis Janin to AS, 1 Dec 1865, Folder 32, Box 6, BANC *Papers*; several other letters from Janin to Sutro in the same folder; Several letters
between Janin and Sutro, Folder 136, SUTRO *Papers*

20   Phillip I. Earl, "Philipp Deidesheimer, Pioneer Engineering Genius,"
California Mining Journal, April 1983, 74-75

21   http://www.onlinenevada.org/Hermann Schüssler and the Comstock Water System; Hugh A. Shamberger, *The story of the water supply
for the Comstock; including the towns of Virginia City, Gold Hill, and Silver City, Nevada, together with other water-related events for the period
1859-1969,* (Washington: Geological Survey, U.S. Govt. Print. Off.,
1972), 8-22

NOTES FOR CHAPTER 4

22   AS to Emma Sutro, 6 Oct 1876, Folder SUT 1192; 17 Oct 1876, Folder SUT 1193; 29 Oct 1876, Folder SUT 1194; AS to Emma Sutro, 14
Nov 1876, Folder SUT 1195; AS to Emma Sutro, and 6 Dec 1876,
Folder SUT 1197; R.S. Raw to AS, 8 Dec 1876, Folder SUT 851, and
16 Dec 1876, Folder SUT 819, all Box 5, HUNT *Papers*; E.J. Moore to
AS, 9 Dec 1876, Folder 38, Box 8, BANC *Papers*

23   AS telegram to McCalmonts, 15 Dec 1876, Folder 1, Box 1, BANC
Papers; Raw to AS, 16 Dec 1876, Folder SUT 819, Box 5, HUNT *Papers* ; L.R. Price to AS, 20 Dec 1876, Folder 1, Box 1, STAN *Papers*; AS
to Emma Sutro, 28 Dec 1876, Folder SUT 1199, Box 5; White Star
Line to AS, 1 Jan 1877, Folder 3, Box 1, Cecil H. Green Library, Special Collections, Stanford University (hereafter STAN *Papers*); Raw
to AS, 28 Dec 1876, Folder SUT 844, Box 6, HUNT *Papers*

24   Price to AS, 2 Jan 1877, Folder 11, Box 2; G.M. Clements to AS, 3 Jan
1877, Folder 10, Box 2, STAN *Papers*

25   Ames to Raw, 5 Jan 1876, Folder SUT 28, Box 5, and Ames to Phillip
Douglas, 10 Feb 1876, Folder SUT 27, Box 5, HUNT *Papers*

26   AS to Ames, 19 Apr, 23 Apr and 24 Apr 1877, letterbook "Superintendants Letters from April 1877 to April 1878," Box 2, Collection NC3,
Sutro Tunnel Company Collection, Nevada Historical Society, (hereafter NHS *Collection*); H.L. Foreman to AS, 1 Sept 1877, and H.L.

Foreman to Ames, 9 May 1877, Folder "Sutro Material," Carton 3, Collection BANC 93/97c, *Oscar Lewis Papers,* Bancroft Library, University of California - Berkeley; "The Human Battery." (author not identified), *California Farmer and Journal of Useful Sciences,* vol. 46, number 24, 2 Aug 1877, 1

27 Raw to AS, 21 Feb 1877, Folder SUT 856; Raw to AS, 21 Feb 1877, Folder SUT 845; Raw to AS, 6 Mar 1877, Folder SUT 846; Raw to AS, 1 Apr 1877, Folder SUT 859; Raw to AS, 6 Apr 1877, Folder SUT 862; Raw to AS, 9 Apr 1877, Folder SUT 864; telegram Raw to AS, 9 Apr 1877, Folder SUT 849, Box 6, HUNT *Papers*

28 AS to Emma Sutro, 6 Mar 1877, Folder SUT 1209, Box 6, ibid

29 Brush to AS, 13 Sept 1877, Folder 30 "Brush '77," Box 3, BANC *Papers*

30 AS to Joseph Aron, 14 Sept and 29 Sept 1877, Letterbook vol. 29, Carton 2, BANC *Papers*

31 Brush to AS, 27 Sept 1877, Folder 30, Box 3, BANC *Papers*

32 Simon Ingersoll to AS, 22 Oct 1874, Folder 28 "I – Misc.," Box 6, BANC *Papers*

33 "The Burleigh Rock Drill Co.," *The Engineering and Mining Journal,* vol. XXII, July to Dec 1876, (Scientific Publishing Co., NY), 230

34 Michael H. Piatt *Bodie: the mines are looking well...,"* (El Sobrante, CA: North Bay Books, 2003), 275-6; Rossiter W. Raymond, *Statistics of Mines & Mining in the States and Territories West of the Rocky Mountains,"* (Washington, DC: Government Printing Office, 1870), 503-512

35 AS to Burleigh Rock Drill Co, 6 Dec 1876, Folder 9, Box 2, STAN *Papers*

36 L.C. Parke to AS, 22 Jan 1877, Folder 11, Box 2, STAN *Papers*

37 J.B. Reynolds to Raw, 30 Jan 1877, Folder 12, Box 2, STAN *Papers*

38 Raw to Reynolds, 8 Feb 1877, Folder SUT 827, and 12 Feb 1877, Folder SUT 828, Box 6, HUNT *Papers*

39 Reynolds to AS, 16 Feb 1877 and H.B. Hanmore to AS, 15 Feb 1877, Folder 10, Box 2, STAN *Papers*

40 Raw to AS, Apr 1-12, 1877, Folders SUT 859, SUT 860, SUT 861, SUT 862, SUT 864, SUT 847, SUT 848,and SUT 849; Baldwin Hotel

bill, 10 Apr 1877, Folder SUT 72, all Box 6, HUNT *Papers*; AS to D.E. McCarthy, 23 Apr 1877, Folder 1 "AS outgoing 1864-93," Box 1, BANC *Papers*; Reynolds to AS, 27 Apr 1877, Folder 12, Box 2, STAN *Papers*

41 *Silver Slate*, (Humboldt County, NV), "Mines & Mining," 4 May 1877

42 Ethel H. Van Vick Manter, *Rocket of the Comstock: the Story of John William Mackay*, (Caldwell, Idaho: Caxton Printers, 1950),138-142; Grant Horace Smith, *The history of the Comstock lode, 1850-1920*, (Reno, NV: Nevada State Bureau of Mines and the Mackay School of Mines, 1943), 204-206; http://www.insidemydesk.com/, history data desk, Richard L. Garner *The Comstock: an economic history of a mining Bonanza, 1865-1885*, (accessed November 20, 2011), Chapter 18, 8-14; Supreme Court of the United States of America, 94 US 762, *Forbes v. Gracey*, October Term, 1876; AS to Brush, 9 May 1877 and 11 May 1877, Letterbook "Superintendent's Letters from April 1877," Box 2, NHS *Collection*

43 Robert Warner to AS, 1 Jun 1877, Folder 7:4, SUTRO *Papers*

44 *Stock Reporter,*(San Francisco), "The Sutro Tunnel," 1Jun 1877; *New York Times*, "The Sutro Tunnel," 3 Jun 1877; G.J. Griffith to AS, 14 Jun 1877, Folder SUT 416, Box 6, HUNT *Papers*; Griffith, who had made a fortune in a mining venture, was famous for having given 3,015 acres in Los Angeles to the city for use as a park and later leaving funds in his will to build a theater and a scientific observatory. Griffith Park, the Greek Theater and the Griffith Observatory thrive today. http://en.wikipedia.org/wiki/Griffith_J._Griffith

45 Brush to AS, 21 Jun and 23 Jun 1877, Folder 30 "Brush '77," Box 3, BANC *Papers*

46 *New York Times*, "A Sensation at Saratoga," 19 Jun 1877; *Sutro Independent*, untitled, 20 Jun 1877; Stephen Birmingham, *Our Crowd, the great Jewish families of New York*, (New York, Evanston and London: Harper & Row, 1967), 141-149

47 Brush to AS, 13 Sept and 27 Sept 1877, Folder 30 "Brush 77," Box 3, BANC *Papers*; *Sacramento Daily Union*, "The Sutro Tunnel," 8 Oct 1877; "The Sutro Tunnel and the Comstock Mines," 12 Oct 1877 and "The Sutro Tunnel – Colonel Fair Interviewed," 15 Oct 1877; (The

last two articles in the Sacramento paper were taken from the *Virginia Evening Chronicle,* Oct 11, 1877 and Oct 15, 1877.)

48 Knox, *Who's Who,* 5; *Time* (magazine), 27 May 1929, cover story; AS to Ames, 30 Nov 1877, Letterbook "Superintendent's Letters From April 1877," Box 2, NHS *Collection*; Sutro Tunnel Co. Indenture, 7 Dec 1877, Folder 3.5, Carton 3 and Adams to AS, 29 Oct 1877, Folder "ED Adams," Box 2, BANC *Papers*; Ames to AS, 7 Apr 1879, Folder ll/15, Box 2, UN-R *Records*

49 AS to Ames, 12 Dec 1877, Folder "Sup't's Letters," Box 2, NHS *Collection*; J.A. Williamson to AS, 17 Dec 1877, Folder 13, Box 2, STAN *Papers*

50 AS to Ames 7 Dec and 10 Dec 1877, Folder "Sup't's Letters," Box 2, STAN *Papers.* Dr. Abram C. Renninger was graduated from Bellevue Hospital Medical College in 1872

51 H.M. Yerington to AS, 1 Oct 1877, Folder SUT 1701, Box 7, HUNT *Papers,* (Henry Yerington was an important figure in the Comstock as proprietor of the largest lumber company in the region, an officer of the Virginia & Truckee Railroad Company and on the boards of several mining companies. He was both a friend and a business associate of Ralston, Sharon, and the leaders of the Comstock silver fraternity making his contentious relations with Sutro quite understandable); U.S. House of Representatives Bill H.R. 1202, 6 Nov 1877, Folder ll/3, UN-R *Records*; Shellabarger & Wilson to AS, 30 Nov 1877, Folder 13, Box 2, STAN *Papers*

NOTES FOR CHAPTER 5

52 AS to Emma Sutro, 31 Jan 1877, Folder SUT 1205; 6 Feb 1877, Folder SUT 1206 and Feb 16, 1877, Folder SUT 1207, Box 6, HUNT *Papers*

53 Rosa [Sutro] to Dearest Papa [Adolph Sutro] 16 Dec 1872, Folder 22, Box 11, *Sutro Business Collection,* San Francisco History Center, San Francisco Public Library (hereafter SFPL *Collection*)

54 Mother [Leah Sutro] to My Dear Emma [Sutro], 21 Feb 1873, Folder SUT 1424, Box 4, HUNT *Papers*

55   AS to Rosa Sutro, 21 Mar 1873, Folder SUT 1267, Box 4; Rosa V. Sutro to Dear Papa [Adolph Sutro], 9 Apr 1873, Folder 22, Box 11, SFPL *Collection*

56   Leah Sutro to My Dear Emma [Sutro], 13 Jul 1873, Folder SUT 1441, Box 4, HUNT *Papers*

57   ibid, AS to My dear Emma [Sutro], 22 Jul 1873, Folder SUT 1153, Box 4

58   ibid, AS to My dear Emma [Sutro], 4 Nov 1873, Folder SUT 1160, Box 4

59   AS to Emma Sutro, 28 Feb 1877, Folder SUT 1208, Box 6; St. Matthew's School Bill, 15 Apr 1877, Folder SUT 933, Box 6; [Kate Sutro] Poem *To My Father on his 47th birthday*, 29 Apr 1877, Folder SUT 757, Box 6, HUNT *Papers*; Sketch of musicians by Kate Sutro, Folder 18, Box 11, SFPL *Collection*

60   AS to Emma Sutro, 31 May 1877, Folder SUT 1213 and Baldwin Hotel bill, 1 Jun 1877, Folder SUT 72, Box 6, HUNT *Papers*

61   AS to Emma Sutro, 20 Apr 1877, Folder SUT 1210, Box 6, HUNT *Papers*; State of Nevada Public School Teacher's Certificate, 1 Sept 1877, Folder 1.7, BANC 2006/347 *Collection of Adolph Sutro Papers, 1870-1913* (hereafter BANC *Collection*); *Nevada State Journal (Reno)*, 25 Aug 1877, untitled, p. 3, col. 3

62   AS to Emma Sutro, 16 Oct 1877, Folder SUT 1216, Box 7, HUNT *Papers*

63   Telegram AS to Emma Sutro, 18 May 1878, Folder 1, "AS outgoing 1864-93," Box 1; J. Aron to AS, 17 Jun 1878, Folder 22, "J. Aron," Box 2, BANC *Papers*

64   PW Ames to AS, 23 Apr 1878, Folder II/8, Box 1, UN-R *Records*

NOTES FOR CHAPTER 6

65   AS to Ames, 4 Jan 1878, 9 Jan 1878, and 11 Feb 1878, Letterbook "Sup't's Letters," Box 2, NHS *Collection*; Adams to AS, 8 Jan 1878, 10 Jan 1878, 14 Jan 1878, 15 Jan 1878, 17 Jan 1878, and 19 Jan 1878, Folder "ED Adams," Box 2, BANC *Papers*; Ames to AS, 17 Jan 1878, Folder ll/7, Box 1, NHS *Collection*

66 Knox, *Who's Who in New York,* 5

67 *Sacramento Bee,* "The Wily Adolph Brings Suit to gain Possession of the Bonanza Mines," 29 Mar 1878; also folder 23:3, SUTRO *Papers*

68 Brush to AS, 18 Apr 1878, Folder 31 "Brush '78," Box 3, BANC *Papers*

69 Attorneys of the Sutro Tunnel Company to Department of the Interior, General Land Office, undated c1877, Folder 14, Box 2, STAN *Papers; Sacramento Bee,* "Sutro and the Bonanza," 29 Mar 1878; Brush to AS, 18 Apr 1878, Folder 31, "Brush '78," Box 3, BANC *Papers*; Henry N. Copp, Ed., *United States Mineral Lands; Laws Governing Their Occupancy and Disposal,* (Washington, D.C: Published by the editor, 1881), "Land Office Rulings, Sutro Tunnel vs Occidental," 243-247

70 Probate Notice, will of John B. Felton, 24 Apr 1878, Folder SUT 866, Box 7, HUNT *Papers*; Certificate of Incorporation of the Sutro Tunnel Company, 29 Nov 1869, Call Number TN413N3A191, History Room, California State Library, Sacramento; Certificate of Incorporation of the Sutro Tunnel Company, 5 May 1873, Folder 3.1, Carton 3, BANC *Papers*; Adams to AS, 6 Mar, 19 Mar, 1 Apr, and 27 Apr 1878, Folder "ED Adams," Box 2, BANC *Papers*; William D. Cohan, *The Last Tycoons: the secret history of Lazard Frères & Co.,* (New York: Doubleday, c2007), 18-21 and passim; Ames to Messrs. McCalmont Bros. & Co., 2 Dec 1878, Folder ll/13, Box 2, UN-R *Records*

71 Aron to AS, 7 May 1878, Folder 22 "J. Aron," Box 2 and AS to Aron, 8 May 1878, Folder 1, Box 1, BANC *Papers*

72 Stephen Birmingham, *Our Crowd; the great Jewish Families of New York* (New York, Evanston, and London: Harper & Row, 1967), 148; The book has no notes or reference citations; the author has donated his papers to the Mugar Memorial Library at Boston University and believes the letters between members of the family in that collection were the source of his statements. Inquiries to the library have not yielded confirmation. A list of early Sutro Tunnel Company stockholders shows Seligman family members owning a total of 101,728 shares of the two million originally issued. The list of owners includes the banking firm, the brothers and some wives and children as well. (HUNT *Papers,* Box 5, Folder SUT1533, pp.1-20). A second list, dated 2 Sept 1878, shows Seligman fami-

ly-owned stock totaling 98,828 shares out of two million although holders of fewer than 200 shares were not identified. (Folder 1.7, BANC *Collection*).

73   George R. Wells to C.J. Hillyer, 6 Jun 1878, Folder ll/3, Box 1, NHS *Collection*; Brush to AS, 8 Jun 1878, Folder 31 "Brush '78," Box 3, BANC *Papers*

74   Brush to AS, 11 Jun and 12 Jun 1878, Folder 31 "Brush '78," Box 3, BANC *Papers*

75   G.D. Robel (?) to AS, 24 Jun 1878, Folder 36 "Savage Consolidated Mine," Box 10, BANC *Papers*; McCalmont Bros. & Co. to AS, 2 Jul 1878, Folder "Correspondence 1878," Box 1, NHS *Collection*

76   Brush to AS, 16 Jul and 23 Jul 1878, Folder 31 "Brush '78," Box 3, BANC *Papers*; McCalmont Bros. & Co. to AS, 25 Jul 1878, Folder "Correspondence 1878," Box 1, NHS *Collection*

77   McCalmont Bros & Co to Brush, 25 Jul 1878, Folder "Correspondence 1878," Box 1, NHS *Collection*

78   Coulter to AS, 5 Aug 1878, Folder 27 "GT Coulter," Box 4; Brush to AS, 29 Aug 1878, Folder 31 "Brush '78," Box 3, and telegram AS to McCalmonts Bros., 11 Sept 1878, Folder 1, Box 1, BANC *Papers*; Ames to Messrs McCalmont Bros & Co. (copy), 2 Dec 1878 with enclosure (original letter and enclosure dated 8 Nov 1878), Folder ll/13, Box 2, NHS *Collection*

79   Williamson to Messrs. Shellabarger & Wilson, 14 Aug 1878, Folder 16 "US General Land Office," Box 19, BANC *Papers*; Sutro Library *Sutro Papers* Folder 4:17 Shellabarger & Wilson to AS, 3 Sept 1878, Folder 4:17, SUTRO *Papers*

80   Brush to AS, 23 May 1879 and 27 May 1879, Folder 32 "Brush '79," Box 3; and Loan Agreement between David Cahn and Sutro Tunnel Company, 14 Jun 1879, Folder 1 "AS outgoing 1864-93," BANC *Papers*; *Sutro Independent*, "Discharge of Tunnel Employees," 9 Jun 1879; Ames to AS, 23 May 1879, Folder ll/19, Box 2, UN-R *Records*; Aron to AS, 24 Jun 1879, Folder "J. Aron 77/79," Box 2, BANC *Papers*

81   A[lexander] Weil to AS, 5 Jul 1879, Folder 38 "A.Weil," Box 19 and AS to Aron, 6 Jul 1879, Vol. 33, Carton 2, BANC *Papers*; AS to Ames, 3 Jul 1879, Letterbook "Superintendent's Letters Dec 1879," Box 3, NHS *Collection*

82   McCalmont Bros Co. to AS, 2 Sept 1879, Folder 2 "McCalmont Bros Co.," Box 8, and AS to McCalmont Bros. Co., 9 Aug 1879, (this is a letterpress copy in a ledger book and defies reading comprehension; what we know about the contents is drawn from the McCalmont response of 2 Sept 1879), Vol. 33, Carton 2, BANC *Papers*; AS to McCalmont Bros. Co., 15 Oct 1879, Folder SUT 1114, Box 7, HUNT *Papers*

NOTES FOR CHAPTER 7

83   *San Francisco Alta* Article "The Sutro Tunnel" Jul 10, 1878 p. 4 col 1

84   *The Sutro Independent* issue of July 13, 1878 identified the man as Aaron A. Sargent, United States Senator from California; Chairman of the U.S. Senate Committee on Mines and Mining

85   *Sacramento Daily Union,* Articles "Rejoicing at Sutro" and "Through Sutro Tunnel," Jul 11, 1878, p.1 col. 4; *Sutro Independent* Jul 13, 1878 see entire issue headed by "At Last," p.3, column 1 and Jul 20, 1878 p. 3, column 3

86   *Sutro Independent* Jul 13, 1878 p.3, column 2 "Sutro and Savage"

87   Ibid column 3

88   *Sutro Independent* Article "Julia-Sutro" Sept 7, 1878 p. 2, column 3

89   BANC Carton 3 Folder 3.1 "List of Trustees at various incorporations," Trustee list Nov 1878; UN-R NC7 Box 1 Folder II/12 Letters PW Ames to AS Nov 4, 1878, Nov 14, 1878, Nov 19, 1878

90   Nevada State Library and Archives *John Skae Papers* Website Biography of John William Skae; Alfred Doten *The Journals of Alfred Doten, 1849-1903,* Ed. Walter Van Tilburg Clark (Reno: University of Nevada Press, 1973) v. 2, pp. 1324-5; Joseph L. King *History of the San Francisco Stock and Exchange Board: by the chairman, Jos. L. King* (San Francisco: J.L. King, 1910), p. 278

91   Doten *Journals* v. 2, pp. 1323-4; BANC Box 5 Folder 22 Letter TA Edison to AS Nov 18, 1878

92   UN-R NC7 Box 2 Folder II/13 Letter PW Ames to AS Nov 14, 1878; BANC Box 1 Folder 1 (AS outgoing 1864-93) telegrams "Swagger" (AS) to CW Brush Dec 4, 1878 and Dec 6, 1878.

93 BANC Box 10 Folder 6 (Isaac L. Requa) Letter IL Requa to President, Superintendent and Assistant Superintendent of the Sutro Tunnel Company Dec 12, 1878; Box 1 Folder 1 (AS outgoing 1864-93) telegram AS to CW Brush Dec 14, 1878

NOTES FOR CHAPTER 8

94 John Adams Church, *The Comstock Lode; its formation and history* (New York: J. Wiley & Sons, c1879), 134

95 Ames to AS, 30 Dec 1878, Folder ll/14, Box 2, UN-R *Records*; Brush to AS, 1 Jan 1879, Folder 32 "Brush '79," Box 3, BANC *Papers*

96 Kidder, Peabody & Co., to AS, 16 Dec 1878, Folder 10 "Kidder, Peabody," Box 7, BANC *Papers*

97 Ibid, Kidder, Peabody to AS, 4 Jan 1879

98 AS to McCalmonts, 4 Jan 1879, Letterbook Vol. 34, Carton 2, BANC *Papers*

99 AS to McCalmonts, 5 Jan 1879, Folder 1 "AS outgoing 1864-93," Box 1, BANC *Papers*

100 Ames to AS, 6 Jan 1879, Folder ll/14, Box 2, UN-R *Records*

101 Telegram Aron to AS, 17 Jan 1879, Folder 22 "Joseph Aron '77-'79," Box 2, BANC *Papers*

102 McCalmont Bros. to AS, 21 Jan 1879 and McCalmont Bros to Brush, 30 Jan 1879, Folder 9, Box 1, NHS *Collection*

103 John J. Kiernan to AS, 23 Jan 1879, Folder SUT 510, Box 7, HUNT *Papers*

104 *Sutro Independent*, "The Sutro Tunnel," 6 Feb 1879

105 *New York Times*, "The Sutro Tunnel Contest," 18 Feb 1879

106 Hotel Receipt, The Baldwin for Mrs. A. Sutro, 1 Feb 1879, Folder 1.9, BANC *Notes*

107 *New York Times*, "The Sutro Tunnel Company," 19 Mar 1879

108 Brush to AS, 9 Apr 1879, Folder 32 "Brush '79," Box 3, and General Superintendent to the President, Superintendent, and persons in charge of the Mines of the Julia Consolidated Mining Co., [9] Apr 1879, Folder "AS outgoing '64-'93," Box 1, BANC *Papers*

109 Aron to AS, 10 Apr 1879, Folder 22 "Joseph Aron '77/'79," Box 2, BANC *Papers*

110 Theodore Sutro to AS, 26 Apr 1879, Folder 14, Box 2, CHS *Papers*

111 Aron to AS 10 May 1879, Folder 22 "Joseph Aron '77/'79," Box 2, BANC *Papers*

112 Frank Young to John Watson Simonton, 21 May 1879, Folder 1 "AS outgoing '64/'93," Box 1, BANC *Papers*

113 *Sacramento Daily Union* , "A Visit to the Sutro Tunnel – The Town of Sutro," 28 Apr 1879; Lease Agreement between AS and William Hewlett, 28 Apr 1879, Folder 9, Box 1, UN-R *Records*; Adams to AS, 26 Apr 1879, Folder "ED Adams," Box 2, BANC *Papers*; Ames to AS, 6 May 1879, Folder 17, Box 2, UN-R *Records*

114 [I.J.] Benjamin *Three Years in America, 1859-1862,* 2 vols., (Philadelphia: The Jewish Publication Society of America, 1956), v.1, 216, 225-227

115 AS to My dear Emma [Sutro], 7 May 1879, Folder SUT 1220, and telegram AS to Miss Emma Sutro, 18 June 1879, Folder SUT 1222, Box 7, HUNT *Papers*; Ames to AS, 29 May 1879, Folder ll/19, Box 2, UN-R *Records*

116 Ames to AS, 6 Jun 1879, Folder 9 "Sutro Tunnel Co. Sec'y," Box 12, BANC *Papers*

117 Ames to AS, 6 Jun 1879, Folder ll/20, Box 2, UN-R *Records*

118 *Sacramento Daily Union,* "Sutro Tunnel Ready for the Comstock Water," 28 Jun 1879 and "Completion of the Sutro Tunnel – Rejoicing over the Event," 1 Jul 1879; *Sutro Independent,* "It is Finished!," 30 Jun 1879 and "Veni! Vidi! Vici!," 3 Jul 1879; Ames to AS, 1 Jul 1879, Folder ll/20, Box 2, UN-R *Records*

119 Leah Sutro to My Dear Emma [Sutro], 3 Nov 1873, Folder SUT 1451, Box 4, HUNT *Papers*

120 *San Francisco Chronicle,* "Scandal in High Life," 9 Jul 1879; *Daily Alta California,* "A Comstock Scandal," 9 Jul 1879; *Sacramento Daily Union,* "Scandalous Affair on the Comstock," 9 Jul 1879 and "Rough and Tumble Fight," 21 Jul 1879; *Silver State* [Humboldt Co., NV], "Sutro's Sounding," 12 Jul 1879; *Sutro Independent,*

"Scandalous Charges...," 14 Jul 1879; AS to Lazard Fréres, 30 Oct 1879, Letterbook Vol. 34, Carton 2, BANC *Papers*. In this letter, the phrase, "which he refuses," is confusing. Sutro appears to be talking about Leah throughout the message but may be referring to her attorney who had possibly contacted Lazard Frères. It may also have been the result of Sutro's handwriting and/or the vague press copy which survives; Mary Germain Hountalas and Sharon Silva *The San Francisco Cliff House*, (Berkeley, CA: Ten Speed Press, c2009), 70-71

121 List of Adolph Sutro Deeds, Safe Book, Box 2, STAN *Papers*; E.B. Holmes, Secretary of the Savage Mine to AS, 23 Jul 1879, Folder 22, Box 5, BANC *Papers* ; AS to Ames, 7 Aug 1879, Letterbook "Superintendent's Letters Dec 1879," Box 3, NHS *Collection* ; Thomas Alva Edison to AS, 23 Jul 1879, Folder 22, Box 5, AS to Edison, 31 Jul 1879, Vol. 33, Carton 2, and Theodore Sutro to AS, 2 Aug 1879, Folder 49 "Sutro, Theodore," Box 11, BANC *Papers*; George A. King to AS, 11 Aug 1879, Folder SUT 513, Box 7, HUNT *Papers*; *Daily Alta California*, "The Sutro Tunnel," 12 Aug 1879

122 Brush to AS, 24 Sept 1879, Folder 32 "Brush '79," Box 3, BANC *Papers*

123 Ames to AS, 4 Oct, 7 Oct, 8 Oct, and 17 Oct 1879, Folder 21, Box 2, UN-R *Records*; Young to AS, 16 Oct 1879, Folder 8 "Sutro Tunnel Co. 1879," Box 13, BANC *Papers*

124 AS to Mrs. [Adelaide] Aron, 25 Oct [18]79, Letterbook Vol. 34, Carton 2, BANC *Papers*

125 Ames to AS, 1 Nov 1879, Folder 9 "Sutro Tunnel Co – Sec'y," Box 12, BANC *Papers*

126 Mother [Leah Sutro] to My dear Emma [Sutro], 2 Nov 1879, Folder SUT 1471, Box 7, HUNT *Papers*; *Sutro Independent*, "General Grant" and "Mere Mentions," 3 Nov 1879; *Sacramento Daily Union*, four articles under the general heading "Nevada," 30 Oct 1879

127 In New York City, Sutro invariably stayed at the Gilsey House Hotel which is described as "luxurious" with rosewood and walnut finishing, marble fireplace mantles, bronze chandeliers and tapestries in Christopher Gray, "Streetscapes: The 1871 Gilsey House; Re-Restoration in the Offing," *New York Times* 29 Dec 1991; Leah

Sutro to My dear Emma [Sutro], 18 May 1873, Folder SUT 1434, Box 4 and J. Hemings London Apartments Room and Board bills, May and June 1873, Folder SUT 440, Box 4, HUNT *Papers.* In Leah's letter, the term "Do" means "ditto."

128   Indenture of Lease Sutro Tunnel Co. to William Hewlett, 28 Apr 1879 and Ames to AS, 19 May, 20 May, and 29 May 1879, Folder 9, Box 1, UN-R *Records*; H.H. Sheldon to AS, 2 Nov 1879 and FS Young to AS, 5 Nov 1879, Letterbook "Letters," Box 3, NHS *Collection*; *Sutro Independent,* "A Huge Conflagration," 3 Nov 1879

129   Unspecified source: memoranda of ore assays at Sutro Tunnel Company's Assay Office , 26 and 30 Oct 1879

130   Ames to AS, 6 Nov 1879, Folder 21, Box 2, UN-R *Records*; Brush to AS, 10 Nov 1879, Folder 32 "Brush '79," Box 3, BANC *Papers*

131   *Sutro Independent,* "The Sutro Tunnel," 15 Dec 1879; Ames to AS, 6 Nov, 11 Nov and 18 Nov 1879, Folder 21, Box 2, UN-R *Records*; AS to Adams, 10 Dec 1879, Letterbook Vol. 34, Carton 2, BANC *Papers*

132   Robert Sigel, Steinway & Sons to AS, 19 Nov 1879, Folder 22 "S – Misc," Box 10, BANC *Papers*

133   Telegrams AS to Leah Sutro, 17 Nov and 23 Nov 1879, Letterbook Vol. 34, Carton 2 and Receipt from Straus, Kohnstamm & Co. for crockery, china and glassware, 13 Nov 1879, Folder 25, Carton 4, BANC *Papers*

134   AS to Louis [Sutro], 22 Nov 1879, Folder 124, SUTRO *Papers*; AS to Hugo [Sutro], 17 Dec 1879, Letterbook Vol. 34, Carton 2, BANC *Papers*

135   AS to Adams, 10 Dec 1879 and AS to Theodore Sutro, 17 Dec 1879, Letterbook Vol. 34, Carton 2; AS to PW Ames, 17 Dec 1879, Folder 1 "AS outgoing 1864-1893," Box 1; telegram Rosa Sutro to AS, 17 Dec 1879, Folder 48, Box 1, BANC *Papers*; Theodore Sutro to AS, 5 Dec 1879 and Adams to AS, 12 Dec 1879, Folder 14, Box 2, CHS *Papers*; telegram Frank B. Mercer to AS, 24 Dec 1879, Folder SUT 649, Box 7, HUNT *Papers*

136   Telegram AS to McCalmont Bros & Co., 29 Dec 1879, Letterbook Vol. 34, Carton 2, BANC *Papers*

NOTES FOR CHAPTER 9

137 Ella Beck Childs was the mother of Evander Childs, Jr. famous school-teacher for whom a whole school complex was named in The Bronx, NY.

138 Telegram AS to Theodore Sutro, 4 Jan 1880, Letterbook Vol. 34, Carton 2, BANC *Papers*. The reference to "San Francisco 1000's" meant the new Sutro Tunnel stock certificates, in small denominations, that he had Ames prepare to replace those Sutro held of 50,000 or 100,000 shares. This had been accomplished in advance to make sales of the stock easier and faster.

139 Ibid, telegram AS to Ernest Kempton, 4 Jan 1880

140 AS to McCalmont Bros & Co., incorrectly dated 5 Jan 1879, which should be 5 Jan 1880, Folder 1 "AS outgoing 1864-93," Box 1, BANC *Papers*. Sutro often misdated items at the turn of the year by using the previous year's date instead of the new one.

141 Ibid, AS to McCalmont Bros & Co., incorrectly dated 7 Jan 1879, which should be 7 Jan 1880, Letterbook Vol. 34, Carton 2

142 Ibid, AS to Adams, 1 Feb 1880

143 Ibid, AS to Theodore Sutro, 9 Jan 1880

144 AS to Dear Rosa [Sutro], 20 Jan 1880, Folder SUT 1279 and Leah Sutro to My dear Emma [Sutro], 25 Jan 1880, Folder SUT 1473, Box 7, HUNT *Papers*

145 AS to Theodore Sutro, 5 Feb, 9 Feb, and 29 Feb 1880, and telegrams AS to Theodore Sutro, 9 Feb, 10 Feb, 11 Feb, 15 Feb, 17 Feb and 18 Feb 1880, Letterbook Vol. 34, Carton 2, BANC *Papers*; Theodore Sutro to AS, 18 Feb and 21 Feb 1880, Folder 15, Box 2, CHS *Papers*

146 Mother [Leah Sutro] to My dear Emma [Sutro], 27 Feb 1880, Folder SUT 1474, Box 7, HUNT *Papers*

147 AS to Theodore Sutro, 29 Feb 1880, Letterbook Vol. 34, Carton 2, BANC *Papers*; this portion of the letter may have been intended as a telegram; much of this message is unreadable in the letterbook

148 ibid, AS to Adams, 28 Jan, 30 Jan, 1 Feb, 5 Feb, and 5 Mar 1880, cipher

telegrams AS to Ernest Kempton, 30 Jan, 1 Feb, 10 Feb, 11 Feb, 12 Feb, 15 Feb, two on 17 Feb, and 18 Feb 1880, AS to Kempton, 18 Feb, two on 22 Feb, 29 Feb, and 2 Mar 1880 and telegram AS to Winslow, Lanier & Co., 1 Feb 1880. Sutro spent an exceptionally long period of time poring over the letterbook and trying to make acceptable press copies. He didn't always succeed but the effort to read these entries is worthwhile offering considerable detail about the man's character and intentions.

149 Sutro Tunnel Company Annual Report, 1 Mar 1880, Folder 3.9, Carton 3, BANC *Papers*; *Sacramento Daily Union*, "Sutro Tunnel Company – Resignation of Sutro," 2 Mar 1880; *The Sutro Independent*, "The Sutro Tunnel," 8 Mar 1880; the two newspaper accounts differed in that one told of Sutro's resignation having taken place one week earlier while the other said it had occurred three weeks before.

150 AS to H. Jenison, 2 Mar 1880 and AS to Adams, 5 Mar 1880, Letterbook Vol. 34, Carton 2, BANC *Papers*

151 Coulter to AS, 11 Mar 1880, Folder 27 "GT Coulter," Carton 4, BANC *Papers*; Theodore Sutro to AS, 16 Mar and 21 Apr 1880, Folder 15, Box 2, CHS *Papers*

152 Theodore Sutro to AS, 5 May 1880, Folder 15, Box 2, CHS *Papers*

153 AS to Adams, 5 Mar 1880, Letterbook Vol.34, Carton 2, BANC *Papers*; cipher telegrams "Georgia" [Edward D. Adams] to AS, 4 Apr, 6 Apr, 11 Apr, 12 May and 21 Jul 1880, Folder SUT 4, cipher telegram Charles Walter Kempton to Moore, 20 Nov 1880, Folder SUT 503, Box 7, HUNT *Papers*

154 AS to My Dear Emma [Sutro], 24 May 1880, Folder SUT 1231, Box 7, HUNT *Papers*

155 Theo[dore] Sutro to AS, 26 May 1880, Folder 15, Box 2, CHS *Papers*

156 Safe Book, list of Deeds, 1-8, Folder 15, Box 2, STAN *Papers*

157 Deed transferring property from Michael Reese to AS, 1 Jun 1880, Folder 4.21, Carton 4, BANC *Papers*; Deeds transferring property from John H. Baird to AS, 25 Jun 1880, Folder SUT 69,

and 26 Jun 1880, Folder SUT 698, and Deed transferring property from La Societè d'Espargnes et de Prévoyance Mutuelle to AS, 10 Jul 1880, Folder SUT 1025, Box 7, HUNT *Papers;* 1880; Deed in Trust from AS to Elliott J. Moore and W.K. Van Alen, 27 Aug 1880, Folder 15, Box 2, CHS *Papers*

158 *Sutro Independent,* "What the Sutro Tunnel is designed to accomplish," "The company's title to valuable ore bodies," and "Positive value of the property," 16 Aug 1880; cipher telegram [Ernest] Kempton to Moore, 20 Nov 1880, Folder SUT 503, Box 7, HUNT *Papers;* Thompson & West, *History of Nevada...* , 309; AS to Louis [Sutro], 20 Dec 1880, Folder 124, SUTRO *Papers*

NOTES FOR CHAPTER 10

159 Typescript numbered "56112" consisting of notes of interview with Adolph Sutro, author not identified, undated, c1891 (date based upon quoted number of grandchildren at the time of interview), 19 pages total, quoted portion on 13-14, Folder C-D 799:5, BANC *Notes;* AS to Ludwig [Louis] Sutro, 3 Jan 1894, Folder 125, SUTRO *Papers.* Adolph Sutro's brother Ludwig used the name "Louis" after coming to America. Adolph addressed correspondence to him using both names from time to time. Files at the Sutro Library store letters to and from Ludwig/Louis separately despite the fact that both are one person.

160 Thomas Thompson and Albert West, *History of Nevada, with illustrations and biographical sketches of its prominent men and pioneers* (Oakland, CA: Thompson & West, 1881), 92, 93 and 97; Grant H. Smith and Joseph V. Tingley, *The History of the Comstock Lode, 1850-1997* (Reno, NV: Nevada Bureau of Mines and Geology, c1998), 112; United States Constitution, Amendment 17; *Sacramento Daily Union,* "The Senatorial Situation," 7 Jan 1881; *New York Times,* "Nevada's Past and Future," 22 Jan 1881

161 United States Census of 1880, city and county of San Francisco, California, Enumeration District No. 225, Supervisor's District No. 1, p. 8, dated 7 Jun 1880; Contract for purchase of Cliff House Ranch from Samuel Tetlow, 2 Mar 1881, Folder 4.7, Carton 4, BANC *Papers;* "Cliff House Project" sections "1863," "1896" and "1909," (http://www.

cliffhouseproject.com/history); *Sacramento Daily Union,* "Pacific Coast Items," 7 May 1881 and "Prosperity," 7 Jan 1882; Safe Book, "Deeds," 5, Folder 15, Box 2, STAN *Papers*

162 Cecilia Hardman, *Adolph Sutro, Builder, as told by his daughter,* typescript marked "Received May 23, 1931," Folder SUT 429, Box 15, and Contract for sale of house contents, Samuel Tetlow to AS, 23 Mar 1881, Folder SUT 1549, Box 8, HUNT *Papers*

163 Receipts for services rendered by J.J. Robbins for AS, 29 Mar and 3 Oct 1881, Folder 26, Carton 4, BANC *Papers*; *Daily Alta California,* "Superior Court. Proceedings in the General Departments.," 30 Aug 1881; *Silver Slate* (Humboldt Co., NV), "Divorces," 22 Sept 1881

164 United States Census 1880, Enumeration District 225, Supervisor's District 1, Page 8, City of San Francisco, 7Jun 1880; AS to Louis Sutro, 10 Mar 1882, Folder 124, SUTRO *Papers*

165 Richard H. Dillon, "Adolph Sutro Finds a Librarian," *The Journal of Library History (1966-1972),* Vol. 2, No. 3 (July 1967), 225-234

166 Richard H. Dillon, "The Sutro Library," *News Notes of California Libraries,* Vol. 51, No. 2 (April 1956), 338-352

167 AS to My Dear Emma [Sutro] and George [Merritt], 5 Apr 1882, Folder 1 "AS outgoing 1864-93," Box 1, BANC *Papers*

168 AS to Louis Sutro, 16 Apr 1882, Folder 124, and AS to Frank B. Mercer, 3 Sept (girls accompanying AS spelled out here) and 15 Oct 1883 (more information about the girls travels), Folder 121, SUTRO *Papers*; AS to Moore, 2 Sept 1882, Folder SUT 1253, Box 8, HUNT *Papers*

169 Moore to AS, 4 Oct 1882, Folder 38 "Elliott J. Moore," Box 8, BANC *Papers*; Robert Warner to AS, 4 Nov 1882, Folder 163, SUTRO *Papers*

170 AS to Moore, 28 Nov 1882, Folder SUT 1255, Box 8, HUNT *Papers*

171 Ibid, AS to Moore, 3 Dec 1882, Folder SUT 1256

172 Ibid, AS to Moore, 2 Feb 1883, Folder SUT 1257 and fragment of note George Merritt to Emma Sutro, undated (This note is Merritt's marriage proposal to Emma and had to have been prepared and delivered between his arrival in Paris and the day of the wedding.), Folder SUT 681

173   *New York Times,* "Mrs. Sutro's Birthday Celebration," 15 Mar 1883; *Sacramento Daily Union,* "Electric Flashes," 16 Mar 1883; Witness certification of marriage by Edwin A. Merritt, 27 Mar 1883, Folder SUT 653, and Marriage Certificate of George Merritt and Emma Laura Sutro, 27 Mar 1883, Folder SUT 890, Box 8, HUNT *Papers* (certificate contains listing of witness attendees including AS); Irina Narell, *Our City, The Jews of San Francisco,* (San Diego, California: Howell-North Books, 1981), 255

174   AS to Messrs. Adamson & Moore, 19 May 1883, Folder 83, SUTRO *Papers*

175   Ibid, AS to Messrs. Moore & Adamson, 12 Jul and 7 Aug 1883

176   Ibid, AS to Adamson & Moore, 16 Aug 1883; *New York Times,* obituary "Mrs. Rosa Sutro," 5 Aug 1883

177   AS to Messrs. Moore & Adamson, 14 Oct 1883, Folder 83, SUTRO *Papers*

178   Ibid, AS to Messrs. Adamson & Moore, 5 Nov 1883

179   Ibid, AS to My dear Emma [Sutro Merritt] and George [Merritt], 6 Nov 1883, Folder 123; A.V.E. Young to Thomas A. Edison, 12 Dec 1883, Document File Series – 1883, #D8313, AS to Thomas A. Edison, 20 Jan 1884, Document File Series –1884, #D8413, and Samuel Insull to A.V.E. Young, 10 Feb 1884, Document File Series – 1884, #D8416, Archibald S. Alexander Library, Special Collections, Rutgers University, New Brunswick, *The Thomas Edison Papers*

180   AS to Messrs. Adamson & Moore, 3 Dec and 10 Dec 1883, Folder 83, SUTRO *Papers*

181   Ibid, AS to Messrs. Adamson & Moore, 11 Dec 1883, 21Jan, 5 Feb, and 23 Mar 1884

182   Ibid, Folder 171, Moore to AS, 27 Apr 1884, Folder 171 and AS to Messrs. Adamson and Moore, 17 May 1884, Folder 83

183   Ibid, Robert Warner to AS, 22 May 1884, Folder 163, several letters in German from Langstaff, Ehrenberg & Pollak during June 1884, Folder 161, and H.T. Moore of Brooks Wharf to AS, 10 Jul 1884, Folder 163

184 George Aston to AS, including sketches and estimate for conservatory building, 11 May 1884, Folder 1 "Incoming Correspondence –A," Box 2 and L. Tasheira to Adamson, 1 Feb 1884, Folder 1, "Incoming Correspondence – T-Z," Box 19, BANC *Papers*; Manuel Peralta to AS, 2 Mar 1884, Folder 150, SUTRO *Papers*; T.W. Morgan to AS, layout plan for railroad, 3 Jul 1884, Folder SUT 717, Box 8, and accounting data of Chinese laborers working on trees, 14 Aug 1884, Folder SUT 1355, Box 8, HUNT *Papers*; *Survey of Cliff House and Sutro Heights*, Call Number 091 S966 v.2, Main Branch, California State Library, Sacramento

NOTES FOR CHAPTER 11

185 Benjamin, *Three Years in America*, 225-7; Joseph Aron, *History of a great work (preceded by a letter to the Union Trust Co. of New York) and of an honest miner...* (Paris: E. Régnault, 1892), 6

186 Sutro Tunnel Company Document of Incorporation, 1 Aug 1865, Folder 3.1, Carton 3, BANC *Papers*; Folder 22 "J.Aron," Box 2, contains 116 letters Aron sent to Sutro during the period 1870-1879; Aron, *History*, 16, 21, 22

187 Aron to AS, 2 May 1874, Box 5, Folder SUT 53, HUNT *Papers*

188 Aron to AS, 29 Dec 1875, and 15 Jun 1877, Folder "J. Aron '75-'77," Box 2, BANC *Papers*; AS to Emma Sutro, 13 Aug 1876, Folder SUT 1189, Box 5, HUNT *Papers*

189 Aron to AS, 28 Sept 1874, and 20 Jun 1877, Folder "J. Aron '73-'74," Box 2, BANC *Papers*

190 Sutro Tunnel Company Board of Trustees minutes, 4 Nov 1878, Folder 3.7, Carton 3, BANC *Papers*

191 Aron to AS, 20 Mar 1878 and 17 Jun 1878, Folder 22 "J.Aron '77-'79," Box 2; and AS to Aron, 8 May 1878, Folder 1, "A. Sutro outgoing correspondence '64-'93," Box 1, BANC *Papers*

192 *Sacramento Daily Union*, "California, Railroad Commissioners – Sutro Tunnel," 7 Apr 1881

193 Edmund Tauszky and W.E.F. Deal, *Synopsis of the answer of the Comstock Tunnel and of others in the suit of Frank J. Symmes and others against the Union Trust Company of New York and others pending in the Circuit Court of the United States, District of Nevada (1890),* (San Francisco: s.n., 1890), 3-24

194 Ibid, passim; Joseph Aron, *To the Comstock Tunnel Shareholders,* (Paris, France: Published privately, 1890), 12 pages including attachments, not numbered, Rare Books #2762, HUNT; *San Francisco Call,* "Upheld By The Court," 7 Mar 1894; *New York Times,* "Victory for Theodore Sutro et al," 9 Mar 1894

195 *Evening Post,* (Washington, DC), "The Cornelius Herz of the Pacific Coast," 1Feb 1895, (Can be found in Box 22, BANC *Papers*)

196 "Chronology of Joseph Aron," (http://joseph.aron.free.fr/chronologie.htm), 1-8

NOTES FOR CHAPTER 12

197 *Daily Alta California,* "Real Estate Review," 1 Jan 1885

198 *Sacramento Daily Union,* "Social and Personal," 15 Jan 1885; Shipping Manifest, *Phasis* from Liverpool to San Francisco, Robert Warner, shipper, 11 May 1885, Folder 163, SUTRO *Papers; Daily Alta California,* "A Rare Library," 28 Mar 1885, "The City," 6 Jan 1885 and "Real Estate," 16 Feb 1885

199 *Daily Alta California,* "A New Railroad," 8 May 1885

200 *Daily Alta California,* "Auction Sales," 8 Apr 1885; "Real Estate," 20 Apr and 27 Apr 1885; "Real Estate Transactions," 7 May 1885; and "Personals," 27 Apr 1885; AS to Adamson, 27 Sept 1885, Folder 84, SUTRO *Papers; NewYork Tribune, New York Times* and *New York Evening Post,* Advertisements to sell or lease house in Inwood, NY, 28 Mar 1884

201 *Daily Alta California,* "The County Hospital," 17 May 1885; "The City," 20 Mar 1886; University Notes," 22 May 1886; State Board of Regents," 26 May 1886; "The City," 19 Jun 1886;"Arbor Day," 23 Sept 1886, "A Berkeley Villa: Arbor Day," 13 Nov 1886; "Arbor Day" and "At the Presidio," 28 Nov 1886; Sister Stanislaus to AS, 29 Aug 1886, Folder SUT

980; Andrew J. Moulder to AS, 8 Sept 1886, Folder SUT 727; Sarah B. Cooper to AS, 13 Sept 1886, Folder SUT 231; Abbot Kinney to AS, 14 Sept 1886, Folder SUT 517 and J.R. Martin to Virgil Williams, 14 Dec 1886, Folder SUT 937, Box 8, HUNT *Papers*; Robert Sewers to AS, 6 Jan 1886, Folder 11, Box 1, YALE *Papers*; *New York Times*, "Sutro's Generous Offer," 12 Dec 1886

202 *United States Congressional Record, Forty-Ninth Congress, Second Session, Vol. XVIII* Senate Bill S.2428; *Journal of the House of Representatives of the United States, Forty-Ninth Congress, First Session, Volume II (May 13-Aug 5, 1886)*, Committee on Public Lands Bill HR.8107

203 *Daily Alta California*, "A Terrific Explosion," 16 Jan 1887; "The Explosion," 17 Jan 1887; "Sutro Heights," and "John A. Hynes, and What He Knows About the Late Wreck," 17 Jan 1887; *New York Times*, "Ruin in the Golden Gate," 17 Jan 1887

204 *Daily Alta California*, "Engagements," 30 Jan 1887, and "The Social World," 6 Feb 1887

205 *Sacramento Daily Union*, "Social and Personal," 27 Jul 1887

206 Folder 84, SUTRO *Papers*, there are 84 notes sent throughout the year 1887; many of these are referenced in the paragraphs shown

207 AS to Adamson, 14 Oct 1887, Folder 84, SUTRO *Papers*

208 *Daily Alta California*, "The Bay City – Local Attractions," 24 Aug 1887

209 *Daily Alta California*, "Thanksgiving Holiday," 23 Nov 1887 and "On Mount Olympus," 25 Nov 1887; *Los Angeles Herald*, "Our Own State – Sutro's Statue," 25 Nov 1887

210 The story of the Pacific Railway Commission was culled from two principal sources: (1) *Report of the United States Pacific Railway Commission [and Testimony taken by the commission]* , (Washington: Govt. Printing Office, 1887-88) 10 volumes; and (2) nearly one full year's newspaper accounts including *Daily Alta California* , 11 Apr, 14 Apr, 28 Apr, 24 Jul, 26 Jul, 28 Jul, and 1 Dec 1887; *Los Angeles Herald*, 28 Jun, 28 Jul 28 and 21 Sept 1887; *Sacramento Daily Union*, 4 Jan 1888. This is but a sampling of the media coverage.

211 Robert Emory Pattison, *Extracts from the report of the U.S. Pacific Railway Commission, 1888*, (Washington, 1887), Rare Books #247924, HUNT; also Folder 22.2, Box 22, BANC *Papers*

212 Adams to AS, 12 Mar 1888, Folder 13, Box 1, YALE *Papers*; twenty-three letters between 24 Mar and 6 Jul 1888, Winslow, Lanier & Co. to AS, dealing with sale of the Inwood house, Folder 54, Box 19, BANC *Papers*

213 Albert Sutro to AS, 29 Feb, 24 Mar and 29 May 1888 with attachment letter Vicar Albert Battandici to Albert Sutro, 5 May 1888, Folder 13, Box 1, YALE *Papers*

214 George Moss to Mr. [David R.] Sessions, 30 Aug 1888, Folder 174, SUTRO *Papers*

215 *Daily Alta California*, "Articles of Separation," 12 May 1888; *San Francisco Call*, "An Amicable Separation," 12 May 1888; *New York Times*, "An Amicable Separation" (from the *San Francisco Call*), 23 May 1888

216 Most of the information about the trip to Mexico comes from a diary which Sutro dictated to his secretary, Archibald C. Unsworth, along the route consisting of four sections with a total of 58 pages. This was found in Folder SUT 1353, Box 9, HUNT *Papers*; also AS to My dear Emma [Sutro Merritt], 3 Mar 1889, Folder SUT 1233; AS to Dr. Emma Merritt, 12 Mar 1889, Folder SUT 1234; and AS to Dr. Emma Merritt, 18 Apr 1889, Folder SUT 1235, Box 9, HUNT *Papers*

217 Russ Davidson, "Adolph Sutro as Book Collector; A New Look," *The California State Library Foundation Bulletin*, Issue Number 104 (2012): 22, originally published in Issue Number 75, (Spring/Summer 2003); "Garrett of Baltimore" was John Work Garrett, president of the B&O Railroad.

218 Notes from Dr. George Merritt to AS between early February and late June 1889 during the period AS was in Mexico, Folder 2, Box 1, STAN *Papers*; (There was a report issued about every two or three days during that time dealing with real estate management and family issues.)

219 Ancestry.com. *U.S. Passport Applications, 1795-1925* [database on-line]. (Provo, UT, USA: Ancestry.com Operations, Inc., 2007)

220 *New York Times*, "A Library for San Francisco" (reprinted from the *Baltimore American*), 22 May 1889

221 The Mansion House, London, Plan of Tables at Banquet, 31 Jul 1889, Folder 26:8 and AS to Louis Sutro, 19 Sept and 1 Nov 1889, Folder 124, SUTRO *Papers*; Wendell Easton to AS, 26 Nov 1889, Folder 1, Box 1, STAN *Papers*; *Daily Alta California*, "Sutro's Purchase of Books," 29 Nov 1889; *Sacramento Daily Union*, "Electric Flashes," 4 Dec 1889

NOTES FOR CHAPTER 13

222 Carl Wilhelm Schlegel, *American Families of German Ancestry in the United States,* vol. 2, (New York: Genealogical Publishing Co., Inc., 1918-26), 22; Donald G. Miller, *The Scent of Eternity* (Macon, GA: Mercer University Press, 1989), 247-9; Receipt from Otto Sutro & Co., 17 Feb 1892, Folder SUT 1505, Box 10, HUNT *Papers*

223 Schlegel *American Families,* vol. 2, 23-25

224 The history is sprinkled throughout this text.

225 Theodore Sutro *The Sutro Tunnel company and the Sutro tunnel: property, income, prospects, and pending litigation. Report to the stock-holders* (New York: Press of J.J. Little & Co., 1887), 96-105; *Los Angeles Herald,* "The Sutro Tunnel," 12 Jan 1887, and "Sutro Tunnel Company," 10 Mar 1894 ; *Daily Alta California,* "A New Mining Corporation," 31 Aug 1889; A Former President of the Sutro Tunnel Company [Joseph Aron], *Is it the duty of an Attorney to defend his Client's honor when it is attacked?* (New York: Published privately, 1894), 13

226 Schlegel *American Families,* vol. 2, 25-26; *New York Times,* "Victory for Theodore Sutro et al," 9 Mar 1894

227 Elizabeth was Steinway's second wife; he divorced his first wife, Regina, after discovering her adultery.

228 Theodore Sutro to AS, 30 Sept 1895, Folder SUT 1519, Box 12, HUNT *Papers*

229 http://en.wikipedia.org/wiki/United_States_Senate_election_in_ New_York_1911

230 Schlegel *American Families,* vol. 2, 28-34; *National German-American Alliance, Hearings before the Subcommittee of the Committee on the Judiciary, United States Senate, Sixty-Fifth Congress, Second Session on S. 3529, a bill to repeal the act entitled "An Act to Incorporate the National German-American Alliance," approved February 25, 1907,* (Washington: Government Printing Office, 1918), 134-179 and 623-649

231 Schlegel *American Families,* vol. 2, 27-34

NOTES FOR CHAPTER 14

232 AS to Louis Sutro, Esq., 18 Feb 1890, Folder 124, SUTRO *Papers*

233 *Daily Alta California*, "Real Estate," 27 Mar 1890; Advertisement, 5 Apr 1890; "Clarendon Heights," 6 Jun 1890; "Real Estate – Adolph Sutro About to Place More Land on the Market," 19 Jun 1890

234 *Daily Alta California*, "The Social World," 4 May 1890; *San Francisco Call*, "The Social World – The Sutro Dinner Party" and "Birthday Celebration at Sutro Heights," 5 May 1890

235 Joseph Aron, "To the Comstock Tunnel Shareholders," letter with attachments, 12 pages not numbered, Rare Book #2762, Huntington Library

236 *Daily Alta California*, "The Social World – Personals," 7 Sept 1890

237 *Daily Alta California*, "Funeral Ceremonies," 18 Sept 1890 and "The Hebrew Home," 29 Dec 1890; *San Francisco Call* , "To the Home of Peace," 18 Sept 1890; Receipt from Jewish Publication Society of America, 1 Oct 1890, Folder 17, Box 1, Collection BANC mss 2010/613, Bancroft Library; Cyrus Adler to AS, 17 Oct 1890, Folder 1, Box 1, STAN *Papers*; Receipt, 6 Dec 1890, Folder 1.2, BANC *Collection*

238 *San Francisco Call*, "Street Matters," 14 Nov and 12 Dec 1890; "Sutro Wrathy," 16 Dec 1890; *Daily Alta California*, "Public Highways," 14 Nov 1890; "The Public Streets," 21 Nov 1890; "The Public Streets," 12 Dec 1890; "New Advertisements – Lakeview," 23 Aug 1890; *Evening News*, (Gold Hill, NV), "Sutro Tunnel" (connections of tunnel and shafts), 28 Oct 1873

239 Luncheon Bill of Fare, 27 Apr 1891, Folder 22.7, Box 22, BANC *Papers*; *San Francisco Call*, "The Sutro Luncheon," 28 Apr 1891

240 *Daily Alta California*, "Real Estate Transactions," 20 Mar 1891; *San Francisco Call*, "Real Estate Transactions," 21 Mar, 3 Jun, 12 Jul and 18 Aug 1891

241 *San Francisco Call*, "A Great Bath-House," 6 Aug 1891

242 *San Francisco Call*, "Real Estate Transactions," 5 Jan 1892; Bill of Sale from Otto Sutro & Co., Baltimore, MD, 17 Feb 1892, Folder SUT 1505, Box 10, HUNT *Papers*; Bill of Sale from Matthias Gray Co., San Francisco, CA, 1 Mar 1892, Folder 13:3, SUTRO *Papers*

243 *San Francisco Call,* "Mr. Sutro's Mob," 26 Jan 1893

244 Receipt for purchase of cemetery lot, 5 Apr 1893, Folder "Cemetery Lots," Box 2, SFPL *Collection;* General Electric Company to AS, 20 Jun 1893, Folder 41, Box 5, BANC *Papers*

245 AS to My dear Louis [Sutro], 14 Aug 1893, Folder 124; AS to My dear Louis [Sutro], 26 Oct 1893 and AS to Louis Sutro, 23 Nov 1893, Folder 3:12, SUTRO *Papers*

246 Home of Peace Cemetery receipt for funeral expenses, 10 Dec 1893; United Carriage Company receipt for transportation expenses, [10] Dec 1893; Halsted & Co. receipt for undertakers goods and services, 12 Dec 1893; M. Michelson & Co. receipt for transportation services, 12 Dec 1893; Southern Pacific Co. receipt for transportation services, 12 Dec 1893; Carbone & Co. receipt for floral decorations, 13 Dec 1893; Check for funeral services, 13 Dec 1893; Check to Temple Emanu-El sexton for various other services attendant to the funeral, 13 Dec 1893, Folder "Funeral, wife Leah," Box 2, SFPL *Collection; San Francisco Call,* "Funeral of Mrs. Sutro," 12 Dec 1893 and "All to her Children," 15 Dec 1893; *Sacramento Daily Union,* "Cruise of the Theodora," 10 Dec 1893; *San Francisco Examiner,* "After Days of Illness," 10 Dec 1893

NOTES FOR CHAPTER 15

247 David Max Eichhorn, *The Joys of Jewish Folklore; the journey from New Amsterdam to Beverly Hills and beyond* (Middle Village, New York: Jonathan David Publishing, Inc., 1981), 473

248 Stewart, Jr. and Stewart, *Adolph Sutro,* 32

249 John P. Marschall, *Jews in Nevada, a history* (Reno & Las Vegas, NV: University of Nevada Press, 2008), 76

250 Robert Ernest Stewart, Jr. *Adolph Sutro: A Study of his Early Career,* Dissertation submitted in partial satisfaction of the requirements for the degree of Doctor of Philosophy in History in the Graduate Division of the University of California, (typescript), 14 Jul 1958, Doe Library, University of California - Berkeley

251 Irena Narell, *Our City; The Jews of San Francisco* (San Diego, CA: Howell-North Books, 1981), 242

252 Leah Sutro to My dear Children [Emma and Rosa Sutro], 11 Apr 1871, Folder SUT 1477, Box 3, HUNT *Papers*

253 Mother [Leah Sutro] to My Darling Emma [Sutro], 22 Aug 1871, Folder SUT 1415, Box 3, HUNT *Papers*

254 ibid, L[eah] Sutro to My Dear Emma [Sutro], 10 Sept 1871, Folder SUT 1416

255 ibid, Leah Sutro to My Dear Emma [Sutro], 21 Sept 1871, Folder SUT 1417 and L[eah] Sutro to My dear Rosy [Rosa Sutro], 21 Sept 21, 1871, Folder SUT 1486

256 ibid, Leah Sutro to My Dear Emma [Sutro], 18 Oct 1871, Folder SUT 1418

257 ibid, Leah Sutro to My Dear Rosy [Rosa Sutro], 30 Nov 1871, Folder SUT 1492

258 ibid, L[eah] Sutro to My Dear Emma [Sutro], 2 Dec 1871, Folder 1419

259 ibid, L[eah] Sutro to My Dear Emma [Sutro], 1 Jan 1873, Folder SUT 1421

260 ibid, L[eah] Sutro to My Dear Emma [Sutro], 10 Jan 1873, Folder SUT 1422

261 ibid, Your loving Mother [Leah Sutro] to My Dear Emma [Sutro], 21 Feb 1873, Folder SUT 1424

262 ibid, Leah Sutro to My Dear Emma [Sutro}, 2 Mar 1873, Folder SUT 1426

263 *Daily Alta California,* "Superior Court," 30 Aug 1881 and "Articles of Separation," 12 May 1888; *Silver Slate,* "Divorces," 22 Sept 1881; Mrs. C. Howard to AS, undated (c1879), Folder 1 "H – Misc," Box 6, BANC *Papers*; Emma Allen to AS, 23 Mar 1897, Folder SUT 17, Box 13, HUNT *Papers*

264 Receipt from Friedman & Wolf Bakers, 23 Mar 1893, Folder 15, Box 1, Collection 2010/613, *Magnes Collection on Adolph Sutro, 1858-1893,* Bancroft Library; Receipt to Congregation Emanu-El, 5 Apr 1893,

Folder "Cemetery Lots," SFPL *Collection*; AS to My dear Louis [Sutro], 14 Aug, 26 Oct, and 23 Nov 1893, Folder 124, SUTRO *Papers*; *San Francisco Call*, "Death's Harvest," 10 Dec 1893

265 Letter and enclosure Collis P. Huntington to C.E. Bretherton, 1 Jan 1894, "Central Pacific-Railroad Company. Mr. Huntington's explanation of the Revised Lease to the Southern Pacific Company," Rare Book #384887, Huntington Library

266 Oscar Lewis, *The Big Four; The Story of Huntington, Stanford, Hopkins, and Crocker, and the building of the Central Pacific,* (New York, London: Alfred A. Knopf, 1938), 211, 212, 214; David Lavender, *The Great Persuader,* (Garden City, New York: Doubleday & Company, 1970), 66 including accompanying note 8

267 *San Francisco Call*, "At Sutro Heights," 2 Jan 1894; "Richmond District," 11 Jan 1894; "Brokers in Arms," 3 Mar 1894; "Adolph Sutro's Loan," 6 Mar 1894; AS to Ludwig [Louis] Sutro, 3 Jan 1894, Folder 125, SUTRO *Papers*

268 *San Francisco Call*, "Sutro's Fence," 11 May 1894; "A Five-Cent Fare," 13 May 1894; "A Point That May Grow," 16 May 1894

269 Unsigned draft of agreement to deed Sutro Heights to a Board of Trustees, 17 May 1894, Folder SUT 1346, Box 10, HUNT *Papers*; Receipts from C.A. Sumner, J.M. Bassett and F.B. Perkins for advances in payments for services connected with the Pacific Railroad Funding Bill, all dated 18 May 1894, Folder 25 "Railroad War," Box 1, SFPL *Collection*

270 *San Francisco Call*, "Down Monopoly," 18 May 1894; "Sutro's Railway," 22 May 1894 and "Sutro is Wroth," 24 May 1894; L.R. Ellert to Col. C.F. Crocker, 22 May 1894, Folder SUT 314 and L.R. Ellert to AS, 23 May 1894, Folder SUT 315, Box 10, HUNT *Papers*

271 *San Francisco Call*, "Sutro's Railroad," 25 May 1894

272 ibid, "Scheel's Benefit Today," 21 Oct 1894 and "Scheel's Benefit," 22 Oct 1894

273 AS to Col. Charles A. Sumner, 6 Jun 1894, Folder "AS out '94," Box 1, BANC *Papers*; Form letter from William C. Little to addressees, 16 Jun 1894, Folder SUT 569, Box 10, HUNT *Papers*; *San Francisco Call*, "Direct Talk," 20 Jun 1894

274 *San Francisco Call,* "Sutro Expanding," 22 Jun 1894, "Sutro to Cleveland," 30 Jun 1894, "Gavigan Is Out," 3 Jul 1894; "Sutro's Gift," 6 Jul 1894; "The Supervisors," 10 Jul 1894; "In Aid of Sutro," 17 Jul 1894; and "Sutro's Acceptance," 19 Jul 1894; *Mariposa Gazette,* "Pacific Coast News," 28 Jul 1894

275 AS to Ludwig Sutro, 4 Sept 1894, Folder 125, SUTRO *Papers*; AS to dear Moritz & Kate [Nussbaum], 13 Aug 1894, Folder "AS out '94," Box 1 and *San Francisco Star,* supplementary section, 21 Jul 1894, 13-20, "How Members of Congress are Bribed," Folder 22.2, Box 22, BANC *Papers,* (The newspaper was a weekly called *The Star* but was often referred to as *The Weekly Star* or *The San Francisco Star* to avoid confusing it with papers from other cities. The listed author is Joseph H. Moore, older brother and law partner of Elliott J. Moore, who served in various legal capacities for Sutro who may have collaborated in writing this document).

NOTES FOR CHAPTER 16

276 *San Francisco Call,* "Sutro For Mayor," 23 Jul 1894 and "Will Accept," 24 Jul 1894

277 *San Francisco Call,* "None For Sutro," 31 Jul 1894; Advertisement "Sutro Railroad" and article "In Four Months," 6 Aug 1894; "Articles of Incorporation," 22 Jul 1894, Collection BANC mss 91/195c, Box 1, Bancroft Library

278 AS to P.O. Chilstrom, 14 Aug 1894, Folder 17, Box 1, YALE *Papers*

279 *Los Angeles Herald,* untitled article, 24 Aug 1894; *Sacramento Daily Union,* "Adolph Sutro," 3 Sept 1894

280 Veteran Soldiers and Sailors Republican Club to AS, 24 Oct 1894, Folder SUT 1608, Box 10, HUNT *Papers*; H.E. Weissig to AS (on Col. Little's stationery), 28 Oct 1894, Folder 176 and G. Moss to AS, 15 Oct 1894, Folder 175, SUTRO *Papers*

281 *San Francisco Call,* "Brought to Time.," 31 Oct 1894

282 *San Francisco Call,* "The New Mayor," 8 Nov 1894; *New York Times,* "Not a Populist Victory," 11 Nov 1894

283 *San Francisco Call,* "Was it a Bluff?," 12 Nov 1894; W.C. Little to AS, 13 Nov and 15 Nov 1894, Folder 11:7, SUTRO *Papers*

284 J. Russell to Hon. Adolph Sutro, 13 Nov 1894, Folder 11:1, SUTRO *Papers*

285 *San Francisco Call,* "Start Smoothly.," 10 Dec 1894 and "On the Record," 21 Dec 1894

286 *San Francisco Call,* "Sutro on the Funding Bill.," 15 Dec 1894

287 *Los Angeles Herald,* "The Cliff House Gone.," 26 Dec 1894

288 *San Francisco Call,* "All Hands Round," 7 Jan 1895 and "The Bomb Markham Threw," 7 Jan 1895; *Sacramento Daily Union,* "Academy of Sciences.," 7 Jan 1895

289 *San Francisco Call,* "In New Hands Now," 8 Jan 1895

290 *San Francisco Call,* "Reformers Defeated," 8 Jan 1895

291 Minutes of California Legislature – Senate, Thirty-First Session, 32, 15 Jan 1895, "Senate Joint Resolution No. 3," Folder 25:8, SUTRO *Papers*; *San Francisco Call,* "The Funding Bill Dead For This Session.," 3 Feb 1895; "As to Refunding the Central Pacific Debt.," 28 Jan 1878 (last date of more than 50 letter fragments quoted; letters from C.P. Huntington to David Colton between 1874 and 1878), Rare Book #245227, Huntington Library

292 AS to Louis Sutro, 18 Feb 1895, Folder 124 and Dan Patten to AS, 28 Mar 1895, Folder 11:9, SUTRO *Papers*

293 *San Francisco Call,* "The Proposed Charter," 5 Feb 1895 and "Repeat the Charges.," 6 Feb 1895

294 *San Francisco Call,* "C.P. Huntington Wants Church Street.," 8 Feb 1895

295 *Los Angeles Herald,* "Has Wearied Of The Work," 16 Feb 1895; *San Francisco Call,* "Mayor Sutro in Explanation," 19 Feb 1895

296 *San Francisco Call,* "Spring Valley And Its Rates," 28 Feb 1895 and "As To The Water Of Lake Merced," 6 Mar 1895

297 *San Francisco Call,* "The Mayor Asked Pointed Questions," 7 Mar 1895; "Lake Merced May Be Abandoned," 11 Mar 1895; "Will

Make A Trip To Lake Merced," 11 Mar 1895; "Lake Merced Water Analyzed," 17 Mar1895 and "May Enjoin The Water Company," 21 Mar 1895; *Sacramento Daily Union,* "Lake Merced Water," 21 Mar 1895

298   *San Francisco Call,* "Mayor Sutro And The Little Joker," 26 Mar 1895; "Against The Car Fare Bill," 27 Mar 1895 and "Two-Fare Bill Dies.," 29 Mar 1895

299   *San Francisco Call,* articles covering the bituminous rock monopoly appeared in issues of the newspaper on 1 Feb, 8 Feb,15 Mar, 19 Mar, 30 Mar, 31 Mar, 2 Apr 2, and 6 Apr 1895

300   *San Francisco Call,* "Sutro's Old Residence.," 22 May 1895; "Real Estate Transactions," 26 Apr and 16 May 1895; "Sutro's New Carhouse., 9 July 1895" and "The New Cliff House.," 10 Jul 1895

301   AS to Regents of the University of California and to the Committee of Affiliated Colleges on the Selection of a Site for the Affiliated Colleges, 5 Sept 1895, Folder 343, SUTRO *Papers; San Francisco Call,* "Real Estate Transactions.," 10 Oct 1895

302   *Sacramento Daily Union,* "The Railroad Builder of the Pacific Coast.," 8 Oct 1895

303   *San Francisco Call,* "The Railroads May Beat the Government.," 18 Oct 1895; "C.P. Huntington on the Railroad's Debt.," 19 Oct 1895; and "Two Mayors on C.P. Huntington's Answers.," 21 Oct 1895

304   Receipt for final payment to Campbell & Pattus for Cliff House work, 17 Oct 1895, Folder 13:3, SUTRO *Papers;* Pfister Knitting Co. to AS, 2 Nov 1895, Folder SUT 794, Box 12, HUNT *Papers;* Joseph Krauskopf to AS, 30 Oct 1895, Folder 18, Box 7, BANC *Papers;* Receipt from Home of Peace Cemetery, 5 Nov 1895, Folder 17, BANC *Magnes Collection;* Indenture from Hibernia Bank to AS, 1 Dec 1895, Folder 4, Box 1, BANC *Papers*

305   *San Francisco Call,* "Protest Against Funding," 7 Dec 1895 and "Thousands Are Against the Funding Bill," 8 Dec 1895; List containing Committee of Fifty appointees, 7 Dec 1895, Folder 25:5, SUTRO *Papers*

NOTES FOR CHAPTER 17

306 Typescript interview notes of AS telling about himself (probably to his secretary Archibald C. Unsworth), c1891 (dated from statement in the text that he had four grandchildren; that would be the only year that fits), 11-12, Folder 799:5, Collection BANC mss C-D 799, Bancroft Library, University of California – Berkeley (hereafter BANC *Notes*)

307 Alexander Saxton, *The Indispensable Enemy; labor and the anti-Chinese movement in California* (Berkeley: University of California Press, 1971), 55-59; *Indianapolis Times,* Dennis Kearney address "Appeal from California. The Chinese Invasion. Workingmen's Address," 28 Feb 1878; Henry Kittredge Norton, *The Story of California From the Earliest Days to the Present,* (Chicago: A.C. McClurg & Co., 1924 (7th ed.), Chapter XXIV, 283-296; *Sutro Independent,* (Sutro, NV), "Anti-Chinese Meeting," 15 May 1876

308 Rudolf Glanz, *Studies in Judaica Americana,* (New York: KTAV Pub. House, 1970), 318 and 320; Reva Clar and William M. Kramer, "Chinese-Jewish Relations in the Far West: 1850-1950," *Western States Jewish History,* October 1988, 24-25

309 Glanz, *Studies,* 319

310 Interview , 11-12, Folder 799:5, BANC *Notes*

311 *San Francisco Call,* "Ten Thousand for a Swim," 1 Aug 1897

312 ibid, "Negroes Claim Civil Rights," 2 Aug 1897; and "A Judgment Against Sutro," 17 Feb 1898

NOTES FOR CHAPTER 18

313 *San Francisco Call,* "Opening of the Cliff House," 3 Jan 1896; "The Storm at the Beach," 27 Jan 1896

314 ibid, "San Francisco Water is Pure," 14 Feb 1896; "Adopted the Reports," 5 Mar 1896

315 ibid, "Almost Ended in a Row," 4 Feb 1896; "Mayor Sutro and Auditor Broderick Have a Lively Tilt in the Election Commission," 11 Feb

1896; "Said Sutro Was Insane," 25 Mar 1896; "They Baited the Mayor," 1 Apr 1896; "Mayor Sutro on Rings," 8 Apr 1896

316   ibid, "The New Road to the Cliff," 2 Feb 1896; "The Sutro Celebration," 2 Feb 1896; "Twenty Thousand," 7 Feb 1896

317   ibid, "Collis Did Not Swear," 3 Feb 1896

318   ibid, "Almost Ended in a Row," 4 Feb 1896

319   Fred B. Perkins to AS, 20 Feb 1896, Folder "Fred B. Perkins," Box 9 and J.T. Gordon to Honl. Mr. [Adolph] Sutro, 22 Feb 1896, Folder "G – Misc.," Box 5, BANC *Papers*

320   *San Francisco Call*, "Thousands Cheer Sutro," 15 Mar 1896

321   ibid, "Sutro to Budd," 31 Mar 1895

322   ibid, "Accuses the Railroad," 9 Apr 1896

323   ibid, "Sutro's Raid on the Regents," 15 Apr 1896; "Governor Budd and Mayor Sutro," 17 Apr 1896

324   AS to Louis Sutro, 11 Apr 1896, Folder 124, SUTRO *Papers*

325   *San Francisco Call*, "Sutro May Go East," 21 Apr 1896 and "Who is Mayor of this Town?," 3 Jul 1896;   Perkins to AS, 21 Apr, 27 Apr, 18 May, and 27 May 1896, Folder "Fred B. Perkins," Box 9, BANC *Papers*

326   *San Francisco Call*, "Old Glory Waves," 5 Jul 1896; List of Allowances to be paid by William C. Little for AS, 10 Jul 1896, Folder 15:1, SUTRO *Papers*

327   *San Francisco Call*, "After the Mayor's Scalp," 21 Jul 1896

328   ibid, "How the Mass Meeting Lashed 'The Seven'" and "A Public Chastisement," 29 Jul 1896

329   AS to The Municipal Convention of the Peoples Party, San Francisco, 30 Sept 1896 (unsigned but positively identifiable as Sutro's handwriting), Folder SUT 1317, Box 13, HUNT *Papers*

330   *San Francisco Call*, "Huntington Getting Ready to Force the Funding Bill," 17 Nov 1896

331   ibid, "Supervisors Study," 7 Dec 1896

332   *Sacramento Daily Union*, "Pacific Railroads Funding Bill," 8 Jan 1897; "Funding Bill Debate Continues in the House," 9 Jan 1897; *San Francisco Call*, "Powers' Poor Plea," 8 Jan 1897; "Refunding is Argued," 9

Jan 1897; *Los Angeles Herald,* "Debate on Funding Gets Sensational," 9 Jan 1897; Transcript of speech by Hon. Samuel G. Hilborn of California in the House of Representatives, 9 Jan 1897, Folder 342, SUTRO *Papers*; Sumner to AS, 11 Jan 1897, Folder "Charles A. Sumner," Box 11, BANC *Papers*

333   AS to the People of the United States entitled "The True Question Before Congress," 18 Feb 1897, Folder 1.1, Box 1, BANC *Collection*; Adolph Sutro to unspecified newspaper editor, 16 Feb 1897 (possibly a form letter sent to many editors) with responses from U.S. Senators George C. Perkins and Stephen M. White, Folder "Adolph Sutro outgoing '96/'97," Box 1, BANC *Papers*

334   AS to Ludwig Sutro, 8 Jan 1897 (notice date correction!), Folder 125, SUTRO *Papers; San Francisco Call,* "Eulogy on August Helbing," 20 Aug 1896; "Life and Death of Gustav Sutro," 13 Mar 1897; and "Adolph Sutro's Cousin Dies," 26 Aug 1897

335   Receipt for Tallac House hotel stay, 27 Aug 1897, Folder 1.9, BANC *Collection; San Francisco Call,* "Sutro Quite Ill," 7 Sept 1897; "Ex-Mayor Sutro Ill," 20 Oct 1897; "Adolph Sutro Better," 21 Oct 1897; "Real Estate Transactions," 2 Nov 1897; "Real Estate Transactions," 9 Dec 1897; Deed, 30 Oct 1897, Folder 5, Box 22, BANC *Papers*

336   *San Francisco Call,* "Ten Thousand for a Swim," 1 Aug 1897; "Negroes Claim Civil Rights," 2 Aug 1897; "A Judgment Against Sutro," 17 Feb 1898; W.C. Little to AS, 21 Dec 1897, Folder "Wm. C. Little," Box 7, BANC *Papers; San Francisco Call,* "Adolph Sutro Incompetent," 8 Feb 1898; *Los Angeles Herald,* "Adolph Sutro Insane," 8 Feb 1898; *Sacramento Daily Union,* "Sutro Mentally Incompetent," 8 Feb 1898; *New York Times,* "Adolph Sutro Deranged," 8 Feb 1898

337   Edgar E. Sutro to Mrs. Emma L. Merritt, M.D., 7 Feb 1898, Folder SUT 1371, Box 14, HUNT *Papers; Los Angeles Herald,* "The Sutro Estate," 11 Mar 1898

338   *San Francisco Call,* "Adolph Sutro's Estate," 4 Mar 1898; Memo (unsigned) recording agreement for real estate management, 22 Apr 1898, Folder SUT 675, Box 14, HUNT *Papers; New York Times,* "Woman a Railroad President" (From the *San Francisco Examiner*), 2 May 1898

339 *San Francisco Call,* "Adolph Sutro Forcibly Taken From His Home," 6 May 1898

340 ibid, "Peace Overtures Were Refused," 7 May 1898; "Rupture in the Family of Sutro," 29 May 1898; "Sutro May Now Recover," 31 May 1898; "Miss Sutro is Engaged," 2 Jun 1898; and "Death Claims Adolph Sutro, Philanthropist," 9 Aug 1898

NOTES FOR CHAPTER 19

341 AS dictated interviews Folders 799:3, 799:4 and 799:5, BANC *Notes*

342 Lance J. Sussman, *Isaac Leeser and the making of American Judaism,* (Detroit, MI : Wayne State University Press, 1995) pp. 21-29

343 S. Stern to AS, 2 April 1896, Folder "S –Misc.," Box 10, BANC *Papers*

344 Schlegel *American Families* v. 2, 19

345 AS to My dear Emma [Sutro Merritt] and George [Merritt], 5 April 1882, Folder "AS outgoing 1864-93," Box 1, BANC *Papers*

346 AS to Emma Sutro, 20 Dec 1873, Folder SUT 1167, Box 4, HUNT *Papers*

347 AS to Emma Sutro, 31 Jan 1877, Folder SUT 1205, Box 6, HUNT *Papers*

348 AS to My dear Emma [Sutro], 21 May 1871, Folder SUT 1121, Box 3, HUNT *Papers*

349 Angelika Pauels, Aachen City Archivist to Helmut W. Ganser, 12 May 2009, Aachen City Archives

350 AS to My dear sister Juliane [Sutro], 11 Feb 1850, Folder 2:1, SUTRO *Papers*

351 AS dictated interview, "56111," Folder 799:4, BANC *Notes*

352 AS to Emil & Otto Sutro, 1 Dec 1850, Folder 2:8, SUTRO *Papers*

353 Benjamin *Three Years in America,* vol. I, 210-227

354 *San Francisco Call,* Obituary of August Helbing, 20 Aug 1896

355 AS to Emil & Otto Sutro, 1 Dec 1850, Folder 2:8, SUTRO *Papers*; Carl B. Glasscock & Pauline Jacobson *Adolph Sutro – Pioneer,* Part I, (un-

published typescript text), Alice Phelan Sullivan Library, Society of California Pioneers, 45; AS to Sali [Emmanuel] Sutro, 12 Jun 1851, Folder 2:8, SUTRO *Papers*; George Henry Tinkham, *A History of Stockton from its organization up to the present time...* (San Francisco: W.M. Hinton & Co., printers, 1880), 364, 384

356   David Max Eichhorn *Joys of Jewish Folklore; A Journey From New Amsterdam to Beverly Hills and Beyond*, (New York: Jonathan David, 1981), 473; Rabbi Eichhorn passed away in 1986 – his son, also a rabbi, retired and donated his father's papers to the American Jewish Archives. An archivist scoured the collection without finding notes to cite for the Sutro marriage. No other source has been found.

357   Memorandum of Carlo Morbio, 2 June 1959, Folder 1, Box 1, CHS *Papers*

358   Leah Sutro to Emma Sutro, 21 Sept 1871, Folder SUT 1417, Box 3, HUNT *Papers*

359   Leah Sutro to Rosa Sutro, 21 Sept 1871, Folder SUT 1479, Box 3, HUNT *Papers*

360   Leah Sutro to Emma and Rosa Sutro, 15 Jun 1871, Folder SUT 1447, Box 3, HUNT *Papers*

361   Leah Sutro to Emma Sutro, 10 Sept 1873, Folder SUT 1447, Box 4, HUNT *Papers*

362   *Popular Science Monthly*, July 1906, 12, Charles Sedgwick Minot "The Relations of Embryology to Medical Progress"; *The Anatomical Record*, v. 6 (1912), 149

363   Dr. Heinz Schott, Address at University of Bonn, 18 Jun 2007; the new spelling of Nussbaum's first name probably came from Dr. Schott who was unaware of the correct version

364   Hugo D. Ruys, Address for the International Ihagee/Exacta Convention, Dresden, 17 Sept 2012, "Johan Steenbergen, the Man"

365   Carlo Morbio memorandum, CHS *Papers*; Receipt from J.A, Conbie Co., 20 Oct 1894, Folder "Re-interment of Son's Body," Box 2, SFPL *Collection*

366   *The Journals of Alfred Doten: Book No. 47*, v. 2, pp. 1221-2 recording events between Mar 25-Apr 1, 1874

367 Ibid, pp. 1233-4 recording events between Aug 18-24, 1874

368 S.M. Pettengill & Co. *Pettengill's newspaper directory and advertiser's handbook...* (New York: S.M. Pettengill & Co., 1877), 218

369 List of Shareholders in the Sutro Tunnel Company, 2 Sept 1878, Folder 1.7, BANC *Collection*

370 Subscription renewals (selected from group), 10 May 1885, 2 Jan 1887, 1 Sept 1896, Folder 12:6, SUTRO *Papers*; Joseph Krauskopf to AS, 1 Apr 1892, 31 Jul, 13 Aug and 30 Oct 1895, Folder 18 "Joseph Krauskopf," Box 7; Oscar Klonower to AS, 11 Jun 1892, Folder 15 "Oscar Klonower, Box 7; H. Weinstock to AS, 15 Jun and 19 Jun 1892, Folder 40, Box 19, BANC *Papers*

371 Receipt from Home of Peace Cemetery, 5 Apr 1893, Folder "Cemetery Lots," Box 2; Receipts from Halsted & Co., M. Michelsen & Co., and Southern Pacific Company, 12 Dec 1893 and Accounting Record, 13 Dec 1893, Folder "Funeral, wife Leah," Box 2, SFPL *Collection*; *San Francisco Examiner,* "After Days of Illness," 10 Dec 1893; *San Francisco Call,* "Death's Harvest; Mrs. Adolph Sutro," 10 Dec 1893 and "Funeral of Mrs. Sutro," 12 Dec 1893

372 Receipts from J.A. Conboie, Dr., 20 Oct 1894 and Home of Peace Cemetery, 22 Oct 1894, Folder "Re-interment of Son's Body," Box 2, SFPL *Collection*;

www.findagrave.com/cgi-bin/fg cgi?page =pv&GRid=8071279

NOTES FOR CHAPTER 20

373 Family records do not show a "Mrs. E.E. Schücking." It was most likely Elise Sutro Schücking, a younger sister of Adolph. Elise was not found to have a middle name in any document seen. Newspaper reports were often incorrect in spelling names and this appears to be one example.

374 *San Francisco Call,* "Laid to Rest with Little Ceremony," 11 Aug 1898

375 ibid, "Sutro's Will Is Read To His Children," 12 Aug 1898

376 In the event certain people predeceased Sutro, he specified the amounts could be given to children of those named. Heydenfeldt was one.

377 *San Francisco Call,* "Sutro's Will Criticized," 13 Aug 1898

378 ibid, "Heirs to Contest Adolph Sutro's Will, 31 Aug 1898; "Will Administer Sutro's Estate," 2 Sept 1898; "Will Of Sutro Now Attacked," 7 Sept 1898

379 ibid, "Persecution Alleged By Mrs. Sutro," 15 Oct 1898, (Henrietta Sutro's maiden name had been Elbe. Often, she was incorrectly identified as "Henrietta L.B. Sutro." This article is one example.); "Miss Clara Sutro Will Be Married To-day," 25 Dec 1898; *Los Angeles Herald,* "Sutro—English, A San Francisco Heiress to be Married Here Today," 25 Dec 1898

380 *San Francisco Call,* "Mrs. Kluge-Sutro a Borrower," 18 Jan 1899; "Sutro's Heirs Will Enjoy His Wealth," 19 Jan 1899; *Los Angeles Herald,* "The Sutro Estate," 19 Jan 1899; *New York Times,* "Adolph Sutro's Will," 19 Jan 1899

381 *Sacramento Daily Union,* "Sutro's Will," 20 Jan 1899; *San Francisco Call,* "Railroad Men Scramble For Sutro's Line," 18 Oct 1899; "Heirs To Over Twenty Millions Await Judgment," 10 Dec 1899

382 *Sacramento Daily Union,* "Supreme Court Decisions," 11 Dec 1899; *San Francisco Call,* "Final Assault Now Made On Sutro's Will," 19 Jan 1900; "Sutro Family Skeleton Will Walk To Light," 18 Mar 1900; "Opposition To Sale Of Sutro's Library," 7 Jun 1900; "Settle Claim Of Mrs. Kluge," 24 Dec 1901; *New York Times,* 26 Apr 1901; *Los Angeles Herald,* "Sutro Contest Settled," 24 Dec 1901; C. P. Pomeroy, Reporter, *"Reports of Cases determined in the California Supreme Court,"* vol. 134, (San Francisco: Bancroft-Whitney Company, 1906), 580-582

383 *San Francisco Call,* "Real Estate Transactions" 19 Jul 1902; 19 Jul 1903; 21 Dec 1904; 13 Jan 1905; 24 Jan 1905; 4 Feb 1905; 15 Feb 1905; 25 Feb 1905; 2 Mar 1905; 13 Jun 1905; 23 Jun 1905; 26 Jul 1905; 15 Feb 1906; "Builder's Contracts," 29 Nov 1904

BIBLIOGRAPHY

ARCHIVES

Archibald S. Alexander Library, Special Collections, Rutgers University, New Brunswick
>Thomas Edison Papers

Bancroft Library, University of California, Berkeley (BANC)
>Adolph Sutro Papers, 1853-1915 (*Papers*)
>Collection of Adolph Sutro Papers, 1870-1913 (*Collection*)
>Adolph Sutro autobiographical notes, biographical and character sketches, etc. for the use of Hubert Howe Bancroft, [1888ca] (*Notes*)
>Magnes Collection on Adolph Sutro, 1858-1893 (*Magnes*)

Beinecke Rare Book and Manuscript Library, Yale University, New Haven (YALE)
>Adolph Sutro Papers(*Papers*)

California Historical Society, San Francisco (CHS)
>Adolph Sutro Papers and Scrapbooks, MS 2115 (*Papers*)

California History Room, California State Library Main Branch, Sacramento
>Manuscripts dealing with Cliff House and Sutro Heights

Cecil H. Green Library, Special Collections, Stanford University, Palo Alto (STAN)
>Adolph Sutro Papers, 1869-1899 (*Papers*)

Huntington Library, San Marino, CA (HUNT)
    Papers of Adolph Sutro, 1835-1931 (*Papers*)
    Louis Janin Papers

Mathewson-IGT Knowledge Center, University of Nevada – Reno (UN-R)
    Sutro Tunnel Company Records, 1861-1935 (*Records*)

Nevada Historical Society, Reno (NHS)
    Sutro Tunnel Company Collection (*Collection*)

Nevada State Library and Archives, Carson City (NSL&A)
    Adolph Sutro, on the bill before Congress to aid the Sutro Tunnel

San Francisco History Center, San Francisco Public Library (SFPL)
    Adolph Sutro Collection (*Collection*)

Alice Phelan Sullivan Library of The Society of California Pioneers, San Francisco
    Adolph Sutro - Pioneer; his life and times

Sutro Library Branch, California State Library, San Francisco (SUTRO)
    Adolph Sutro Collection, 1830-1898 (*Papers*)

PRIMARY SOURCES

Alden, John, ed. *Souvenir and official programme of the centennial celebration of George Washington's inauguration as first president of the United States.* New York: Garnett & Gow, c1889

Aron, Joseph. *History of a great work (preceded by a letter to the Union Trust Co. of New York) and of an honest miner...* Paris: E. Régnault, 1892.

To the Comstock Tunnel Shareholders. Paris, France: Published privately, 1890.

Benjamin, [I.J.]. *Three Years in America, 1859-1862.* Philadelphia: The Jewish Publication Society of America, 5716-1956.

Browne, Ross E. *Water meters: Comparative tests of accuracy, delivery, etc.: Distinctive features of the Worthington, Kennedy, Diemans and Hesse meters.* [San Francisco: G. Spaulding & Co., 1885].

Chilstrom, P.O. *Prostituted manhood: Solemn warning to Populists in California.* San Francisco, 1893

Church, John Adams. *The Comstock lode, its formation and history.* New York, J. Wiley & sons, c1879.

Clark, Walter Van Tilburg, ed. *The Journals of Alfred Doten, 1849-1903.* Reno: University of Nevada Press, 1973.

Collins, Charles, ed. *Mercantile guide and directory for Virginia City, Gold Hill, Silver City and American City; Also containing valuable historical and statistical matter; together with the only accurate mining directory.* San Francisco: Printed by Agnew & Deffebach, [1864].

Constitution of the United States. Amendment 17.

Copp, Henry Norris. *United States Mineral Lands; laws governing their occupancy and disposal; with forms, glossary and rules of practice.* Published by the Editor, Washington, D.C., 1881.

Crockwell, James H. *Souvenir of the Comstock: embracing the principal views of Virginia City, Gold Hill, Silver City and Sutro.* New York: Albertype Co., c1890

De Quille, Dan (William Wright). *History of the big bonanza: an authentic account of the discovery, history, and working of the world renown Comstock silver lode of Nevada including the present condition of various mines situated thereon.* Hartford, CT: American; San Francisco: Bancroft, 1877.

Drinker, Henry Sturgis. *A Treatise on Explosive Compounds, Machine Rock Drills and Blasting.* New York, J. Wiley & Sons, 1883.

Glasscock, Carl Burgess. *The Big Bonanza.* Portland, OR: Binfords & Mort, 1931.

Griffin, George Butler. *The California coast: a bilingual edition of Documents from the Sutro collection.* Norman, OK: University of Oklahoma Press, [1969].

Holmes, Eugenia Kellogg. *Adolph Sutro: a brief story of a brilliant life/*illustrated by Carl Dahlgren. San Francisco: Press of San Francisco Photo-Engraving Co., 1895.

Hopkins, Mark. *Letters from Mark Hopkins, Leland Stanford, Charles Crocker, Charles F. Crocker and David D. Colton, to Collis P. Huntington from August 27th, 1869, to December 30th, 1879.* New York: J.C. Rankin co., 1891.

Howard, George Washington. *The Monumental City: its past history and present resources.* Baltimore: J.D. Ehlers and co., printers, 1873.

Huntington, Collis Potter. *Central Pacific - Railroad Company: Mr. Huntington's explanation of the revised lease to the Southern Pacific Company.* [New York, 1894].

How Congressmen are Bribed: the Colton letters: declaration of Huntington that congressmen are for sale. [San Francisco?, 1894?].

Letters from Collis P. Huntington to Mark Hopkins, Leland Stanford, Charles Crocker, E.B. Crocker, Charles F. Crocker, and D.D. Cotton [sic], from August 20, 1867 to [March 31, 1876]. New York, 1892-94.

The Octopus speaks: the Colton Letters/ edited, with notes and introduction by Salvador A. Ramirez. Carlsbad, CA: Tentacled Press, 1992, c1982.

Huntington's record of fraud and bribery as shown by his letters to David D[outy] Colton. He is trying to buy California's state government. San Francisco: Examiner, 1898.

As to refunding the Central Pacific debt. [S.I., 189?].

Jacobson, Pauline and Carl Burgess Glasscock. *Adolph Sutro - Pioneer; His Life and Times.* Unpublished, ca1938.

King, Joseph Leonard. *History of the San Francisco Stock and Exchange Board.* San Francisco: J.L. King, 1910.

Lloyd & Wood, of counsel for appellant. *William C. Watson, respondent, vs Adolph Sutro, appellant: Appellant's points, authorities and brief.* [San Francisco]: Bosqui eng. & printing co., [1889].

McHenry, George. *Philadelphia and Reading railroad company: its financial history.* Philadelphia: January 1881.

Monaghan, Jay. *Chile, Peru, and the California gold rush of 1849.* Berkeley, University of California Press, 1973.

Pattison, Robert Emory. *Report of the United States Pacific Railway Commission and the testimony.* Washington, Govt. Print. Off., 1887-88.

Pattison, Robert Emory, Charles P. Young, E. Ellery Anderson, David T. Littler, and the Pacific Railway Commission. *Testimony taken by the United States Pacific Railway Commission appointed under the act of Congress approved March 3, 1887: entitled "An act authorizing an investigation of the books, accounts and methods of railroads which have received aid from the United States and for other purposes."* Washington: Govt. Print. Off., 1887.

Richthofen, Ferdinand baron. *The Comstock lode: its character, and the probable mode of its continuance in depth.* San Francisco, Sutro Tunnel Company, 1866.

Robinson, John R. The Octopus; *A History of the Construction, Conspiracies, Extortions, Robberies, and Villainous Acts of the Central Pacific, Southern*

Pacific of Kentucky, Union Pacific, and Other Subsidized Railroads. San Francisco, CA: Bancroft, 1894.

Roubin, Solomon. *A scroll of the law supposed to have been written by Maimonides: explanations.* San Francisco, Calif.: Sutro Library, [188?].

Scharf, John Thomas. *History of Baltimore city and county, from the earliest period to the present day: including biographical sketches of their representative men.* Philadelphia: L.H. Everts, 1881.

Schlegel, Carl Wilhelm. *Schlegel's American families of German ancestry in the United States: genealogical and biographical, illustrated.* Originally published: New York: The American Historical Society, 1918-1926.

Schüssler, Hermann. *The Twin Peaks tunnel problem.* San Francisco, 1911

Shinn, Charles Howard. *The story of the mine as illustrated by the great Comstock lode of Nevada.* New York, [D.] Appleton, 1898

Smith, Grant Horace with new material by Joseph V. Tingley. *The History of the Comstock* Lode, 1850-1997. Reno, NV: Nevada Bureau of Mines and Geology, 1998.

Stewart, Robert Ernest, Jr. and Mary Frances Stewart. *Adolph Sutro: a biography.* Berkeley, CA: Howell-North, 1962.

Sutro, Adolph. *Adolph Sutro to the people; He appeals to them to rise en masse against the Funding Bill.* [San Francisco, 1894].

The Bank of California against the Sutro Tunnel. Argument and statement of facts, showing why the amendments to Senate bill 16, adopted by the House of Representatives, should be concurred in by the Senate. [Washington] M'Gill & Witherow, printers, 1874.

The Bank of California vs. the Sutro Tunnel; [Also, Extract from a speech of Adolph Sutro to the miners of Nevada on the Sutro Tunnel and Bank of California]. [Washington, D.C., 1870].

The California bank ring against the Sutro Tunnel. [Washington, 1874].

Closing argument of Adolph Sutro, on the bill before Congress to aid the Sutro tunnel/delivered before the Committee on Mines and Mining, April 22, 1872. Washington, D.C.: M'Gill & Witherow, printers, 1872.

The mineral resources of the United States, and the importance and necessity of inaugurating a national system of mining, with special reference to the Comstock lode and the Sutro tunnel, in Nevada. Baltimore: J. Murphy & Co., 1868.

The Sutro Tunnel and railway to the Comstock Lode in the state of Nevada: importance of its construction, and revenue to be derived therefrom. London: Edward Stanford: [Printed by C. Roworth and Sons], 1873

A Trip to Washoe. [San Francisco: The White Knght Press, 1942].

Sutro, Theodore. *Is it the duty of an attorney to defend his client's honor when it is attacked?: a few considerations respectfully submitted to the members of the Bar Associations of New York and San Francisco/ by a former President of the Sutro Tunnel Company.* [New York: s.n., 1894].

The Sutro tunnel company and the Sutro tunnel: property, income, prospects, and pending litigation. Report to the stockholders. New York: [Press of J.J. Little & Co.], 1887.

Tauszky, Edmund; W.E.F. Deal; United States Circuit Court (Nevada). *Synopsis of the answer of the Comstock Tunnel Company and others in the suit of Frank J. Symmes and others against the Union Trust Company of New York and others pending in the Circuit Court of the United States, District of Nevada.* San Francisco?: s.n.,1890.

Thompson, Thomas and Albert West. *History of Nevada with illustrations and biographical sketches of its prominent men and pioneers.* Oakland, Cal.: Thompson & West, 1881.

United States. Dept of the Treasury. *Report of J. Ross Browne on the mineral resources of the states and territories west of the Rocky Mountains.* Washington: Govt. Prin. Off., 1868.

United States Census, 1880

Voorsanger, A.W. *Western Jewry: an account of the achievements of the Jews and Judaism in California including eulogies and biographies.* San Francisco: Emanu-El, 1916.

SECONDARY SOURCES

Adams, Edward Dean. *Niagara power: history of the Niagara Falls power company, 1886-1918: evolution of its central power station and alternating current system.* Niagara Falls, NY: Bartlett Orr Press, 1927.

Ambrose, Stephen E. *Nothing like it in the world: the men who built the transcontinental railroad, 1863-1869.* New York: Simon & Schuster, c2000.

Berkove, Ed., Lawrence I. *Insider stories of the Comstock Lode and Nevada's mining frontier, 1859-1909: primary sources in American social history.* Lewiston, NY: Edwin Mellen Press, c2007.

Bullard, Frederick Lauriston. "Abraham Lincoln and the statehood of Nevada." *Journal of the American Bar Association,* March and April, 1940.

Caen, Herb. *Hills of San Francisco.* San Francisco: Chronicle, 1959.

Carosso, Vincent P., Marian V. Sears and Irving Katz. *Investment banking in America, a history.* Cambridge, MA: Harvard University Press, 1970.

Chaky, Doreen. "Sutro's sensational tunnel." *Wild West* 10.n4 (Dec 1997) pp56(6).

Cogan, Ed. Sara G. *The Jews of San Francisco & the Greater Bay Area, 1849-1919; an annotated bibliography.With a foreward by Moses Rischin.* Berkeley, CA: Western Jewish History Center, 1973.

Cohan, William D. *The Last Tycoons: the secret history of Lazard Frères & Co.* New York: Doubleday, c 2007.

Dinkelspiel, Frances. *Towers of Gold: how one Jewish immigrant named Isaias Hellman created California.* New York: St. Martin's Press, 2008.

Doten, Alfred. *The journals of Alfred Doten, 1849-1903. Edited by Walter Van Tilburg Clark.* Reno: University of Nevada Press, 1973.

Drabelle, Dennis. *The Great American Railroad War.* New York: St. Martin's Press, 2012.

Mile-High Fever; Silver Mines, Boom Towns, and High Living on the Comstock Lode. New York: St. Martin's Press, 2009.

Fischel, Walter Joseph. *Semitic and Oriental studies; a volume presented to William Popper, professor of Semitic languages, emeritus, on the occasion of his seventy-fifth birthday, October 29, 1949.* Berkeley: University of California Press, 1951.

Flamm, Jerry. *Good life in hard times: San Francisco's '20s and '30s.*San Francisco: Chronicle Books, [1977].

Glanz, Rudolf. *Studies in Judaica Americana. Foreward by Jacob R. Marcus.* New York: KTAV Pub. House, 1970.

Glanz, Rudolf. *The Jews of California: from the discovery of gold until 1880.* New York: [s.n.], 1960.

Hountalas, Mary Germain and Sharon Silva. *The San Francisco Cliff House.* Berkeley, CA: Ten Speed Press, c2009.

Hughes, Edan Milton. *Artists in California, 1786-1940.* San Francisco, CA: Hughes Pub. Co., c1986.

Jackson, Donald Dale. "One man's soaring stately pleasure dome for the people." *Smithsonian* 23.n11 (Feb 1993) pp120(10).

Jonnes, Jill. *Empires of Light: Edison, Tesla, Westinghouse, and the race to electrify the world.* New York: Random House, 2003.

Kahn, Ava Fran, Ed. *Jewish Voices of the California Gold Rush; a documentary history, 1849-1880.* Detroit, MI: Wayne State University Press, 2002.

Karp, Abraham J. *From the ends of the earth: Judaic treasures of the Library of Congress:[essays].* New York: Rizzoli, 1991.

Kraus, George. *High Road to Promontory -- Building the Central Pacific (now the Southern Pacific) across the High Sierra.* Palo Alto: American West Publishing Company, [1969].

Lavender, David. *The Great Persuader.* Garden City, NY: Doubleday, 1970.

Lewis, Oscar. The Big Four; the story of Huntington, Stanford, Hopkins, and Crocker, and of the building of the Central Pacific. New York, London: Alfred A. Knopf, 1938.

Silver kings: the lives and times of Mackay, Fair, Flood, and O'Brien, lords of the Nevada Comstock lode. New York: A.A. Knopf, 1947.

Lyman, George Dunlap. *Ralston's Ring: California plunders the Comstock lode.* New York, London: Charles Scribner's Sons, 1937.

Makley, Michael J. *The infamous king of the Comstock: William Sharon and the Gilded Age in the West.* Reno: University of Nevada Press, c2006.

Manter, Ethel H. Van Vick. *Rocket of the Comstock: the story of John William Mackay.* Caldwell, Idaho: Caxton Printers, 1950.

Marschall, John P. *Jews in Nevada: a history.* Reno: University of Nevada Press, c2008.

Meyer, Martin A. *Western Jewry: an account of the achievements of the Jews and Judaism in California: including eulogies and biographies.* [San Francisco, CA: Henry Hollander, Bookseller, 2001]

Michelson, Miriam. *The wonderlode of silver and gold.* Boston, MA: The Stratford Company, [c1934].

Myrick, David F. *Railroads of Nevada and eastern California.* Berkeley, CA: Howell-North Books, [1962-1963].

Narell, Irina. *Our City, The Jews of San Francisco.* San Diego, CA: Howell-North Books, 1981.

Norton, Henry K. *The Story of California From the Earliest Days to the Present.* Chicago: A.C. McClurg & Co., 1924.

Piatt, Michael H. *Bodie: "the mines are looking well...": the history of the Bodie mining district, Mono County, California.* El Sobrante, CA: North Bay Books, 2003.

Rasmussen, Louis J. *San Francisco ship passenger lists.* Colma, CA: San Francisco historic record & genealogy bulletin, c1965-1970.

Rickard, Thomas Arthur. *A history of American mining.* New York, London: McGraw-Hill Book Company, 1932.

Rochlin, Harriet and Fred Rochlin. *Pioneer Jews: a new life in the Far West.* Boston, MA: Houghton Mifflin, 1984.

Roland, Carol. *The California Kindergarten Movement: A Study in Class and Social Feminism (dissertation).* Ann Arbor: University Microfilms Intl., [1980].

Rosenbaum, Fred. *Cosmopolitans: a social and cultural history of the Jews of the San Francisco Bay Area.* Berkeley: University of California Press, 2009.

Architects of Reform: congregational and community leadership Emanu-El of San Francisco, 1849-1980. Berkeley, CA: Western Jewish History Center, Judah L. Magnes Memorial Museum, c1980.

Roxburghe Club of San Francisco. *Seven pioneer San Francisco libraries.* San Francisco: The Club, 1958.

Saxton, Alexander. *The indispensable enemy; labor and the anti-Chinese movement in California.* Berkeley: University of California Press, 1971.

Schlegel, Marvin Wilson. *Ruler of the Reading: the life of Franklin B. Gowen, 1836-1889.* Harrisburg: Archives Pub. Co. of Pennsylvania, 1947.

Shamberger, Hugh A. *The story of the water supply for the Comstock; including the towns of Virginia City, Gold Hill and Silver City, Nevada, together with other water-related events for the period 1859-1969.* Washington: U.S. Geological Survey, 1972.

Silver, Mae. *Rancho San Miguel: a San Francisco neighborhood history.* San Francisco, CA: Ord Street Press, c2001.

Sobel, Robert. *The Money Manias: The Eras of Great Speculation in America, 1770-1970.* New York: Weybright and Talley [1974, c1973].

Stampfer, Joshua. *Pioneer Rabbi of the West: the life and times of Julius Eckman.* [Portland, OR ?]: J. Stampfer, [1988?].

Starr, Kevin. *Inventing the dream: California through the Progressive Era.* New York: Oxford University Press, 1985.

Stern, Mark Abbott. *David Franks; Colonial Merchant.* University Park, PA: The Pennsylvania State University Press, 2010.

Stone, Irving. *Men to match my mountains: the opening of the Far West, 1840-1900.* Garden City, NY: Doubleday & Co., Inc., 1956.

Thorpe, James Ernest. *Henry Edwards Huntington: a brief biography.* San Marino, CA: Huntington Library, c1996.

Wilkins, Mira. *The history of foreign investment in the United States to 1914.* Cambridge, MA: Harvard University Press, 1989.

INDEX

-C-

Cadiz 106

Cahn, David 10, 18, 51, 72, 89,

Cairo, Egypt 111

California (general) xii, xv, xvi, 5, 6,
12, 16, 17, 67, 79, 83, 96, 97,
101, 103, 106, 107, 113, 114,
129, 132, 135, 143, 145, 162,
168, 180, 190, 192, 199,
202-204, 207, 211, 213,
218-220, 234, 239, 249, 250,
258, 267, 269, 281, 282,
290-298

California, State of

--Assembly 192, 195

--Attorney General 46, 183

--Board of Regents of University of
California 127, 214, 242, 270

--Chief Justice 242

--Governor 16, 28, 74, 134, 190,
192, 195, 196, 202, 213, 214,
220, 242, 282

--Supreme Court 1, 28, 47, 146,
180, 242, 245, 253, 287

California Academy of Sciences
129, 190

California Mine 27

California State Library xi, 247,
249, 257, 268, 272, 288, 289

Calistoga, California 20

Cambridge University 156

Committee of 50 (opposition to
RR bill) 200, 217, 220, 280

Campbell & Pattus 200, 280

Capon Springs, West Virginia 51

Carnall-Fitzhugh-Hopkins 154,
157

Carnegie, Andrew 149, 160

Carnegie, Louise 149

Carson City, Nevada 23, 28, 43, 98,
235, 289

Carson River 48, 69

Catania 106

catarrh 20, 125

Catholic Church 102

Catholics, Greek 102

Catholics, Roman 102, 125

Catskill Mountains, New York 31

Caspian Sea 103

Caucasian, white 202, 204, 222

Caucuses 103

Central Pacific Funding Bill 199

Central Pacific Railroad Company
(CPRR) 16, 17

Chaky, Doreen xiii, 295

Charlemagne 111

Chicago 162, 225, 244, 281, 297

Chihuahua, Mexico 140

Children's Hospital 1, 142, 216

Childs, Ella Beck 81, 263

Chilstrom, P.O. 186, 278, 290

China, Chinese 103, 204

Chinatown, San Francisco 203

Chinese Exclusion Act 203

Chollar-Potosi Mine 45, 59

-H-

-N-

-R-

-T-